The American Immigration Collection

Two Portuguese Communities in New England

DONALD R. TAFT

Arno Press and The New York Times
NEW YORK 1969

TWO PORTUGUESE COMMUNITIES IN
NEW ENGLAND

MAP OF PORTSMOUTH, R. I., IN 1920.

Small dots show the Location of 184 Portuguese Families.

TWO PORTUGUESE COMMUNITIES IN NEW ENGLAND

BY

DONALD R. TAFT, M. A.

Professor of Economics and Sociology
Wells College

SUBMITTED IN PARTIAL FULFILMENT OF THE REQUIREMENTS

FOR THE DEGREE OF DOCTOR OF PHILOSOPHY

IN THE

FACULTY OF POLITICAL SCIENCE

COLUMBIA UNIVERSITY

NEW YORK
1923

To

MY MOTHER

PREFACE

WHILE the writer alone is responsible for the conclusions of this study, it has been in high degree a co-operative venture. Without the assistance of scores of individuals including relatives, friends, government officials, instructors, officers and social workers in numerous social service organizations, and sundry kindly citizens and aliens —Portuguese and non-Portuguese—it would have been impossible.

Among this large number a certain few have been peculiarly helpful. It would be a duty and a pleasure to acknowledge this help in an extended preface. It happens however that the one who, outside of my immediate family, has contributed most prefers not to be thanked publicly. I shall therefore refrain from mentioning any of these friends by name. To them all I owe a debt which cannot be repaid. I should like also to include in my thanks the hundreds of kindly Portuguese folk whose homes I have invaded, and who have almost without exception received me with gentle courtesy when I was engaged in an inquisitory errand which would have brought me scant welcome in many more cultured households.

AURORA, NEW YORK, MARCH 15, 1923.

TABLE OF CONTENTS

CONTENTS

CHAPTER VII

LIMITATIONS AND CONCLUSIONS 343

LIST OF TABLES

CHAPTER I

INTRODUCTION

THE writer's interest in the Portuguese of New England was first attracted by the contrast between the infant mortality rates for different nationalities in Fall River. Residents of Fall River had called attention to a difference of no less than a hundred and twenty-five points in the rate of mortality of Portuguese infants as compared with those of French Canadian parentage. The notoriously excessive mortality of babies in that city was therefore attributed by some to the presence of about twenty-five thousand inhabitants of Portuguese extraction. But in the absence of more definite knowledge of the characteristics of these people it was difficult to tell whether their infants died because of racial or nationalistic traits, or because the Portuguese chanced to be exposed to peculiarly adverse surroundings. A study of these people was obviously needed.

But the need for studies of particular nationalities is not confined to the problem of infant mortality. The presence of the foreign-born and their descendants in many communities complicates every social problem. Indeed students of society find a need for studies not only of particular problems as related to many nationalities, but of particular nationalities as related to many different problems. We need to know what are the problems of the Italians, for instance, as well as to know how the Italians complicate a particular problem such as that of the criminality of communities. Or rather we cannot know our problems until we know the peoples which figure in them; and similarly we cannot know the lives of these peoples until we know something of each of the social problems which influence their lives. The two needs are reciprocal.

We already possess some studies of the Italians, Greeks, Slavs, Poles, Jews, Chinese, Japanese and other recent immigrants to the United States. The Portuguese, however, have been a neglected group. Aside from a periodical article or two few have thought it worth while to describe the lives of these simple folk. Their relatively small numbers and their high degree of concentration in two regions may in part account for this neglect. In part, too, their high degree of illiteracy and reputed low standard of living may make them relatively unattractive. If these characteristics of the Portuguese complicate our problems, however, the people themselves are the more worthy of study for that very reason.

The Portuguese are also interesting to study because of their peculiar racial composition. Not only are they Southern-Europeans but also, as we shall show, some of them seem to be of a semi-negroid type. This is true not only of the Bravas who are now recognized as " colored " by the United States Census, but in varying degrees of a part, though not all, of the so-called white Portuguese. This fact raises important sociological questions. What is the effect of this infusion of negro blood upon their own social welfare and upon the influence they exert in America? To what extent are they recognized as negroid and therefore subjected to social ostracism? A study of the Portuguese of certain types may throw some light upon the study of the mulatto in the United States.

Assimilation of similar racial stocks with different mores is sufficiently difficult. If these mores are rooted in real racial differences assimilation becomes doubly difficult. As a rule we are all too ready to identify differences in culture with differences in race; but a priori there is more reason to do so in the case of the Portuguese than in that of most of our European immigrants. The Portuguese are worthy of study then as a group which complicates important social problems, as a neglected nationality, and as a people apparently differing somewhat in race as well as in mores, from native Americans and from other elements among the foreign-born.

The present paper does not pretend, however, to meet the need for such a study. So far as intensive study is concerned it is confined to one rural and one urban community which, as is shown later, can hardly be taken as fair samples of the Portuguese as a whole. The communities are probably reasonably representative of the St. Michael Portuguese immigrants engaged in cotton mill work and in small farming in New England. Other limitations of the study are emphasized in Chapter VII below.

It is hoped, however, that this study will throw some light on the problems mentioned above by comparing somewhat similar elements in the Portuguese nationality which are found living under rather different conditions. The study aims to compare two communities of Portuguese— one urban and one rural. In one the occupations are chiefly industrial; in the other they are largely agricultural. In one the Portuguese are one among many immigrant elements; in the other such contacts as they have with non-Portuguese are mostly with the native-born. In one they are trying to adapt themselves to relatively complex social relationships in a city; in the other the environment is that of a simple rural community. In one some degree of effort has been made to solve their problems for them; while in the other the success or failure they have attained has been largely, though not entirely, their own.

The bulk of the material concerning these two communities will be found in Chapter VI. While it is hoped that the other chapters are not without value in throwing light upon the problems of the Portuguese there is little original work in them, and they do not pretend to exhaust their subjects.

Wherever possible the method used has been statistical. The reasons for choosing these two communities, and the method used in the house-to-house study are described at the beginning of Chapter VI. Fully as much labor has been expended, however, upon the compilation and analysis of data from secondary sources, as upon the more intensive study of families. These tables are scattered through the different chapters.

In addition to the use of statistics, books, periodicals and government studies have been freely drawn upon. A considerable number of personal interviews with the leaders in the communities studied and elsewhere have also been invaluable. No attempt was made to learn the Portuguese language either for conversation or for the reading of sources. This is undoubtedly a serious weakness in the study. It is hoped that statements throughout have been sufficiently qualified and that attention has been called to the more important weaknesses. To guard against too sweeping and dogmatic conclusions a special chapter has been devoted to the limitations of the study.

CHAPTER II

THE RACIAL COMPOSITION OF THE PORTUGUESE NATIONALITY

POPULARLY we identify race and nationality. Popularly we think of the observed characteristics of a people as inherent and as permanently associated with them. Even official publications and otherwise scholarly works frequently treat our immigration problem as a problem of race. In some cases and to some degree this is true. In other cases it is more false than true. A recent book on the problem of assimilation [1] has concluded that our immigration is primarily not an influx of different races, but of similar racial stocks which have different mores because they have been exposed to different social environments. On the other hand Professor Ross treats the immigration problem as one of the intermingling and eventual intermarriage of racially distinct stocks.[2]

To insist that a particular group of immigrants differ from the native-born or from other immigrant groups in mores rather than in racial constitution is not to minimize the importance of their distinctive characteristics. Nor does it imply that assimilation will be easy, for the mores are extremely rigid. It does imply, however, that such group differences are not necessarily permanent. It does imply that the process of harmonizing such differences

[1] Park and Miller, *Old World Traits Transplanted* (New York, 1921), p. 302 and *passim*.

[2] *Cf.* his *Old World in the New* (New York, 1914), *passim*.

21

though slow, is not impossible. The question whether group differences are primarily innate or acquired is, then, fundamentally important to ask and extremely difficult to answer.

In order to answer it we must ask three sub-questions:

(1) Is the nationality in question made up of one or of several racial types?

(2) What are the racial characteristics of the type or types represented?

(3) Has the process of emigration selected a fair sample of these types and of the variants within them?

We shall discuss the first two questions in this chapter. The third will be touched upon in the chapter on Emigration. We shall first take up the physical anthropology of the mainland Portuguese, then of the Portuguese of the Islands, and then shall give a little attention to possible differences in the racial types of different islands.

The Physical Anthropology of the Mainland Portuguese[1]

The following brief sketch of the ethnic development of the Portuguese of the mainland is taken from Corrêa's account except where other sources are acknowledged.[2]

We cannot say with certainty that men were living in Portugal in eolithic times. The evidence we have is, as usual, unreliable. But we do know that Portugal was inhabited during the paleolithic period, for discoveries have been made near Coimbra and in southern Portugal. The physical type of this earliest paleolithic man is, however, unknown. Kitchen middens have been found in the Tagus

---

[1] No pretense is made at an exhaustive anthropological study. Scientific studies of special areas are needed to enable us adequately to answer our questions.

[2] Corrêa, "Origins of the Portuguese," *American Journal of Physical Anthropology*, vol. ii, p. 139.

valley with some two hundred skeletons dating from the end of the quaternary and showing an Aurignacian civilization. The people of that time were sedentary, living on game and fish, and were backward in culture. Their origin was perhaps meridional. Physically they were of the Australoid or Proto-ethiopian type with both brachycephalic and dolichocephalic heads. They were not, however, the bringers of the neolithic culture and are to be distinguished from the Mediterranean stock which predominates among the modern Portuguese.

The real beginnings of the modern Portuguese date from neolithic times with the coming of the Mediterranean (Iberian) stock. Indeed Ripley says that they were the primary possessors of the soil.[1] " Whether the Ligurians ever penetrated as far as this beyond the Pyrenees is certainly matter for doubt. Following the Ligurians came the Celts at a very early period, pretty certainly overrunning a very large part of the Peninsula." [2] The builders of the dolmens were a somewhat heterogeneous type physically though predominantly dolichocephalic and below medium in stature. Some lived in villages, some in caves and some, perhaps, in lake dwellings. Among the Ligurian and Celt-Iberian elements which came, the Lusitanians were the most important group and they formed the nucleus of the future Portuguese population. To these elements Rome gave unity of language and of law. Even before the Romans came, Portugal, or what was to be Portugal, was subjected to foreign influences of the Phoenicians, Carthaginians and Greeks. Despite their backwardness at that time, however, the inhabitants maintained many of their ancient customs and much of their individuality.

[1] Ripley, *Races of Europe* (New York, 1899), p. 276.
Ibid., p. 276.

From the fifth century on we have the series of northern invasions—Vandals, Suevi and Alans—whose dominion was short, however. The Suevi and the Visigoths were of more ethnogenic importance than the other northerners but they too assumed gradually the Luso-Roman civilization. From the eighth to the thirteenth centuries Portugal was under Arab and Berber dominion and here too assimilation proved easy. After the fall of the Moorish rule many Saracens remained and formed a permanent element in the population. The Jews came in gradually and remained until their expulsion in 1497.

During the period of the maritime conquests migrations were going on between Portugal and India, Africa and Brazil. The slave trade which is discussed below brought at this time no small element of negro blood. But the visits of English, French, Germans and Flemings counted for little ethnogenically. To make our list of population elements complete we must add the Gypsies. " Portugal ", says Corrêa, " has sheltered people of many different origins; yet in spite of this, Portugal is to-day one of the least heterogeneous countries in Europe from the ethnic point of view." [1] In this view Ripley concurs: " The Iberian peninsula now divided between two nationalities, the Spanish and the Portuguese is . . . . in the main homogenous racially—more so in fact than any other equally large area of Europe." [2]

Ripley describes three physical characteristics of the inhabitants of Portugal—hair color, cephalic index and stature. Referring to a study of 1800 Portuguese women by Dr. Ferraz de Mecedo he says: " Less than two per cent of these were characterized by light hair of any shade; [3]

[1] Corrêa, *op. cit.*, p. 137.
[2] Ripley, *op. cit.*, p. 19.
[3] *Cf.* data on immigrants to Providence, R. I., *infra*, p. 45.

about a fifth were black-haired, the remainder being of various dark chestnut tints." [1]

As for complexion, Corrêa finds that the percentage of brunet varies from 45.9 in Povoa to 74.5 in Beira Alta. The shade oscillates between numbers 23, 24, 25 and 26 of Broca's scale. On the other hand blondes made up from 7.5 to 14.3 per cent of the population.[2]

In cephalic index the Portuguese are still less variable. Ripley speaks of a " variation of the cephalic index, imperceptible to the eye, of scarcely four units from the most dolichocephalic type in Europe." [3] The index varied from .75 to .79 with an average according to Corrêa of .763. He adds that the " cephalic index shows the actual exceptional homogeneity of the people." [4] The per cent of brachycephals does not exceed 8 per cent whereas in Spain it rises to 26.5 per cent and in parts of Italy to 74 per cent.[5]

Turning to stature we find a people below the average. Measurement of 1444 males gave an average height of 164.5 c. m. (about 5 feet, four and three-quarters inches). Ripley does not give separate data for the Portuguese but finds a variation for the inhabitants of the Peninsula of only a little over two inches between extremes.[6]

To these basic characteristics Corrêa adds [7] the following details. The noses of Portuguese are leptorhinic with an average index of 44.4. Their faces are relatively long. Their cranial capacity varies with stature in different parts

[1] Ripley, *op. cit.*, p. 7.

[2] Corrêa, *op. cit.*, p. 139.

[3] Ripley, *op. cit.*, pp. 273-4.

[4] Corrêa, *op. cit.*, pp. 139-40.

[5] *Ibid.*, p. 142.

[6] Ripley, *op. cit.*, map, p. 96.

[7] Corrêa, *op. cit.*, pp. 140-141.

of Portugal with an average of 1573 c. c. for men and of 1399 c. c. for women. They are characterized by marked orthognathism. Their lumbo-vertebral indices are small averaging 98.7 for males and 97.6 for females. The sacrum is exceedingly flat with a male index of 113 and a female of 116.2.

Despite this high degree of uniformity Corrêa distinguishes three racial types in Portugal:

(1) Medium Portuguese type identical with the Ibero-Insular race, which is found in its purest form in the remote mountainous regions.

(2) Nordic type, the presence of which shows plain traces of invasions which were most felt in certain northern regions.

(3) Semito-Phoenician type which is tall, brunet and dolicho-cephalic with aquiline nose and triangular face. This type is most numerous in the south.

Negroid Elements among the Mainland Portuguese

The question of the importance of the negroid element in the Portuguese nationality, is a difficult but important one. There are at least four possible sources from which our Portuguese immigrants may have received an infusion of negro or negroid blood:

(1) From an ancient contact between the white ancestors of the Portuguese and the Negroes in northern Africa.

(2) From contacts in Portugal with the Moors and their African slaves.

(3) From contacts with slaves imported into Portugal, especially during the fifteenth and sixteenth centuries.

(4) From contacts with African slaves and Moors in the Azores and Madeira.

In addition there is the possibility that Portuguese in Brazil or other colonies returning to the mainland or to the Islands brought traits produced by contacts with the Negro and Indian populations abroad. The story of the earliest intermixture of Negro blood is buried far in the past. We need only note that many anthropologists recognize that: " There is an ancient negroid strain underlying the populations of Southern and Western France, Italy, Sicily, Corsica, Sardinia, Spain, Portugal, Ireland, Wales and Scotland." [1] But the same author minimizes the importance of these early contacts as far as the Portuguese are concerned when he says: " There is a strong negroid element in the south of Spain and the south of Portugal, but we are not entitled in default of evidence to assume that this is due to such an ancient negroid immigration as seems to be indicated in France and Italy." [2]

Yet there is according to Ripley, but little doubt that Portugal shares with other European countries the effects of the Negro element in the Mediterranean race. " Beyond the Pyranees begins Africa ", he says, and while much of the negroid element is due to a later intermixture, he considers the inhabitants of the Iberian Peninsula as the purest types of Mediterraneans. He distinguishes this mixed type to-day by their predominant long-headedness, accentuated darkness of hair and eyes, medium stature inclining to be short, and oval facial characteristics.[3]

From the eighth to the thirteenth centuries, as we have noted, we have the period of Arab dominion on the Peninsula. In the Moors we find a people where " upon the soft and wavy-haired European stock has surely been engrafted a negro cross." [4]

---

[1] Johnston, quoted in Reuter, *The Mulatto in the United States* (Boston, 1918), p. 15.

[2] Johnston, in *The Universal Races Congress* (London, 1911), p. 330.

[3] Ripley, *op. cit.*, pp. 272-3.

[4] *Ibid.*, p. 278.

But Ripley says: " There is a profound difficulty in identifying their descendants, owing to their similarity to the native in all important respects. . . . Intermixture with them would not have modified either the head form or the stature in any degree." But the " honey-brown eyes of the south-western quarter of Spain near Granada, and the broader more African nose may be due to their presence." [1]

The third infusion of Negro blood came as a result of the slave trade in the sixteenth and following centuries. If we give weight to the extent of this trade in area and time we must put Portugal first among the slave-trading nations.[2] Jayne, quoting from the account of Azurara says: " Those [slaves] whom they saw fitted for managing property they set free and married to women who were natives of the land." [3] Apparently, then, in Portugal miscegenation was not confined to the usual " illicit relations between men of the superior and women of the inferior race ",[4] though the cases where the white element was the male undoubtedly were the more numerous. Jayne gives us somewhat more definite evidence as follows:

Slaves were imported from the West Coast to till the wasted fields of Estremadura and Alemtejo, and to breed a degenerate race of half-castes in the heart of the Empire, while the freemen of the old stock were daily growing fewer. All the white inhabitants which the kingdom possessed could easily be housed in South London.[5]

Authorities differ in the importance they attach to this influx of negroid stock in Portugal. Some of the more

---

[1] Ripley, *op. cit.*, p. 276.

[2] Johnston, *The Negro in the New World* (London, 1910), p. 83.

[3] Jayne, *Vasco Da Gama and His Successors* (London, 1910), p. 22.

[4] Reuter, *op. cit.*, p. 88.

[5] Jayne, *op. cit.*, pp. 285-6.

extreme assign to it the major rôle in the decadence of the Empire. Morse goes so far as to say: " In Lisbon itself they [the slaves] outnumbered the free men by the middle of the sixteenth century." [1] And Schultz in a somewhat intemperate book declares: " In the fifteenth century the Portuguese acquired African possessions and, carrying negro blood in their veins, elective affinity caused them to cross freely with the Negroes. At first the Negro blood came to Portugal in droplets; later it became a flood." [2] The Portuguese anthropologist, Corrêa, on the other hand, while not denying the numerical importance of the slave influx, minimizes its effects upon the racial characteristics of the people. He writes:

The slave trade of the sixteenth century and afterwards, brought undoubtedly many African Negroes to Portugal . . . . [Some, when they were freed, set up shops and taverns in provincial places.] Their intermarriage had greater effect, however, in some populous centers than in the provinces. Still they left no important traces in any part of the country, either on account of the return of their mixed progeny to the predominant native type, or because of the great dilution of theirs in the great mass of native blood. The affirmation of some authors that, especially in Lisbon, an enormous part of the population is made up of mulattoes, is not true. [3]

Arnold Bennett, however, speaking of the Lisbon population notes wide difference in complexions. He declares that every variety of intermixture from 99 per cent Latin-Moorish and 1 per cent Negro, to 99 per cent Negro and 1 per cent Latin-Moorish can be seen, and that racial purity of any sort is rare. " There is no color prejudice in Portugal; there could not be. . . . You can see the races of the earth in Chicago, if

---

[1] Morse, *Portugal* (New York, 1891), vol. i, p. 182.

[2] Schultz, *Race or Mongrel* (Boston, 1908), p. 148.

[3] Corrêa, *op. cit.*, p. 136.

you visit the different quarters, but in Lisbon you can see the races of the earth in a single individual." [1] We must no doubt allow for considerable exaggeration on the part of casual observers. For our present study it is important to note that the presence of negro blood in some degree in parts of Portugal is universally recognized, even by Portuguese authorities. It is also important to note that the negroid element is more prominent in southern Portugal than in the north; [2] for it will appear that the Azores whence came many of the Portuguese in America, were probably settled more largely from the latter section of the mother country.

The readiness with which the Portuguese interbreed with the colored races, both through illicit relations and in lawful wedlock, has often been emphasized. It is true that no two races have ever lived side by side without some degree of miscegenation taking place. When two races meet there are first illicit unions which break down the barriers of prejudice and open the way to possible blending of races, which in the absence of positive checks, leads to an ultimate fusion of types. [3] But the Portuguese seem to mix most readily of all nationalities and in largest numbers. " They have mixed, moreover, with almost equal readiness with the Malay, the American Indian and the African Negress." [4] " To the Portuguese the idea of personal contact with an Indian or a Negro excites little feeling of personal repulsion." [5]

[1] Bennett, " Some Impressions of Portugal," in *Harper's Magazine*, vol. xciv, Jan., 1922, p. 213.

[2] *Cf.* Crawfurd, " The Greatness of Little Portugal," in the *National Geographic Magazine*, vol. xxi, p. 868. Also Higgin, *Spanish Life in Town and Country* (New York, 1911), p. 286.

[3] Weatherly, " Race and Marriage ", in the *American Journal of Sociology*, vol. xv, p. 434.

[4] Reuter, *op. cit.*, p. 88.

[5] *Ibid.*, p. 36.

" Centuries of slave owning have not kindled among the Portuguese that fierce loathing of colored races which makes intermarriage with them appear a crime." [1] In South America the Portuguese " intermarried with the Indian women with an entire want of restraint" and even more readily than did the Spanish.[2] " The distinction between the races in Spanish America is a distinction of rank or class rather than of color." [3] " In Portuguese East Africa where the Portuguese have no objection to connnections with native women, the half-breeds are absorbed by the negro stocks. This intimate connection between the two races has been alleged as a cause of the unprogressive condition of the dependency." [4]

We have evidence that in India, at least, it was a deliberate policy on the part of the Portuguese officials to promote this intermingling of the races as a method of populating their colonies or for other reasons. Thus of Portuguese slavery under Albuquerque, we read : " To man his ships he encouraged the lower class Portuguese to marry Indian women. It was a practice less distasteful to them than to other peoples of Europe : indeed they were already inured to the embraces of Guinea and Gold Coast beauties. The mother of Albuquerque's own son was a Negress." [5]

Curiously enough Drachsler,[6] in his valuable study of intermarriage in New York City finds that of fifty-five dif-

[1] Jayne, *op. cit.*, p. 105.

[2] Koebel, *South America* (London, 1913), p. 45.

[3] Reuter, *op. cit.*, p. 49, quoting from James Bryce.

[4] Macdonald, *Trade, Politics and Christianity in Africa and the East* (London, 1916), pp. 243-4.

[5] Jayne, *op. cit.*, p. 104. *Cf.* also Keller, *Colonization* (New York, 1908), p. 104.

[6] Drachsler, *Intermarriage in New York City*, in Columbia Studies in History, Economics and Public Law, vol. xciv, no. 2, table v, face p. 98.

ferent nationalities the Portuguese have the highest ratio of intermarriage—88.23 out of every hundred marriages being intermarriages. This can hardly be considered more than an interesting coincidence, however, for closer examination of Drachsler's data shows that he found only seventeen cases of the marriage of Portuguese in the city, fifteen of which were intermarriages. These intermarriages were, of course, between Portuguese and other white nationalities.

We have considered this tendency of the Portuguese to mix readily with the dark races at some length because it gives us some a priori basis for expecting similar intermixture in the Azores and Madeira, where our direct evidence is none too plentiful. The statement above that such intermixture is usually found among the lower classes of the population is also worthy of some emphasis, as it is among them that we find the largest amount of emigration. At least it is not from among the upper social class primarily that our Portuguese from the Azores come.[1]   If this theory is correct then the emigration of the unskilled will tend to tap off the more negroid elements of the Island population. We may add one more bit of evidence along this line from Bryce. To quote: " The Brazilian lower class intermarries freely with the black people; the Brazilian middle class intermarries with the mulattoes and the quadroons." [2]   If similar conditions prevail elsewhere we should expect that the lower the strata of the population emigrating, the greater the degree of negroid intermixture which we should find among them.

We shall presently show some direct evidence of racial intermixture in the Azores and Madeira. The point we are making at present is that we should expect such inter-

---

[1] Cf. infra, p. 107.

[2] Quoted in Reuter, op. cit., p. 36. Cf. also Bryce, South America (New York, 1912), pp. 479-480.

mixture there both because of the racial makeup of the Portuguese themselves and because of what we know of their habits elsewhere. Johnston, seeking to explain the readiness with which the Portuguese immigrants to Brazil interbreed with the Indians and Negroes, says:

Possibly this may spring from two facts: that there is a strong Moorish North-African element in Southern Portugal, and even an old intermixture with those Negroes who were imported thither from north-west Africa in the fifteenth and sixteenth centuries to till the scantily-populated southern provinces; and also that Brazil, the Azores and Madeira were rather colonized from the Moorish southern half of Portugal than from the Gothic north.[1]

This last statement is important, for it helps to support our theory that some at least of the Island Portuguese are more negroid than those of the mainland because they came from those sections of Portugal where the darker-skinned type predominates, and because, as we shall see, they were subjected to further contact with the Negroes in the Islands. Nevertheless, without a scientific anthropological examination of the Islanders, no dogmatic statement can be made on this point.

Physical Types in the Azores and Madeira

Turning now to the Azores and Madeira from which the vast majority of our Portuguese immigrants come, we are chiefly interested in the Azores because few of the members of the groups we have specially studied were from Madeira. In the Islands, of course, the predominating nationality is Portuguese. They are the Portuguese, it is to be remembered, who had been subjected to all the ethnogenic influences described above. As colonists from the mainland they were then presumably a homogeneous Kelt-Iberian variety

[1] Johnston, *The Negro in the New World, op. cit.*, p. 98.

of the Mediterranean stock, except for an indeterminate intermixture of Moorish and Negro blood. As noted above on possibly inadequate evidence they probably came in largest numbers from southern Portugal and may therefore be somewhat more negroid than the average mainland type. To this basic stock there has been added in the Islands a fair amount of Flemish and some additional Moorish and Negro blood; while to complete the list of new ethnic elements we must add Hebrews, a few Spanish and a very few French and English soldiers.[1] All these latter groups are to be thought of, however, as minor elements which cannot have radically affected the Azorean or Island type. But the Flemish, Moorish and Negro admixtures are worthy of more consideration.

A few observers have held that the Azoreans are fairer than the Portuguese of the mainland. Thus Ashe contrasts the two types and says of the former: " Their bodies are tall and well-proportioned, their features are mild and regular, their complexions inclined to be florid."[2] These characteristics bespeak the Teutonic type and would lead one to picture the Islanders as less negroid than the Mainlanders. The explanation seems to be, however, that Ashe is here referring to the upper classes among the Portuguese, for he later contrasts the upper and lower classes, noting that the latter have a " tawney skin ". Another possible explanation of such occasional characterizations is the fact that travellers often visit but one section or a single island. Thus a visitor to the Flemish settlement in Fayal might possibly note such characteristics as Ashe describes.[3]

---

[1] Sandham, ".St. Michael's of the Azores," in the *Century Magazine*, vol. xci, p. 223, Dec., 1915.

[2] Ashe, *History of the Azores* (London, 1813), pp. 114 and 209.

[3] Cf. Boyd, *A Description of the Azores or Western Islands* (London, 1834), pp. 273-289.

The Flemish settlements in the Azores have been the subject of a special investigation by Jules Mees of the University of Gand. He discards as fictitious many of the details of the coming of the Flemings, considers the emigration to have been a private rather than a public venture, and inclines to reduce somewhat the larger estimates of its numerical importance. Yet he more than justifies the early denomination of the island of Fayal as " Ilha dos Flamengos " and permits one to believe that the Flemings were at one time an element of some importance in Fayal, and at least a minor one elsewhere. To quote: " Il paraît certain que l'élément flamand fut clairsemé á Terceira et á San Jorge, en revanche il a été prépondérant á Fayal qu'on a nommée á bon droit ' l'île des Flamands.' " [1]

The emigrants were taken to Fayal by Jose de Ura at the request of the Portuguese. The willingness of the Portuguese to have other foreigners settle in the Azores is explained by the difficulty they had found in colonizing newly discovered lands, by the commercial relations of Flanders and Portugal, and by the relationship of Isabel of Burgundy to Henry the Navigator. A number of conditions in Flanders explain the ease with which the emigrants were induced to settle in the Islands; for to unemployment, rising prices of grain and consequent malnutrition was added in 1438 a pestilence as a driving force to impel the Flemings to emigrate. About this time Bruges lost a fifth of her population through emigration.[2] Estimates of the number of emigrants leaving Flanders for the Azores at this time vary greatly. One authority says Jose de Ura took fifteen people with him while another puts the number

---

[1] Mees, *Histoire de la Découverte des Isles Açores et de L'Origine de Leur Denomination D'Isles Flamands* (Université de Grand, 1901), p. 98.

[2] *Ibid.*, pp. 105-7.

at two thousand. While there were doubtless other ship-loads Mees finds no records of their sailings. For this reason he somewhat minimizes the number of Flemish settlers. Nevertheless he estimates that Pico and Fayal had a total population of 1500 by 1490. These were mostly Flemings although the very first settlers, according to Mees, were Portuguese. Walker states that there were several thousand Flemings in the Azores in 1490, and accepts the larger number of two thousand as the correct figure for the first influx.[1] Mees' study is no doubt the more reliable of the two. Walker, however, admits that there is today no trace of these people in the Islands while Mees speaks more cautiously: "Il serait tout fois téméraire de dire qu'il ne reste plus aucun vestige de l'élément flamand dans la population de Fayal, une étude local pourra seule élucider cette question."[2] He quotes observations to the effect that the Valley of the Flemings in Fayal is still the best cultivated part of Fayal, with cheerful aspect and pretty white houses.

From Mees' careful study one gets the impression that while the importance of the Flemish immigration may have been exaggerated, and while their present importance is uncertain, they at one time were the chief population element in the Islands and that their presence may conceivably be urged as an explanation for local differences in the Island population. The importance of this consideration will appear when we discuss racial, and later social contrasts between the various islands.

In spite of such occasional comments as that of Ashe quoted above most observers stress rather the negroid appearance of the Azoreans and the inhabitants of Madeira. Thus a recent handbook of the British Foreign Office says: "The population of the Azores is mostly white, but as

[1] Walker, *op. cit.,* pp. 2-3.

[2] Mees, *op. cit.,* pp. 109-110.

in the African possessions of the Portuguese there is a large infusion of Negro blood." [1] And Weeks declares the infusion of Moorish blood has tinged the characteristics and customs of the people as well as their faces and their architecture." [2]

We have somewhat more definite information as to negroid admixture in the island of St. Michael's, which as the most populous island and the one from which the majority of the Portuguese in our special study came, is an important one to study. Thus Walker tells us that Santa Maria and San Miguel received their first inhabitants from southern Portugal (Estremadura and Algarvre provinces), a fact which itself would probably mean a more negroid type at the beginning. The former province, it will be remembered, is especially mentioned by Jayne [3] as the scene of the miscegenation of Portuguese and Negroes. Cabral's first settlement in San Miguel consisted in part of African slaves. Thereafter slavery increased until by 1531 in many places the slave population outnumbered the European. [4] Walker even goes so far as to say that this island was the scene of a race war in which " every *male* [5] Negro and Arab was massacred "! " It is owing to the presence of these slaves for so long a period, and the introduction of half-breeds from the Brazils that so many prognathous types are met with amongst the inhabitants of Portugal and her dependencies." In 1775 Pombal decreed the abolition of slavery, but the decree was never carried out and on his fall from power slavery became for a time as regnant

---

[1] British Foreign Office, *Historical Studies,* Handbook No. 116 (London, 1920), p. 26.

[2] Weeks, *Among the Azores* (Boston, 1882), p. 135.

[3] *Cf. supra,* p. 28.

[4] Walker, *op. cit.,* pp. 4, 49 and 54.

[5] Italics the present writer's.

as ever. The governor of San Miguel contracted with the Spanish government for the introduction of 4240 African slaves every year " into the Brazilian Colony " and the contract was carried out from 1603-1611.[1]

Another writer tells us that Cabral left a shipload of Moorish slaves at Provocao in St. Michael's and says: " Even to-day their descendants are more swarthy than the other islanders." They retain many Moorish customs also.[2]

We have reason, then, to expect to find the inhabitants of Fayal exhibiting Teutonic traits to some degree, and to see strong evidence of an African admixture in St. Michael's and St. Mary's. We have found no evidence, however, as to how many Negroes or Moors were settled in Fayal. We shall present later evidence of a different kind to show a difference in type between the inhabitants of that island and those of St. Michael's.

As for the other islands, we have at hand but the scantiest information as to their distinctive racial characteristics. Walker stresses the fact that certain of the islands were first settled from different sources than the others. We have already noted that St. Mary's as well as St. Michael's island was first settled from southern Portugal. Fayal, Pico and St. George are alike in having received their first important group of inhabitants from Flanders;[3] while Flemings from St. George, according to Captain Boyd, first populated Flores.[4] Furlong notices that the inhabitants of Flores are slightly lighter in color than those

[1] *Ibid.*, pp. 54-55. These statistics and others given by Walker leave some doubt, however, as to just how many of these slaves were settled in St. Michael's or in other of the Azores.

[2] Furlong, "On the Crest of the Lost Atlantic", in *Harper's Magazine*, vol. cxxxiv, p. 339, Feb. 1917.

[3] Walker, *op. cit.*, p. 7.

[4] Boyd, *op. cit.*, p. 320.

of St. Michael's, and attributes the difference to the infusion of Flemish blood.[1] The same difference is noted by Mrs. Roundell.[2] She characterizes the folk of the little island of Corvo as particularly good looking and of Moorish descent.[3]

The only deduction which seems justified by the above evidence is that one might expect some difference in type as between Fayal and St. Michael's and St. Mary's, but that the characteristics of the other islands are in doubt. Incidentally we may note that the islands which are most certainly part negroid are those nearest to the continent of Africa.

As for Madeira there is quite as much evidence of a negroid strain there as in St. Michael's so far as written accounts may be used as evidence. Biddle says that the inhabitants of Madeira are very dark of complexion as a rule. " They are not true Portuguese; at least the lower classes are not, as there is an admixture of African blood in their veins." [4] Taylor states that on the west coast the peasantry retain many of the Moorish characteristics, while in the north the negro type prevails.[5] Crawfurd tells us: " A queer race of men are these natives of Madeira. Mainly of Portuguese origin, they clearly are a nation of half-castes, and the negro cross is conspicuous in their good-natured ugly faces, in their stature (they average two or three inches more than the Portuguese of the Continent), in their shambling gait, and in their ill-knit frames." [6] He

[1] Furlong, "Two Mid-Atlantic Isles," in *Harper's Magazine*, vol. cxxxiii, p. 801, 1916.

[2] Roundell, *A Visit to the Azores* (London, 1889), p. 120.

[3] *Ibid.*, p. 127.

[4] Biddle, *The Madeira Islands* (London, 1882), p. 58.

[5] Taylor, *Madeira, Its Scenery and How to See It* (London, 1882), p. 58.

[6] Crawfurd, *Portugal Old and New* (London, 1880), p. 343.

adds that in the seventeenth century there were several thousand negro slaves in Madeira, and to them rather than to the Moors he attributes the dark skin of the inhabitants of to-day.[1] In a more recent work Biddle states that in 1552 there were said to be some 2700 slaves in Madeira, and that when they were freed by decree of Pombal in 1775 they intermarried with Portuguese natives.[2] Koebel informs us that as early as 1419 or thereabouts Madeira was colonized by sending captive Moors and slaves from Africa and the Canary Islands in large numbers together with condemned prisoners.[3] By the first quarter of the sixteenth century the number of retainers and slaves had greatly increased, and in 1578, since so many slaves were " living in sin " a law was passed permitting their marriage.[4]

Undoubtedly our knowledge of the racial type in the Islands lacks a careful anthropological study. But even without it there can be little doubt that the Island Portuguese have received more than negligible infusions of negro blood. Our information would lead us to expect some differences in the degree of intermixture as between the different islands also. On the other hand no one could mistake the Portuguese of Madeira or of the Azores for the decidedly negroid Bravas of the Cape Verde Islands. Immigrants to the United States from these latter have since 1915 been classed as " colored " by the Massachusetts and the Federal Censuses. However, as they are almost unrepresented in the communities we are studying they have been disregarded in this study.

[1] *Ibid.*, pp. 344-5.
[2] Biddle, *The Land of the Wine* (London, 1901), vol. i, p. 89.
[3] Koebel, *Madeira Old and New* (London, 1909), p. 15.
[4] *Ibid.*, pp. 21 and 23.

*Physical Types Among Immigrants Landing at
Providence, R. I.*

The possible differences between the inhabitants of the
different islands suggested above, has led the writer to seek
to confirm them by referring to the manifests of certain
ships docking in Providence, Rhode Island in 1920. The
method used was to begin with the manifest of the ship
which had most recently docked (the latest on file had arrived in October 1920), and work backwards until at least
a hundred records were obtained for each sex from each of
the four island districts of Ponta Delgada, Funchal, Angra
and Horta, as well as from the mainland. All the ships
docked sometime during the year 1920 but not all the ar-
rivals for that year have been included.

Among other data on these manifests are recorded the
color of eyes, color of hair and stature of all immigrants.
By classifying immigrants by the islands of emigration it
was hoped to obtain some indication of the physical type
prevailing among emigrants from each island. The results
of the study, however, as shown in the following tables are
rather disappointing. The manifests are not the work of a
single official, and apparently different officials work with
different degrees of care. A former Vice-Consul informed
the writer that these records of physical appearance are
made by the agents who sell steamship tickets at the various ports—presumably at Lisbon, Funchal, Horta, Ponta
Delgada and Angra. Apparently at one port all except
those with very exceptional features are grouped together
as " fair " or " olive " or " dark "; whereas at another more
careful distinctions are made. Such being the case, the
question arises as to how far the predominance in the records of olive-skinned types among emigrants from Ponta
Delgada is due to real differences in color between them

and the Horta group, and how far to a difference in the care with which records are made at the two Ports. No answer can be given to this question.

Are the records then valueless? The writer believes that with all their imperfections they are of some value, though they must be used with great caution. In the first place, there is little question that the records from Horta are worthy of some confidence for they contain such fine distinctions as those between " brown ", " light brown " and " dark brown " hair. In the second place, distinctions between different types are noted in all the districts, apparently, when they are sufficiently striking. Yet it must be admitted that whole pages of records from Ponta Delgada occur with no classification of complexions except that of " olive ". But why " olive " ? Presumably because to the agent at that port an olive-skinned man or woman is the typical emigrant. With a view to least effort he therefore lumps together under that caption all except the most striking exceptions. Similarly the agent at Angra lists all as of " fair " complexion and as having " chestnut " hair save when he notices one who can obviously not be so listed.

If the above surmises are correct there are doubtless many errors in the tables which follow. Probably, however, they do represent the general tendency for one or another type to predominate among the emigrants of a given district. Certainly the classification of types from Horta is significant.

TABLE I [1]

COMPLEXIONS OF PORTUGUESE IMMIGRANTS ARRIVING AT PROVIDENCE, R. I.—1920 (ADULTS 18 YEARS OF AGE AND OVER)

Number Men

Source	White	Fair	Rosy	Natural	Olive	Dark	Brown	Total
Mainland	2			465		7		474
Ponta Delgada	1	1			121	1		
St. Michael's	1	1			102	1		105
St. Mary's					19			19
Horta	79	59	1		3	57	2	
Pico	19	22			3	20	2	66
Fayal	23	21	1			28		73
Flores	31	15				8		54
Corvo	6	1				1		8
Angra		177	1		1	1		
Terceira		111						111
St. George		36			1			37
Graciosa		30	1			1		32
Funchal (Madeira) ...		7			133			140
Totals	80	246	2	465	258	66	2	1119

Per cent Men

	Light	Natural	Dark	Total
Mainland	.4%	98.1%	1.5%	100.0%
Ponta Delgada	1.6		98.4	100.0
Horta	69.2		30.8	100.0
Angra	98.9		1.1	100.0
Funchal	5.0		95.0	100.0
Total	29.3%	41.6%	29.1%	100.0%

[1] This table and the three following were derived from the manifests of ships docking at Providence in 1920. In figuring percentages in table I "white," "fair" and "rosy" complexions have been combined under the caption "light." "Natural" have been left as an intermediate group which strictly should be divided between the other two, and "olive," "dark" and "brown" have been combined as "dark".

Number Women

Source	White	Fair	Rosy	Natural	Olive	Dark	Brown	Total
Mainland				117				117
Ponta Delgada		2			109			
St. Michael's		2			104			106
St. Mary's					5			5
Horta	54	32				25	3	
Pico	13	13				10		36
Fayal	18	13				12	2	45
Flores	18	6				3	1	28
Corvo	5							5
Angra		111			1			
Terceira		82						82
St. George		19			1			20
Graciosa		10						10
Funchal (Madeira)					87			87
Totals	54	145		117	197	25	3	541

Per cent Women

	Light	Natural	Dark	Total
Mainland		100.0%		100.0%
Ponta Delgada	1.8		98.2	100.0
Horta	75.4		24.6	100.0
Angra	99.1		.9	100.0
Funchal		100.0		100.0
Total	36.8%	37.7%	25.5%	100.0%

TABLE 2

COLOR OF HAIR OF PORTUGUESE IMMIGRANTS ARRIVING AT PROVIDENCE—
1920 (ALL AGES AND BOTH SEXES COMBINED)

Source	Brown	Chestnut	Dark	Dk. Brown	Black	Gray	Red	Golden	Lt. Brown	Fair	Total
Mainland ...	753				78	4	1			14	850
Ponta Del. ..	119	2	288						3		
St. Mi.	118	2	267						3		390
St. Ma. ...	1		21								22
Horta	133	8	1	44		8			49	1	
Pico	48	1	1	10		3			17		80
Fayal	40			9		3			23	1	76
Flores	40	7		21		2			5		75
Corvo	5			4					4		13
Angra	1	268		2		5		2	8	1	
Terceira ..		230				4		1	5	1	241
St. George.	1	28		1		1		1	2		34
Graciosa ..		10		1					1		12
Funchal(Mad)	8	5	34						2		49
Total ..	1014	283	323	46	78	17	1	4	60	16	1842

Percentage of light hair (red, golden, lt. brown and fair) to the total by Districts

Mainland	1.8%
Ponta Delgada	.7
Horta	20.5
Angra	3.8
Funchal	4.1

TABLE 3

COLOR OF EYES OF IMMIGRANTS ARRIVING AT PROVIDENCE—1920
(ALL AGES AND BOTH SEXES)

Source	Brown	Chestnut	Dark	Black	Gray	Green	Blue	Totals	%Blue
Mainland	1031	1	6	8	10	4	33	1093	3.2%
Ponta Delgada.		2	399				1	402	.2
St. Mi.		2	376				1	379	
St. Ma.			23					23	
Horta	201	10					28	239	11.7
Pico	64						12	76	
Flores	64	8					4	76	
Fayal	62	2					10	74	
Corvo	11						2	13	
Angra	2	290		1			1	294	.3
Terceira		242		1				243	
St. George ..		33						33	
Graciosa	2	15					1	18	
Funchal(Mad)		7	40					47	
Total	1234	310	445	9	10	4	63	2075	3.0%

TABLE 4

AVERAGE STATURE OF IMMIGRANTS ARRIVING AT PROVIDENCE, R. I.—1920
(ADULTS 18 YEARS OF AGE AND OVER)

	Men		Women	
Source	Number	Av. Stature	Number	Av. Stature
Mainland	100	5' 5.21"	100	5' 1.36"
Ponta Delgada	110	5' 5.21"	105	5' 2.86"
St. Mi.	100	5' 5.16"	100	5' 2.96"
St. Ma.	10	5' 5.70"	5	5' .80"
Horta	245	5' 5.81"	160	5' 2.38"
Pico	81	5' 6.11"	57	5' 2.89"
Fayal	99	5' 5.87"	67	5' 1.97"
Flores	57	5' 5.07"	32	5' 2.34"
Corvo	8	5' 7.87"	4	5' 2.50"
Funchal (Mad.)	100	5' 5.35"	87	5' 2.18"
Total	713	5' 5.56"	577	5' 2.22"

Making due allowance for difficulties, the tables as they stand, seem to confirm our expectation that somewhat different types of emigrants are be found among those coming from the different islands. The islands which have received a considerable number of Flemish colonists are, it is true, divided between the two districts of Horta and Angra, but the contrast between these two districts and that of Ponta Delgada, containing the two islands of St. Michael's and St. Mary's, is interesting. But since Fayal, Pico and Flores are all located in the Horta district the most significant comparison is between this district and that of Ponta Delgada. Horta shows 69.2 per cent of light-complexioned men and 75.4 per cent of women, as against 1.6 per cent and 1.8 per cent respectively for Ponta Delgada. It is true that Angra has a still larger proportion, but this is quite possibly due to less careful classification. Horta again is decidedly marked out with respect to the color of hair of its emigrants showing 20.5 per cent with various types of light hair as against but .7 per cent for Ponta Delgada. As for eye color it is true that only 11.7 per cent of the emigrants from Horta showed blue eyes, but this proportion was far in excess of that for any other district. The men from Horta also averaged the tallest of those of any district, but their women measured exactly the same height as those from the mainland though taller than those from any of the other island districts. As our investigation does not show whether these emigrants from the mainland came from northern or from southern Portugal we cannot even speculate as to the probable racial composition of that group.

Before leaving this subject it will be interesting to note that Hoffman, writing as early as 1899, suggested the possibility that the Island Portuguese might not prove to be a homogeneous racial group. He says: " For some curious reason the emigrants to the United States have mostly come from Fayal, San Jorge and Flores, while those to the Sandwich Isles have come principally from Madeira, and those to Brazil from the islands of San Miguel, Santa Maria and Terceira.". . . . This distinction of the origin of the American-Portuguese immigration is of some importance in view of the fact that there may possibly be shown to be certain important differences in the racial types of the inhabitants of the different groups of islands.[1] Nevertheless Hoffman concludes tentatively that " This [negro] strain must be considered as unimportant from a physiological point of view, and does not to my mind represent a factor detrimental to the health or longevity of these people at the present time." Indeed he concludes that the Portuguese in America have shown an unusually low death rate.[2]

The interesting points about Hoffman's article for our present study are first that he recognized the possibility of there being heterogeneity among the racial types of the Island Portuguese, secondly that he was considering Portuguese from the islands where we have found evidence of the Flemish intermixture, and, finally, that he found them a healthy people in the United States, and exhibiting traits which he contrasts with those of the Negro.[3] In this connection it may be well to note at this point that the early immigration from the Azores to Boston seems to have been from Fayal largely.[4] Callender, writing in 1911, says:

[1] Hoffman, " The Portuguese Population in the United States," in the *American Statistical Association Publications*, vol. vi, no. 47, p. 328. Sept., 1899.

[2] *Ibid.*, pp. 330 and 334.

[3] *Ibid.*, p. 336.

[4] *Cf.* Caswell, " The Portuguese in Boston," in *The North End Mission Magazine*, and contribution of the Portuguese Consul, M. Borges de F. Henriques, pp. 73-75. Though speaking of Fayal the Consul says, however, that what is said of one island holds good for the others.

" Fifty years ago, Americans, when referring to the Azores, thought only of Fayal." [1]

Our query then is: Does the fact that the more recent immigration from the Azores has been from St. Michael's largely, mean that there has been a significant change in the racial type of Portuguese immigrants, and if so, is this change in racial type correlated with a corresponding change in social characteristics or in susceptibility to disease? This must probably remain a mere query so far as this study is concerned, but we shall keep the racial factor in mind as we study other characteristics of the Portuguese in our particular communities.

Returning to the questions with which we opened this chapter,[2] we can now say in answer to the first that the Portuguese of the mainland have been considered by anthropologists a homogeneous racial group as measured by their variability with respect to stature, head shape and hair color; but that this homogeneity does not necessarily preclude a considerable intermixture of Moorish or Negro blood. We note that the Portuguese of the islands are probably somewhat less homogeneous than those of the mainland since some Flemish blood has been introduced, and perhaps because more of the negroid element is present among them. In answering this question we have also in a measure answered the second question and have noted some of the physical racial characteristics of the island types. We have given practically no evidence of other than physical characteristics. We have only partially answered the third question, but have given some eivdence to show that the earlier immigration did select a type of Azorean which was possibly a bit more Teutonic and a bit

[1] Callender, " Islands of the Hawks," in *Travel*, vol. xviii, p. 24, Nov., 1911.

[2] *Cf. supra*, p. 22.

less negroid than that of the groups which have come more recently. Our answer to these questions, however, has throughout been tentative. A careful anthropological study is required before it can be confirmed.

As for the fundamental question: Is the Portuguese immigration primarily the introduction of types racially different from our other population elements?—our partial answers to the sub-questions have only given us a bare starting point towards the answer. Even if we could say that we have shown that the more recent Portuguese immigration brings us a distinctly negroid type, we have not yet shown that this physical characteristic is correlated with social or cultural traits which cannot be assimilated by the other elements. Our study has shown, the writer believes, the danger of hasty generalizations as to " the Portuguese ". For there are certainly differences between the white Portuguese and the Bravas.[1] There are quite possibly racial differences between the white Portuguese of the mainland and those of the Islands; and as probably there are differences between the immigrants from St. Michael's and those from Fayal. The existence of these differences is perhaps not proven, but enough has been shown to demonstrate the possible existence of differences of real importance. There is not *an immigration* problem, there are *immigration problems,* differing for each nationality. There is, quite possibly, not a Portuguese problem; there is possibly a different problem for each racial element of which the Portuguese are made up. Our further study should throw a little more light on this question.

[1] Not treated in this study.

CHAPTER III

THE CONTINENTAL AND ISLAND BACKGROUND

THE last chapter attempted to determine the racial composition of the Portuguese nationality. From the short-time point of view it is quite as important to understand the social inheritence of these people. Unlike racial characteristics, acquired traits may be greatly modified in the course of generations, but the mores yield but slowly and before they yield and while they are yielding they frequently create serious social problems. The Portuguese mores, traditions and other acquired characteristics are, of course, the product of their racial characteristics as influenced by the physical and social environment of Continental Portugal and of the Western Islands and Madeira. In the present chapter we shall treat a few important aspects of the environment of the mainland and of the Azores. Less frequent reference will be made to Madeira because few of the subjects of our later study came from that island.[1]

The Azores consist of nine inhabited islands and a group of black rocks called the Formigas. Their combined area of 922 square miles and their population of 243,078 were distributed in 1911 as shown in the following table:[2]

[1] The writer is conscious of the superficiality of much of this chapter. It seemed better, however, to summarize such data as had come to his notice rather than to omit altogether this important subject. A scientific study of these backgrounds would involve an examination of Portuguese sources and an extended stay at least in the Azores, both of which were impossible for the present work.

[2] British Foreign Office, Historical Section, *Handbook no. 116, The Azores and Madeira* (London, 1920), pp. 1-7. The Census of 1911 is still (1922) the latest available.

TABLE 5

AREA AND POPULATION OF WESTERN ISLANDS—1911

San Miguel	....	297	square miles	Population	..	116,619	Density	392
Terceira	....	223	" "	"		48,029	"	215
Pico	....	175	" "	"		21,066	"	125
Fayal	....	64	" "	"		20,461	"	319
Flores	....	57	" "	"		7,233	"	127
Santa Maria	....	42	" "	"		6,268	"	149
San Jorge	....	40	" "	"		14,309	"	357
Graciosa	....	17	" "	"		7,447	"	455
Corvo	....	7	" "	"		746	"	106
Azores	....	922	" "	"		243,078	"	264

The Azores as a whole, therefore, are considerably more densely populated than is Continental Portugal with its area of 32,528 square miles and its population of 5,716,978 in 1911 giving a density of 174 per square mile.

Vital Statistics

Vital statistics are available for the years 1913-1917, but unfortunately they do not include data on the important subject of infant mortality. Bell says of infant mortality on the Continent: "The mortality among the children of the poor is enormous: it is quite common for two to grow up out of a family of seven or nine." [1]   And Hoffman wrote in 1899 of the children of the Azores: "The mortality of children would seem to be high though accurate data are wanting." [2]

The Census for 1911 gives the population of Portugal including the islands as 5,960,056 or an increase in fifty years of nearly a third, and "although something must be allowed for the more accurate returns in recent years, [it] is evidently in no danger of diminishing, in spite of increasing emigration." [3]   This latter statement, however, ap-

[1] Bell, *Portugal of the Portuguese*, p. 26.
[2] Hoffman, *op. cit.*, p. 332.
[3] Bell, *op. cit.*, p. 25.

plied at the time only to Continental Portugal for the population of some of the islands was actually decreasing.

Table 6 below shows for the last five years for which data are available the actual net increase or decrease of population in Continental Portugal, in the islands as a whole and in the different island districts:[1]

TABLE 6

AVERAGE ANNUAL NET INCREASE OR DECREASE OF POPULATION 1913-1917[2]
BY POLITICAL DIVISIONS COMBINED CRUDE RATES PER
THOUSAND POPULATION

	Birth Rate	Death Rate	Natural Increase	Emigration	Net Change[3]
Portugal	31.13	20.13	11.00	5.30	+ 5.70
Continental	31.47	20.35	11.12	4.06	+ 7.06
Islands	33.74	21.75	11.99	14.39	— 2.40
Angra	28.98	22.33	6.65	15.13	— 8.48
Horta	26.42	20.92	5.50	11.98	— 6.48
Ponta Delgada ...	36.64	24.06	12.58	21.93	— 9.35
Funchal	35.53	20.23	15.30	9.61	+ 5.69

The above table shows that if we disregard immigration and returning emigrants at the time when Bell was writing Portugal as a whole was losing nearly half her natural increase of population through emigration, but was nevertheless growing. Moreover, it is quite possible that returning emigrants made up the apparent loss in the islands also. Table 12[4] shows that during this period approximately one-fifth as many natives of Portugal left the United States annually as entered. Most of them were undoubtedly returning to their homes. If we may assume that as large

[1] For the names of the islands in each political division see table I, *supra*, p. 43.

[2] Derived from Portugal, *Estatistica Demográfica* (Lisbon, 1911), table 5, pp. 26-7.

[3] Disregarding immigration and return of emigrants.

[4] *Cf. infra*, p. 101.

a proportion of emigrants to South America and elsewhere return, as to the United States, and if these five years are typical, then apparently new births plus returning emigrants just about balance deaths plus emigrants from the islands. Real immigrants to the islands are presumably negligible. This loss of population in the islands, through emigration, is not, however, liable to continue unless increased emigration to South America or elsewhere takes the place of the recently declining emigration to North America. This latter is due, of course, to the illiteracy test established in 1917 and to the three per cent law of 1921.[1] It is also conceivable that emigration, if it does continue, will be offset by an increase in the excess of births over deaths, although this would have to be considerable to make up for the rapid loss in Ponta Delgada.

The difference in rates of natural increase as between the mainland and the islands is not great, the islands having a slightly higher rate due to their higher birth rate and in spite of their higher death rate. As between the different island districts Horta shows decidedly the lowest rate of natural increase, and Funchal, closely followed by Ponta Delgada, the highest. Ponta Delgada leads all divisions in its crude birth rate and also has the highest death rate. It is particularly worth noting that Horta shows a crude birth rate more than ten points lower than that of Ponta Delgada. The possible explanation of this difference in terms of racial composition is discussed elsewhere.[2] Moreover table 7, giving refined birth rates, shows that these differences in birth rates are not altogether due to differences in the age distribution of the population of the different districts. As the official reports give no com-

[1] *Cf.* tables for recent emigration given *infra*, p. 101.
[2] *Cf. supra*, p. 47.

bined rates for the five year period we print separate rates for each year. This table shows the same contrasts

TABLE 7

BIRTHS PER THOUSAND WOMEN OF CHILD-BEARING AGE [1]

	1913	1914	1915	1916	1917
Portugal	128.32	123.51	123.88	120.84	118.26
Continental	127.00	122.15	122.52	119.58	117.21
Islands	141.74	143.71	144.27	140.00	133.12
Angra	132.87	132.80	128.91	122.19	123.35
Horta	116.01	119.76	116.17	112.67	108.32
Ponta Delgada	155.52	150.20	158.97	157.51	147.65
Funchal	156.28	149.41	147.10	141.59	135.99

between the different divisions and is probably the most significant of the different kinds of evidence we have to offer, tending to show different social and, quite probably, different racial conditions in these different divisions. The table also shows a general tendency, though an irregular one, for these birth rates to decline between 1913 and 1917 in all divisions.

The proportion of stillbirths per thousand births are also given in the government tables but are very variable as between the political divisions, and are, in many cases, probably based upon too few cases to be of significance. It is interesting to note, however, that the rate for stillbirths is always much higher for the mainland than for the islands, the lowest rate for the mainland being 38.70 per thousand births in 1913, and the highest for the islands being 28.56 in the same year. The rate for Horta was usually low, being under 20 for three of the five years.[2]

The marriage rates for the five year period were as follows: Portugal 6.10; Continent 6.19; Islands 6.19; Angra

[1] *Estatistica Demográfica, op. cit.,* table no. 1, pp. 6-7. The age limits are not given.

[2] *Estatistica Demográfica, op. cit.,* table 3, pp. 17-20.

5.48; Horta 5.06; Ponta Delgada 6.57; Funchal 6.51. Here again we note that Horta has the lowest rate and Ponta Delgada the highest, though the former is not far separated from Angra nor the latter from Funchal. Apart from these comparisons between divisions these statistics show the Portuguese to be characterized by a high birth rate and a moderately high death rate. Their rate of population increase would be fairly large were it not for the factor of emigration.

These death rates are not greatly different from those given by Hoffman for the years 1895 and 1896 when the mainland rate was 22.6 and that for the islands 22.2. He speaks especially of the high death rate from respiratory diseases among the poor of the islands who "get wet through in the winter months and have no opportunity of drying themselves, and altogether are very thinly clad."[1] It may be added that the Portuguese aversion to fresh air may be another cause of their high mortality from respiratory diseases. Hoffman, as noted above, also surmises that the death rate of children is high.

Climate

It is possible that climatic change may account for some of the difficulties of the Portuguese in New England. We shall therefore note briefly the important characteristics of the physical environment on the Continent and in the Azores.

The climate of Continental Portugal varies considerably in different sections of the country. In the southern provinces the heat of summer may reach 120 degrees Fahrenheit and the winter cold in the north is severe. But the central part of the country is said to have a climate which is "the best in Europe." The mean annual temperature at

[1] Hoffman, *op. cit.*, p. 331.

Lisbon (1856-1900) was 60.2 degrees Fahrenheit, the winter average 51.2, spring 57.9, summer 69.3 and autumn 62.1.[1] Along with these generally moderate changes in temperature we find a country with a genial atmosphere consisting of " a succession of fertile valleys interspersed with rich alluvial plans." [2]

A colonist from central Portugal to the Azores finds little change in the mean annual temperature in his adopted land. At Ponta Delgada this is reported to be but two degrees higher (62.6) than that of Lisbon. But the range in temperature is, in general, considerably less in the Azores than in Continental Portugal, with a minimum winter temperature in the former of 40 degrees and a maximum summer temperature of 82 degrees.[3] In Madeira the mercury may rise somewhat higher with a mean annual of 66 degrees and a range from 46 to 90.[4] The change in temperature in migrating from Portugal to the Azores or Madeira is therefore a change to a region of less extremes.

Ponta Delgada enjoys dry weather from June to September but the winters are unpleasantly wet with an average of 171 rainy days and an annual rainfall of 35.4 inches.[5] The islands are, in general, blessed with extraordinary fertility and a delightful climate, but according to Thomas-Stanford " Nature's bounty has been unavailing against the perversity of man." [6]

---

[1] Bell, *op. cit.* (New York, 1915), p. 80.

[2] Crawfurd, " Portugal," in *Living Age*, vol. 256, p. 215, Feb. 29, 1908.

[3] British Foreign Office, *op. cit.*, pp. 5-6.

[4] Roundell, *op. cit.*, p. 173.

[5] British Foreign Office, *op. cit.*, p. 6.

[6] Thomas-Stanford, *Leaves from a Madeira Garden* (London, 1909), p. 164.

Occupations and Economic Status

Continental Portugal is predominantly agricultural with a little mining, considerable fishing, and some manufacturing. One per cent of the *total* population is said to be engaged in the catching and selling of fish and perhaps three times that proportion in manufacturing. The country is however three-fifths agricultural, and it is with agriculture, therefore, that we are chiefly concerned.[1] In northern Portugal the masses of the population are small tenant farmers, and in the south they are employees on large estates. In Minho the average size of holdings is under an acre " and many of them are mere patches the size of a pocket handkerchief ". In 1908 for a little less than six million inhabitants the number of holdings was given as 11,430,740. This small size of holdings is in spite of the existence of properties in the south containing as many as 20,000 acres, with an average size fifty times greater than in the north.[2]

The chief products of the farms are grapes, olives and other fruits, and cattle, together with maize which is grown chiefly in the north. Wine, fruits, cork and olive oil are exported, but strangely enough wheat, maize and rice are imported, despite the fact that whole regions remain untilled, and the population is emigrating.[3]

Moreover, the farming which is done is of the most unprogressive kind in many parts. " The wine is still made to-day [1910] just as the Roman agricultural writers directed it to be made two thousand years ago." [4] The only

[1] Bell, *op. cit.*, pp. 35-7.

[2] *Ibid.*, pp. 30-31.

[3] Bell, *op. cit.*, pp. 38-39.

[4] Crawfurd, " The Greatness of Little Portugal," in *The National Geographic Magazine*, vol. xxi, p. 881. *Cf.* also the same author's article on " Portugal " in *The Living Age*, vol. cclvi, p. 520.

great change since Roman times seems to have been the introduction of maize as a cereal crop.

Alemtejo, under the Romans flourishing with corn, has large tracts of waste land, and when the land is cultivated modern machinery is rarely in use. When introduced by the owner of the land it is allowed to fall out of use if possible by the workmen, and at harvest time one has the picturesque sight of an interminable row of laborers at work without any of the noise and bustle of machinery.[1]

Portugal does, however, suffer from droughts which, in the absence of irrigation, are a real handicap to the extension of agriculture. Whether the cause of this backwardness be chiefly nature, or chiefly man, the result is deplorable, for according to Young's careful study: " Instead of the Portuguese population producing its own food and sufficient surplus of produce, raw or manufactured, to pay its creditors abroad, and for such commodities as it cannot produce at home, it is dependent on foreign supplies for its food, and pays for this and the rest by exporting its own national labourers and by exploiting the native labour of its imperial possessions." [2]   Similarly the backwardness of the individual peasant is pictured by Bell:

One need not go many leagues from Lisbon to find a look of immemorial age about the life of the peasantry. One might be in pre-Roman times. The peasant in black peaked woolen cap, black shirt or blouse and knee-breeches and woolen leggins, walks slowly, goad in hand, in front of his ox-cart with its spokeless wheels of solid wood, or is jolted along as he stands against the tall crooked stakes that form the sides of the cart.[3]

[1] Bell, *op. cit.*, pp. 31-32.
[2] Young, *Portugal Old and Young* (Oxford, 1917), p. 255.
[3] Bell, *op. cit.*, p. 49.

The apportionment of the blame for this backwardness is not so easy. " Indolence, ignorance, mistaken finance and lack of capital have hitherto fettered agriculture in Portugal, neglect on the part of the state and of private landowners going hand in hand with illiteracy and distrust on the part of the peasants." [1] The system of excessive protection according to Bell " fills the Exchequer and ruins the country." It is powerless to make industries flourish and it seriously injures agriculture. [2] That this short-sighted financial policy is at least an immediate cause of the economic backwardness of the Azores and Madeira as well as of Continental Portugal is the opinion of not a few observers, as we shall see below.

The result of this inefficiency and low productivity is, naturally, low incomes and a poverty-stricken peasantry and laboring class. Miss Clare, observing northern Portugal in 1907, gives some interesting data on wages. The head carter at a Qunita received twelve pounds a year and food and lodging. Girls working in the fields had seven pence a day without food and with irregular employment. Their work was from sunrise to sunset with a half hour for breakfast and one or two hours during the noonday heat for lunch and a siesta. A laundress expected six shilling sixpence per month, while male laborers on the farm might get as high as one shilling one pence per day. [3] The following paragraph from Bell's account gives more recent wage data, characteristic, apparently, of conditions just before the rise in prices and wages attendant upon the World War:

[1] *Ibid.*, pp. 39-40.
[2] *Ibid.*, p. 230.
[3] Clare, "A letter from a Portuguese Country House," in *The Living Age*, vol. cclv, pp. 592-3.

In Portugal the salaries are low and give no incentive to labour especially as they have remained almost stationary, while the price of food and rent has risen. Even during the long harvest days the women receive a shilling a day or even less for working perhaps sixteen hours in the fields, the men two shillings or less. . . . A day labourer of the Duora district receives 200 reis (equal to tenpence), an agricultural labourer in Alemtejo 250 (500 in time of harvest), a carpenter of the Serra da Estrella 320 reis, a miner in a lead mine near Aveiro 350, a mason of Minho 400, a carpenter of Braga 400, a weaver of Guimaraes 500, a mason of Lisbon 700, a shoemaker's assistant in Coimbra from 220 to 440, a carpenter in Alemtejo 400, a dressmaker's assistant in Lisbon 240.[1]

A moment's consideration of the above figures leaves no doubt of the fundamental reason why the Portuguese leave home. Data on American wages will be given in another chapter, but, in passing, we may note that if we take pre-war laborers' wages in the United States as from $1.50 to $2.00 a day, the Portuguese day laborer could expect to see his money wage multiplied from seven to ten times on emigrating to New England. That costs of living would be higher there also is undeniable but the change undoubtedly represented to him a genuine rise in status, and if he were no better informed than the average workman as to the difference between money and real wages the outlook would seem bright indeed.

The peasant class in Portugal proper, then, are poverty-striken despite reasonably fertile land. What of their fellows in the Azores?

The inhabitants of the Azores like those of the mainland are chiefly agriculturalists. Fruit is raised in abundance, the largest single export of the islands being pineapples.

[1] Bell, *op. cit.*, pp. 27-8.

The once fruitful orange trees have been destroyed but bananas and apricots are exported and figs, lemons, loquats and pomegranates are found. The leading farm products, however, are maize, beans and wheat. Barley and millet are also raised, while the beet-sugar industry is found in the islands of San Miguel and Terceira. In Pico and San Miguel the grape vines have now (1920) recovered from the blight which ruined them. Terceira raises bulls for the Continental ring and exports as well sheep, cheese and butter.[1]

The land being fertile artificial irrigation is rarely necessary, and three or four crops a year are often harvested. The land, however, is " largely in the hands of big landed proprietors living in Portugal who let out their estates in small lots." This land was reported a few years ago as renting for from $5 to $15 an alqueire (less than an acre), while a typical peasant's holding was said to be from twenty to thirty alqueires.[2]

An exception to this predominance of renters is, however, found in the island of Fayal where " independent proprietorship is here and there found." [3] As is usual elsewhere such a system of large estates owned often by absentee landlords, and worked by ignorant peasants, has apparently meant in the Azores the exploitation of the tenant. The peasantry are, at any rate, abjectly and miserably poor, and are described by one investigator as a " people little removed from a condition of serfdom." [4] It will be interesting to remember later that this peasant pauperism was found

---

[1] British Foreign Office, *op. cit.*, pp. 27-28.

[2] Haeberle, " The Azores," in *The National Geographic Magazine*, June, 1919, p. 531.

[3] P. T. L., "Azorean Economics and the Peasantry," in *The Nation*, vol. 73, p. 356, Nov. 7, 1901.

[4] *Ibid.*, pp. 355 and 356.

to exist in its worst form in the island of San Miguel and that independent farming and generally better conditions have been noted in the island of Fayal. Captain Boyd, writing as early as 1834, reported: " I found the surrounding country [in Fayal] in a better state of culture than at the other islands. . . . I observed a remarkable difference in all the fruits in favor of this island." The crops of the Flemish inhabitants of Fayal were reported as good and " their valley has continued from one age to another in superior cultivation."[1] The same writer speaks of the natives at St. Mary's, on the other hand, as oppressed by the morgados, or large landowners, and as forced to work without remuneration.

In general, however, the inhabitants of the Azores are poor indeed. Though patient and laborious they are " almost without exception underfed."[2] Walker, speaking of the period when emigration to North America was in its early stages, says: The " oft recurring failures of crops are aggravated by the whole land being held and owned by the rich to the utter exclusion of the laborer who, unable to rise above his tenpence a day wage, is condemned to a lifetime of ill-paid labour, and when the maize crops, their staple article of food, fail and grain has to be imported at high prices, the labourer and his numerous progeny have a hard time of it here."[3] Mrs. Roundell writing a few years later speaks of men's wages as varying from tenpence to two shillings and of women working for sixpence a day.[4] Yet even on such wages some men apparently saved money, for Weeks tells us: " I knew a common workman who was working for \$1.50 per week. Out of this amount every

---

[1] Boyd, *op. cit.*, pp. 273 and 286. *Cf. supra*, p. 54.
[2] P. T. L., *op. cit.*, p. 355.
[3] Walker, *op. cit.*, p. 104.
[4] Roundell, *op. cit.*, p. 48.

Saturday night he left fifty cents with his employer, and supported himself, wife and three children on the balance until he had saved sufficient to purchase a house." [1] It will be objected that these low wages were found at a very early period and are no longer typical. No evidence has been secured as to wages since the Great War. But Furlong reports as late as 1917 that farm hands in the Western Islands would work for twenty cents a day.[2] About 1900 when immigrants were beginning to come in large numbers to the communities in which we are especially interested, wages in San Miguel would fall in bad times as low as twenty cents a day. Servants in private families earned three dollars a month. In a large tobacco factory " girls rolling three thousand cigarettes a day can actually rise to a little below twenty-five cents. . . . The chief bookkeeper (also a woman) gets a trifle more. The care of the driving engine intrusted to a woman describable as a skilled worker, procures her the magnificent return of a little less than forty cents." [3] At the same period the Portuguese soldier's pay was eight cents a day less a deduction for his uniform.

The above account shows that there is little difference between the income of the peasant and day laborer in Continental Portugal and that of his brother in the Azores. Such information as is at hand for Madeira indicates a similar situation there.[4] Wages in all three regions have long been at the bare subsistence level and up to the outbreak of the European War at least, there had been little tendency for them to rise.

[1] Weeks, *Among the Azores* (Boston, 1882), p. 146.

[2] Furlong, "With Columbus in the African Isles," in *Harper's Magazine*, vol. cxxxv, p. 749, Nov., 1917.

[3] P. T. L., *op. cit.*, p. 356.

[4] *Cf.* Thomas-Stanford, *op. cit.*, p. 161.

The causes of this economic backwardness are variously given as ignorance of the people,[1] injustice of the system of land tenure in the past and continued exploitation to-day,[2] heavy taxation,[3] domination in the Azores and Madeira by the mother country in determining the fiscal policy of the islands,[4] excessive customs duties making the importation of machinery impracticable,[5] and the general over-regulation of industry by the government.[6] Here, as so often in social problems, we are faced with the difficulty of determining which is antecedent and which consequent as between the personal and impersonal factors in the situation. Are the peasants exploited because they are ignorant, or are they kept ignorant because they are economically exploited? And if the former, is their ignorance due to innate low intelligence or to lack of a fair chance in life?

Housing, Home Life and Standard of Living

The low economic and social status of the people of Portugal is further reflected in their home life and in the position of woman among them. A few descriptions of their homes will show living conditions on the Continent. Says Bell:

Many families live from day to day and from hand to mouth by odd jobs. . . . They live on little or nothing and devote their energy and wits to pay arrears of rent sufficient to prevent them from being turned out of their houses, which often

[1] Thomas-Stanford, *op. cit.*, p. 68.

[2] P. T. L., *op. cit.*, p. 356 and *passim*.

[3] Roundell, *op. cit.*, p. 49.

[4] Johnston, "The Portuguese Colonies," in *The Nineteenth Century and After*, vol. lxxi, p. 499, March, 1912.

[5] P. T. L., *op. cit.*, p. 355.

[6] Thomas-Stanford, *op. cit.*, p. 11.

consist of but one or two rooms. In one instance a family of seven lives in a single room, the entire furniture consisting of an old mattress in one corner. . . . The cooking is done over three stones. . . . In many houses such a thing as a bed is unknown, but in houses that can afford it the articles are far more numerous (and ugly) than, for instance, in Spain, and in the kitchen an infinite variety of pots and pans fills up the room to the exclusion of cleanliness. . . . Their state has not changed much since the sixteenth century . . . . Overcrowding in unhealthy quarters in the towns and gnawing poverty in the country [1]

is the typical situation.

The same author in another book speaks of the houses in Alemtejo as low and windowless but whitewashed. Of those in Algarve, in extreme southern Portugal, he writes:

Many houses are low and miserable but scrupulously whitewashed sheds of only two rooms, one containing a table, a bed, a few graceful one-handled bilhas and small chairs set all around the walls; the other a shed for the donkey which . . . . is almost considered one of the family. Children, naked and baked by the sun sprawl in the doorway.[2]

Miss Clare, describing what is apparently northern Portugal, pictures peasant life in similar terms:

The house of the ordinary peasant is bare to destitution, his windows are unglazed and he and his family eat squatting on the clay floor of what is little better than a hovel, gathered round a central bowl into which each dips his or her spoon without further ceremony. . . . The wretched hamlets that lie along the crest of the green-fluffed ridge are not the collection of pigsties and stables for which it would be easy to mistake them, but the abodes of human habitation, swarmed

---

[1] Bell, *op. cit.*, pp. 28-30.
[2] Bell, *In Portugal* (London, 1912), pp. 31 and 61.

over by tribes of Murillo-like children, of gaunt half-famished dogs, of lean and ever-hungry goats. There is lack indeed of common decency.[1]

This wretchedness is, however, not unrelieved by a touch of the aesthetic. " The humblest, most ramshackle cottage will have an old tin of carnations on its window ledge or hanging anyhow from the wall."[2] The same writer, however, maintains that the Portuguese are not truly artistic.

This is shown in a thousand ways, in the curve of a chair, the finish of a bookcase, in their buildings, in the color of their dress and of the wash for their houses, in which squashed hues and especially pink predominate; in the shape of the water-jars, in which the soul of a Latin people is often expressed.[3]

It must be admitted, however, that testimony is not unanimous on this last point, and that what is ugliness to one observer may be beauty to another.

The food of these peasants is likewise simple. In Estremadura it consists mostly of potatoes, cabbage and other vegetables, bread of maize or rye, ham, wine and brandy. All dip out of the same pot of sausage or the fat of ham. In the hotter weather they eat salads of oil and pimento, lettuce, garlic and olives.[4]

Poverty is also indicated by the extent to which women are constantly engaged in severe labor. They work regularly in the fields and even in the quarries, and they row heavy barges.[5] They work much harder, it is said, than the men.

[1] Clare, "Another Letter from a Portuguese Country House," in *The Living Age*, vol. cclxii, p. 417.

[2] Bell, *Portugal of the Portuguese*, p. 16.

[3] *Ibid.*, p. 21.

[4] Bell, *In Portugal*, p. 69.

[5] *Ibid.*, p. 13.

The position of women in Portugal is another instance of vague ideals. Woman is set on a pedestal, but women are not always treated with consideration, and in some parts of the country are little better than slaves. Over and over again you will meet a man and a woman, husband and wife perhaps, the man in lordly fashion carrying a small parcel or nothing at all, the woman bowing under a huge load. . . . The peasant women continue to do twice the work of men, and to receive half the wages.[1]

Home life in the Azores presents few contrasts to that described above, according to the reports of visitors to the islands. Thus Miss Baker describes a peasant's hut in the interior of Fayal in the eighties as follows:

The interiors are bare and poor: one room; rafters visible above; a floor of earth; woven work of willow boughs sometimes partitioning off one end of the room as a bedroom; a loft above it reached by a ladder and on the floor a pallet of straw. There is neither chimney nor stove. The fireplace is without crane or andirons, and is merely a broad stone shelf built out from the wall, and on this a fire of furze and faggots. For cooking utensils there are an iron pot and trivets, and one or two red pottery jars and saucers.[2]

The same author pictures the interior of a peasant's hut in San Miguel. It was of:

one room with floor of earth strewn with rushes or pine needles. Its furniture—two beds touching foot to foot, and occupying one end of the room; two Eastlake chairs, . . . a deep stone window seat under the high window; a niche in the opposite wall usually containing a bambino; and a table. The beds are made up high with ticks of homespun linen, filled with husks, moss or a soft silky fibre . . . ; a hard

[1] Bell, *Portugal of the Portuguese, op. cit.*, pp. 7-8.
[2] Baker, *A Summer in the Azores* (Boston, 1882), pp. 58-9.

round bolster and no pillows. When the family is too numerous to stow away in two beds, others are made up under them and trundled out at night. A loft is also made in the peak of the roof for the big boys.[1]

An apparently lower standard of living is described on the same island:

Halfclad women with folded arms, idle and inane but for the look of stolid despair on their otherwise expressionless faces, crouched on the floor of their squalid huts which they shared with the hens and pigeons. Naked babies crawled about the floors, and an army of brutal and savage children ran clamoring after us for alms.[2]

The above descriptions are the most intimate that have come to our notice and were written in the eighties before the Azores had experienced the influence of the returning emigrant to any great extent. Still earlier observers report conditions, if anything, still more primitive. Captain Boyd in the thirties speaks of the exterior of the houses as attractive, but of the interiors as uncomfortable and uncleanly beyond description. The habitual filth resulted in the prevalence of cutaneous diseases.[3] In the fifties Weston reports a peasantry living in miserable houses made of the rudest-shaped stones, with roof thatched with straw and leaves covered with mud, having neither windows, floors nor furniture; and with pigs, hens and people sharing the same room.[4] Henriques writing in 1867 says that the peasants lived in stone houses with no wooden floors, tile or straw roofs, no chimneys and few glass windows.[5]

[1] *Ibid.*, p. 110.
[2] *Ibid.*, p. 96.
[3] Boyd, *op. cit.*, pp. 60 and 214.
[4] Weston, *A Visit to a Volcano* (Providence, 1856), p. 21.
[5] Henriques, *A Trip to the Azores* (Boston, 1867), p. 37.

Conditions have probably changed somewhat for the better more recently. Emigrants returning in large numbers have brought with them somewhat higher standards together with their savings. The Republican government has perhaps had a good influence. But the change comes slowly so far as we can judge from the unsatisfactory evidence at hand. Thus Callender in 1911 still records one-story stone huts without flooring other than the bare earth and without chimneys. His description of the preparation of the family meal is not different from that of earlier observers: " When the Azorean peasant is hungry and needs a stew, he gathers a few faggots, places them on the ground, sets on the kettle or stew-pan, lights the fire; then when the dish is cooked the doors and windows are opened and the smoke allowed to escape." [1]

Similarly Sandham writing only seven years ago tells of animals living in the same house with the peasants of St. Michael's although they have stalls in the garden: " The morning light is sure to discover all the animals nestling in and about his bed, from the huge black pig and the tiny donkey, down to cats, dogs, sheep and calves, half-starved hens, clean fat rats, and cosmopolitan fleas." [2]

The average diet in the Azores is of the simplest, consisting principally of stew, fish, corn-bread, cabbage and potatoes, all of which, according to some writers, are insufficient in amount and kind.[3] Ashe, in an early book, describes a visit to " the best informed islander I ever met " and reports her as glad to be invited to use her fingers in place of knife and fork.[4] In the eighties, at least, meat

[1] Callender, *op. cit.*, in *Travel Magazine*, vol. xviii, p. 50.

[2] Sandham, *op. cit.*, in *The Century Magazine*, vol. xci, p. 224, Dec., 1915.

[3] P. T. L., *op. cit.*, p. 355.

[4] Ashe, *op. cit.*, p. 258.

was a rare item on Portuguese menus, and Miss Baker reported coarse corn bread with a bit of cheese, fish or peppers and a cup of cold water as their principal foods. In another place she adds: " Their food is corn bread and a drink of spring water, with now and then a few bitter beans and a bit of dry fish as luxuries." [1] Mrs. Roundell speaks of meat as a Christmas luxury.[2]

In Madeira likewise, Miss Taylor reported in the eighties that the peasants ate meat rarely and lived on vegetables, maize meal boiled like porridge, yams, Spanish chestnuts and brown bread, while near the coast much fish was used.[3]

We undoubtedly need more recent and satisfactory evidence on this matter of diet, but if there has been as little change in this direction as in other respects we can think of the Azorean peasant as still living on the simplest of fare. Observations of his fellows in the United States tend to confirm this idea.

In the islands as on the Continent the peasant woman is a hard-working drudge. In the thirties Captain Boyd described the women of Pico as " positive slaves " who, by hard labor, soon became decrepit and infirm.[4] If they are not slaves to-day there can be no doubt that they do their share of the hard labor in the fields and that they are bearers of the heavy burdens. Many observers, however, attribute the erect carriage of these peasant women to their habit of carrying water-jars and other burdens on their heads.

Imperfect as are the above pictures and unsatisfactory as are our sources for scientific purposes, it is apparent that the Portuguese peasant on the Continent or in the Islands is habitually poverty-stricken except, perhaps, when return-

---

[1] Baker, op. cit., pp. 59 and 111.

[2] Roundell, op. cit., p. 170.

[3] Taylor, op. cit., p. 61.

[4] Boyd, op. cit., p. 305.

ing emigrants bring greater prosperity with them. Fortunately his home life is not utterly devoid of the picturesque as seen in beautiful flowers outdoors, bright colored dresses, gay festivals, or exquisite embroidery. It is in these picturesque aspects of life rather than in material welfare that the Portuguese peasant is the loser when he emigrates to "the land of plenty." It is not to be wondered at if he brings with him much of the squalor and untidiness of some of the homes abroad.

Religion, Superstition and Recreation

It may seem incongruous to discuss these three topics together but with the Portuguese they are closely related.

Bell describes the Portuguese of the Continent as often intensely religious but not priest-ridden.[1] In his later book he says:

Portugal has been fortunate in possessing an enlightened clergy. Many priests were liberal in politics, and only a few of them in some remote parts of the country were fanatics. The mass of the people is equally unfanatic. But only a section of the population of a single city—Lisbon—is non-Catholic. Indeed, according to one calculation, there are only six thousand non-Catholics in Portugal, or one in every thousand inhabitants. To the mass of the people religion is a pleasant show, and a refuge from the grinding reality of their lives; the church ceremonies, the processions and pilgrimages are the notes of holiday and gaiety in the villages. . . . The cry of anti-clericalism in Portugal . . . . is not in any sense national, but has been imported bodily from abroad. . . . In the public schools religion has been forbidden by law, in the private it has only been given at the expense of denunciation and persecution. When it is remembered that in many parishes the priests have been de-

[1] Bell, *In Portugal*, p. 8.

prived of all authority, it will be seen how little chance there is of the children receiving any religious instruction. . . . In Portugal many children are being brought up to regard material prosperity as the only good.[1]

But if the people are naturally religious their religious beliefs seem to be vague:

Many prefer an undefined Pantheism and mystic love of Nature or Humanity to dogmatic beliefs. The ostentatious art of Roman Catholic ceremonies and the exact precision of Protestant services are both in a sense congenial to them, the former appealing to their fondness for pomp and show, the latter to their quiet thoughtfulness. But neither the one nor the other affects them with sufficient force to fasten upon their minds a fanaticism which is foreign to dreamy and comfortable natures. . . . Perhaps [Protestantism] is too clear and reasonable for them.[2]

Perhaps this very vagueness of religious beliefs and influence permits the perpetuation of popular superstition and folk-lore. At any rate we find no lack of such elements in the lives of these simple people. Crawfurd tells us that the Portuguese ballads, myths and folk-lore are partly Moorish, partly Latin and partly, (apparently) more strictly Portuguese or native in their origin. He finds the fishermen still believing in sirens and the peasants dreaming of enchanted maids in their springs, and putting faith in many tales of giants, gnomes, warlocks, sorceresses and spirits; while they attribute their ills largely to Brux or omnipresent spirits of the air.[3]

The intermingling of religion and superstition is seen more clearly in the lucky days. Miss Clare tells how the

[1] Bell, *Portugal of the Portuguese*, pp. 64-65.

[2] *Ibid.*, pp. 9-10.

[3] Crawfurd, *Portugal*, pp. 528-9.

Portuguese cut flowers on Ascension Day to ensure prosperity.[1] She confirms Bell's opinion, however, that priestly intervention plays a lesser part among the Portuguese than among the Spaniards.

. . . . Portuguese literature is full of superstitions and in few countries can there be more legends and charms and incantations, ignorance thus fostering an immense popular literature in prose and verse. The varieties of sorcerers and diviners are many: there are *benzedores* and *imaginarios, magicos* and *agoureiros, bruxas* and *feiticeiras* et cetera.[2]

The connection between religion and recreation consists in the fact that religious *festas* and pilgrimages are perhaps the chief form of popular amusement in Portugal, or at least they have a recreative as well as a religious aspect. Says Bell:

The villages themselves, their streets and houses are often miserable enough, but they are enlivened by a large number of *festas* through the year. The pilgrimage or *romaria* is usually to some shrine in the hills or by the sea, and combines the character of a profane picnic with a religious motive. The most famous shrine is that of *Bom Jesus* near Braga, but every village has its small church or hermitage to go to which a yearly procession is organized. In some parts of the country the year begins with the *janeiras,* when groups go from house to house with songs special to the occasion, after the fashion of waits in England. . . . It ends, of course, with the festivities of Christmas, which in Portugal, where the ties of family life are strong, is observed with a peculiar devotion, and all the rites of the yule log and other ancient customs, as the *consoada* or odd meal to pass the time while waiting for the midnight mass called *a missa do gallo.* . . .

[1] Clare, "Another Letter from a Portuguese Country House," *op. cit.,* p. 419.

[2] Bell, *Portugal of the Portuguese, op. cit.,* p. 15.

Between the Day of Kings and Christmas comes a long series of feast days and pleasant customs. . . . But above all June is the month of rustic merriment, with the fêtes of St. Anthony, St. John the Baptist, and St. Peter.[1]

St. John is the greatest of the Saints and his day is celebrated in a manner in keeping with his importance.   No one reading an account of these *festas* and *romarias* can fail to note the intermingling of piety and festivity which they illustrate.

St. John's Day has also superstitions which are peculiar to it.

Its hours between midnight and dawn are among the most precious of all the year, and no witch who has the least inkling of her business will waste a single instant of them. The dews (orvalhadas) then gathered have a special virtue, as also rosemary and other herbs and water brought from the mountains and streams.   By the fountains appear enchanted Moorish maidens combing their hair with combs of gold, and many other spirits are abroad.   It is the night, too, of the great blue thistles or Jerusalem artichokes (alcachofras) and other auguries of love.   Next morning on St. John's Day, the sun dances at its rising, et cetera.[2]

These religious festivals and processions are far " more popular than the bull fight about which in Portugal there seems to be something a little artificial."   Indeed these bullfights cost too much for the peasants.   Miss Clare tells us that the pre-war prices for the worst seats were 2 1/2d. each. She found each village with a barn-like theatre, however, with either seats free to members or a charge of 4 1/4d. or 5 1/4d. which again excluded peasants.[3]

In the islands we find a similar relationship between re-

[1] Bell, *Portugal of the Portuguese*, pp. 50-51.

[2] *Ibid.*, p. 54.

[3] Clare, "Letters from a Portuguese Country House," pp. 418-9.

ligion, superstition and recreation. According to the testimony of Portuguese priests in America the island population is more religious than that of the mainland. This difference may be a recent development, however, associated with the revolution which was as much religious as political and which had a more profound effect in Continental Portugal than in the Azores. Webster, writing a century ago, describes medieval religious customs in the Azores, with processions of penitent friars beating themselves, with even the poor eager to put their children into the convents, with penance done by means of prayer, fasting and walking barefoot all over the island, and with indulgences sold in the shops.[1]

If this is no longer a true picture of life to-day, nevertheless religion forms a very large part of the lives of the islanders. Koebel says of Madeira: " The Madeira peasant is essentially a churchman. His average intelligence not being of a high order, it is to be doubted whether his devotion partakes of much real understanding." [2] Mrs. Thomas-Stanford found a strong pagan survival in the creed of the common people of Madeira but she did not regret the influence of the church upon the otherwise humdrum lives of the people. The church, she says, " with her happy use of dramatic and picturesque art in services and processions " does " much to infuse some interest and variety into " them.[3] The peasant prays to different saints according as he conceives them to be peculiarly able to satisfy specific desires. The peasant also vows to perform unpleasant tasks such as carrying a bar of iron a distance or, in the case of women, shuffling over sharp stones barefooted.

[1] Webster, *Description of the Island of St. Michael* (Boston, 1821), pp. 55-58 and 83-84.
[2] Koebel, *Madeira Old and New* (London, 1909), p. 145.
[3] Thomas-Stanford, *op. cit.*, p. 31.

Here the church is "still [1909] whispering from her towers the last enchantments of the Middle Ages." [1]

The present writer has not seen similar accounts of penance in the Azores in the writings of recent observers. The processions, however, still form an important part of the religious and recreational life of the people. In Ponta Delgada the Procession of Santo Christo is one of the most important, when, on the fifth Sunday after Easter, the Image is taken from the convent and carried in procession through the streets while a crowd of fifteen thousand people participate or look on. To-day with the large number of returned emigrants from the United States in the island, this celebration is said to be the occasion for the production of the American flag in a pyrotechnic display in the Park of San Francisco. This and other processions form the chief amusements of the populace here as in Portugal proper. The peasants come from the rural districts far and wide and en route to the city they play their violas, sing and dance. At specified places also, they have sham battles with wax balls filled with water. [2] As Mrs. Thomas-Stanford says of Madeira, " the holyday and holiday are still one." [3]

The statement that these *festas* are the sole amusement of the people is, of course, not quite literally true. Koebel adds to the carnival: kite-flying in infancy, courtship, guitar-playing and the explosion of fireworks, gossip and, to-day, the moving picture, to complete the list of popular diversions. In Terceira, at least, a modified form of bull-fighting also is in vogue. [4]

In the Islands, as on the mainland, superstitions abound. In Madeira " The state of fear in which the lower classes

[1] *Ibid.*, p. 32.

[2] Haeberle, *op. cit.*, pp. 527-8, June, 1919.

[3] Thomas-Stanford, *op. cit.*, p. 233.

[4] Haeberle, *op. cit.*, p. 539.

here, though they are by nature of a cheerful temperament, pass their lives is inconceivable to the educated northerner." They live in fear of the powers of darkness, of the authorities and of each other. Witches abound who go to the hills to meet the devil. To avoid their influence one opens a pair of scissors in the form of a cross. Charms are worn to ward off the evil eye. A sprig of rosemary laid on the pigstye will protect that important animal.[1] To find a hairball in the stomach of an animal is a stroke of particularly good fortune. One need only bake bread, put the ball into it, and hide the loaf under an altar, to have one's fondest wish gratified. If your hair falls out, cut off a lock on St. John's night and bury it under a quick-growing plant such as a pumpkin and throw it to a pig but do not eat the pig. On important matters it is always well to consult the wise woman or the wizard.[2] It is no wonder, indeed, that physicians both in Madeira and in the United States find it difficult sometimes to win these people to the use of modern medicine.

Both on the Continent and in the Islands, then, we find the Portuguese devout, superstitious and fond of the pleasures of the *festa* and the procession. They are probably more dependent upon the church for their pleasures and for encouragement in the Islands than on the mainland, and recent political changes have, to a slight degree, perhaps, weakened this dependence. It is unfortunate that our evidence of superstitious beliefs and practices comes so largely from Madeira, but their prevalence among the immigrants from San Miguel in Fall River, indicates that they exist in no little degree in that island. It is unfortunate, also, that we cannot compare this trait among the people of Fayal with the superstitions of San Miguel.

[1] Thomas-Stanford, *op. cit.*, pp. 126-8.
[2] *Ibid.*, pp. 129-30.

Educational Status and Illiteracy

The curse of Portugal is popular ignorance, and the simplest, though not the most satisfactory measure of ignorance, is adult illiteracy. The general situation in Continental Portugal is described by Miss Clare as follows: "The majority of laboring men only acquire the rudiments of education during their terms of compulsory military service; while . . . . by far the greater number of women go through life unable to sign their own names or read that of another." Therefore we find no newspapers among the peasants.[1] A traveller is made aware of this situation by noting that the clothing shops have picture signs to accommodate their illiterate customers.[2] The same situation is brought out in the following table, which gives the latest available information:

TABLE 8

PORTUGAL: PER CENT ILLITERATE OF POPULATION OVER SEVEN YEARS OLD [3]

	Total	Men	Women
1911	69.7	60.8	77.4
1900	74.1	65.0	82.1
1890	76.0	67.6	83.5

Thus in 1911 roughly three out of five adult men and three out of four adult women were illiterate, which was an improvement of only six or seven points over the figures for twenty-one years previous. In 1911 the per cents of illiteracy for the total population including children were: men 68.4 per cent, women 81.2 per cent, total 75.1 per cent. The same fact is brought out in Table 9 even more strikingly for here illiteracy is defined as inability to sign one's name to the marriage papers.

[1] Clare, "Another Letter from a Portuguese Country House," *op. cit.*, p. 418.

[2] Peixotto, *op. cit.*, p. 628.

[3] Portugal, *Censo da População*, 1911, vol. i, p. xxii (Lisbon, 1915).

TABLE 9

PERCENTAGE OF MEN AND WOMEN APPLYING FOR MARRIAGE LICENSES
WHO SIGNED THE MARRIAGE PAPERS—1917 [1]

		Per cent Signing	
District	Number of Marriages	Men	Women
Portugal	34,210	53.68	34.58
Continent	31,606	54.89	33.71
Islands	2,604	38.90	45.12
Ponta Delgada	894	36.13	49.55
Funchal	1,063	33.30	28.98
Angra	403	43.42	57.57
Horta	244	66.98	78.69

The somewhat better showing evident in this last table
is perhaps in part due to improvement between 1911 and
1917; but it also is probably due to the simpler definition of
illiteracy which it implies. In table 9, of course, the percentages given are those for the literate. The literacy of
emigrants as compared with that of the general population
is discussed later.[2]   Our present interest in the above table
is in the high degree of illiteracy it reveals and in the differences between the several political divisions. Continental men are more literate than the islanders, nearly sixteen
percent more of men seeking matrimony there in 1917, sign-
ing the papers.   Curiously enough, however, the situation
is the reverse, with respect to women, the island women
being more literate than those of the Continent in every
division except that of Funchal.   Except in Funchal, again,
island women who marry appear to be more literate
than men.   On the mainland they are considerably less
so.   Finally, we note as in other tables, the relatively high
standing of the district of Horta where practically twice as

[1] República Portuguesa, Ministério das Finanças, Direcçâo Geral de
Estatistica, Repartiçâo Central, Estatistica Demográfica, Movemento da
Populaçâo, 1917, table 1, p. 7.

[2] Cf. infra, p. 114.

large a proportion of women marrying were literate as on the mainland.

If we had more recent figures we should probably find some improvement as a result of the efforts of the Republican government. Yet it is not certain that the change would be great, for authorities differ somewhat in the importance they attach to the plans and accomplishment of the new régime. Young, speaking of conditions in 1916, is optimistic and finds " a national desire for literacy." He notes the decline in illiteracy shown by recent figures, calls attention to the increased educational budget and emphasizes the ambulatory and night schools established. As against 5500 primary schools in 1910 he finds 7000 in 1914, with 125 ambulatory schools and 160 night classes. He also stresses the fact that grants to secondary schools, museums, libraries and art schools have been increased " with excellent results." [1]

Bell, however, writing two years earlier is more cautious in his acceptance of figures and less optimistic as to the immediate future.

The Republic, [he says] was ushered in with pompous phrases concerning education. In a few years there were to be no more illiterates, in a few years there was to be a school for every two kilomètres throughout the country. But there has been danger of more attention being given to the show than to the substance of reform, and of education becoming more and more a whited sepulchre. Yet . . . . one must admit that the Republicans realize the importance of education and have a sincere desire to diminish the number of illiterates (as though that in itself were a great gain). The institution of night schools and of itinerate masters is no doubt a step in the right direction. . . . The decree of 29th March, 1911, reforming primary education is little more [than a piece of

[1] Young, *op. cit.*, p. 303.

paper]. Primary education was transferred from the control of the State to that of the local authorities, which tend to neglect it altogether.[1]

So-called compulsory education has existed in Portugal since 1878, and to fix on a room or a house in a village which might be used for educational purposes is often sufficient to add one more to the schools enumerated, but it does not of itself educate the peasants. " There the matter generally ends. Neither books nor furniture nor masters are provided, and that not from any carelessness or indifference, but because there is no money to pay for them." [2] The existing schools were poor enough and it would have been better to improve them. " They were for the most part in hired unhealthy buildings, and the ill-paid or unpaid schoolmasters taught as badly as they were paid."

As we are not so much interested in very recent changes but rather in conditions which surrounded those who later went to New England, our chief concern is to note that facilities for securing education were far from adequate in the Portugal which they knew. So far as we have evidence they were no better if as good in the Azores. The figures for illiteracy seem to indicate that they were worse.

It is important for us to note, however, that there was apparently little popular demand for education in Portugal at that time. To say this is not to say that such a demand could not have been stimulated under different conditions. But it did not exist even though Young may be correct in saying that it does exist to-day. Bell tells us:

There is indeed little inducement for the peasants to send their children to school, and considerable inducement to keep them at home where they can be useful in the fields. In a

[1] Bell, *Portugal of the Portuguese, op. cit.*, p. 68.
[2] *Ibid.*, p. 69.

land of few industries where a large majority of the inhabitants live by agriculture and fishing, there is but little need of book-learning, nor is there any universal book to be found in the peasants' houses as the Bible in England. . . . If illiterates are disfranchized they look upon that rather as a blessing than as a penalty. . . . Some of the children are quite keen to learn, and after being kept at work all day willingly attend night classes; but there is many a family in which the parents not only do not encourage the children to write and read, but deliberately forbid it, considering that the drawbacks of education exceed its advantages.[1]

If we may trust Mr. Bell's account then, the Portuguese do not learn, and there is some evidence that they do not want to learn. School attendance is not a part of their mores and they have not been taught its advantages. Considering the quality of their schools and the conditions surrounding their lives they may not be so short-sighted as they appear at first thought. It is not surprising, therefore, that we find a total of but 6,947 students in the eight lycées.[2] Nor would one expect a people with such standards, such lack of opportunity, and such a background to rush eagerly into our schools in America.

The fact of ignorance and illiteracy in the Islands is noted by practically all observers. Captain Boyd back in 1834 spoke of the inhabitants as mild dispositioned and quick to perceive, " but in every class so deeply ignorant, and in such a state of mental debasement that their existence is not many degrees elevated above that of unreasonable [sic] animals." [3] Fifty years later Walker reported only 125 elementary schools in the whole archipelago with little progress in thirty years time.[4] At the turn of the century

[1] *Ibid.*, p. 71.
[2] *Ibid.*, p. 72.
[3] Boyd, *op. cit.*, p. 48.
[4] Walker, *op. cit.*, pp. 126-7.

an anonymous writer in the Nation calls illiteracy the greatest handicap of the inhabitants, speaks of school houses as rare features, gives the salary of the lycée professor as 75 francs a month, and tells a story of a schoolmaster who was also a servant and whose salary was 35 francs a year.[1] It is not surprising, therefore, that he found it the exception for the peasant to have a newspaper. In Madeira in 1909 Mrs. Thomas-Stanford speaks of the laboring class as " utterly illiterate and incapable of organization or of expressing its wants or grievances." She found the inhabitants of the northern part of the island as ignorant of the rudiments of education as of the outside world. Many died without even visiting Funchal.[2]

Ignorance is then the curse of the Portuguese before they come to America. Ignorance, we shall find, is likewise their handicap after they arrive.

Other Characteristics

Thus far we have seen that the Portuguese peasant class is poor and often poverty-stricken though living under fairly favorable climatic conditions; that they have a very low standard of living, dwelling in humble cottages which are sometimes uncleanly and usually devoid of the barest necessities, and eating the plainest of food; that they lack knowledge of hygiene and sanitation; that they are usually devout though somewhat less so in parts of the mainland than on the Islands; that their religious ideas are somewhat vague and associated with many superstitions; that their recreation is limited and semi-religious in some of its aspects; and that they are grossly ignorant, illiterate, often lacking in a desire for education, though not unintelligent. We noted also, some evidence of a slight change in this last respect.

[1] P. T. L., *op. cit.*, p. 355.
[2] Thomas-Stanford, *op. cit.*, pp. 212-3.

It remains to list very briefly a number of other characteristics of the Portuguese peasants before following them across the Atlantic.

Bell tells us that if we " take the Irish peasant, add hot sun and spice of the East, and perhaps something of the Negro's vanity ", we have the Portuguese. " The quick intelligence, the dreamy melancholy, the slyness and love of intrigue, the wit and imagination are here, and the power of expression in words." [1] They are a people " hardworking, vigorous and intelligent, increasing fairly rapidly, content with little, not willingly learning to read or write but in [their] own way eagerly patriotic." On the other hand, they love lottery, have a perpetual tendency to exaggerate, a vague good-nature, an absence of discipline, a belief in the efficacy of words and rhetoric. But their chief general characteristic, according to this authority, is vagueness. " They think in generalities and abstractions." " They have no love of bloodshed, but it is a state of mind, rather than a course of action, and can be curiously combined with cruel persecutions in practice." Ideally they place woman on a pedestal, but in practice they grind her with toil. Similarly their love of liberty is an ideal of which they fall far short in practice. The same vagueness pervades their business relations. We have already shown that they are equally vague in their religious tenets and to this vagueness they add a strong element of fatalism. They do not know exact justice for they are too impulsive and vindictive. They are devoted to music, flowers, dance and song. Yet they " are not artistic though they love nature." [2]

Crawfurd reports the Portuguese law-abiding citizens,[3] and Miss Clare tells of the mutual confidence between them

[1] Bell, *Portugal of the Portuguese*, p. 1.
[2] *Ibid.*, chap. i, *passim*.
[3] Crawfurd, *op. cit.*, p. 521.

which leads a peasant to sell his oxen to a stranger on his mere promise to pay.[1] They are reputed to be hospitable, courteous and tolerant. As workmen they are industrious, ignorant and willing.[2] They are reported by different observers both cleanly and dirty, and no doubt differ among themselves in this respect. " The daily bath is not an institution among the Portuguese, but they do wash their clothes."[3]

Though wine drinkers, they are not intemperate either in eating or drinking.[4] Their standards of morality seem to vary. " In the interior the men are upright and self-respecting; the women chaste and faithful." In the mountains a girl who has been led astray has her locks clipped completely short and kept so until marriage.[5]

In their dress the styles vary in different communities, but they show a love of bright colors which are sometimes praised and sometimes ridiculed by observers. Some visitors report the women fond also of heavy gold necklaces which even the very poor wear; while others note a tendency toward cheap adornment. The solid gold ornaments are apparently a characteristic of the north of Portugal. The poor go generally barefoot although in Pico and Fayal either rawhide sandals or wooden shoes are worn. In Madeira, according to one writer, the peasants habitually walk barefoot, but carry boots for use in church, often making one pair go for several members of the same family.[6] Callender

---

[1] Clare, "A Letter from a Portuguese Country House," *op. cit.*, p. 595.

[2] Bell, *In Portugal*, pp. 6 and 24.

[3] " Portuguese Vignettes," in *The Living Age*, vol. cclxvi, p. 349.

[4] *Cf.* Clare, "A Letter from a Portuguese Country House," p. 418.

[5] *Ibid.*, p. 418.

[6] Ramsey, "Levada Walking in Madeira," in *The Living Age*, vol. cccvii, p. 661.

declares that the social classes are marked out by the type of footgear : the poorest class going barefoot, the next wearing wooden shoes, and the higher class assuming sandals.[1] For the rest, the style of dress is variable, and except for the universal kerchief worn by women is changed on emigrating.

A single characteristic of the Azoreans must complete this list. They show little regard for family names. Children may take the name of either parent, and the mother of a family will use her maiden name or that of her husband indiscriminately. Nicknames are very common and result from some trivial incident. Once applied, however, the nickname may quite replace the family name of the recipient. One writer even reports that in the post-office in one of the islands mail is sorted not by family names but by given names, a pile of Antonios here and one of Michaels there. This custom of frequent changes of name is most confusing to the student who tries to follow a single family, as the writer's experience demonstrates.

Many of the above-mentioned characteristics of the Portuguese are highly desirable traits; others are less commendable. Perhaps the Portuguese may be characterized as an industrious, simple-minded, ignorant people of kindly but somewhat melancholy disposition.

Such are the Portuguese of the homeland. How does emigration to New England affect them, and how do they influence the social life of the American communities to which they flock?

[1] Callender, *op. cit.*, p. 25.

CHAPTER IV

IMMIGRATION AND DISTRIBUTION IN THE UNITED STATES

No student of history need be reminded that the Portuguese are a migrating people. South America, Asia and Africa have felt the Portuguese influence since the fifteenth century. In South America, at least, the Portuguese influx has been very large and is continuing at the present time. But, except for a few fishermen and seamen, it was not until the middle of the nineteenth century that the Portuguese turned to North America in appreciable numbers. Even in recent years, as the table below shows, only one in four of Portuguese emigrants has been destined for North America, and only one in ten of those from the Continent. In very recent years, however, there has been an increased emigration from the mainland to the United States.

TABLE 10

DESTINATION OF EMIGRANTS FROM PORTUGAL,[1] 1913-1917

Born in	Total Emigrants Number		Destined for North America Number		Per cent
Continent		133,252		14,002	10.5
Islands		29,811		26,499	88.9
Ponta Del.	13,234		12,764	96.4	
Funchal	8,492		6,210	73.1	
Angra	5,199		4,709	90.6	
Horta	2,886		2,816	97.6	
Ultramarine		348		33	9.5
All Portugal		163,411		40,534	24.8

[1] *Estatistica Demográfica, op. cit.,* pp. 30-55.

On the other hand, during the period covered by this table, at least, nearly nine-tenths of the emigrants from the Islands sought the United States or other North American countries. Indeed the total emigration from the Islands to North America exceeded by more than 12,000 the number coming from all of Continental Portugal. Moreover, since the emigration from the mainland to North America is mostly of recent origin it is probable that the above table exaggerates considerably the usual number and proportion of Portuguese emigrants from Continental Portugal to North America. At any rate during this five year period the majority of Portuguese immigrants to the United States came from the Islands and nearly all the Island emigration went to North America.

In earlier years, also, the Islands undoubtedly sent a much larger proportion of their emigrants to Brazil. Hoffman, writing in 1899, speaks of the majority of Azoreans entering the United States as coming from Fayal, St. George and Flores while most of those to Brazil came from San Miguel, Santa Maria and Terceira.[1] All of these islands are in districts which now, according to our table, send most of their people to the United States. In the vicinity of Fall River today by far the majority of the Portuguese come from San Miguel, in the district of Ponta Delgada. There has therefore been something of a change in the source and direction of Portuguese emigration and our table should be taken as characteristic of the period which it covers only.

The latest official reports of Portuguese emigration which are available are those for 1917. For the eleven year period from 1907-1917 between thirty and forty thousand emigrants were usually recorded as leaving Por-

---

[1] Hoffman, *op. cit.*, p. 328.

tugal each year. In addition, according to Bell, there was a considerable clandestine emigration which escaped record. " It is impossible to keep count of those who cross the frontier into Spain, and many even of those who emigrate by sea succeed in escaping registration." [1] Up to 1914 there had been for many years a steady increase in emigration but following that year there was something of a falling off. 1912 was apparently the banner year for Portuguese emigration when the total number " bordered on 100,000."

The importance to the home country of this population movement is seen in the following table.

TABLE II

PORTUGAL: [2] EMIGRANTS PER THOUSAND POPULATION

	1908-1912	1913-1917
Continent	6.75	4.06
Islands	10.58	14.39
Ponta Delgada	13.19	21.93
Funchal	8.25	9.61
Angra	11.07	15.13
Horta	16.64	11.98
Portugal	7.03	5.30

Thus the loss by emigration was, relatively to total population, 50 per cent greater in the Islands than in Continental Portugal during the five year period 1908-1912, and three and one half times as great from 1913-1917.

We note also that the Island districts, with the exception of Horta, did not share the falling off in emigration which the mainland experienced during the second half of the ten year period. On the contrary, they lost more inhabitants than before. If the United States should experience as

[1] Bell, Portugal of the Portuguese, pp. 26-7.
[2] Estatistica Demográfica, op. cit., pp. 30-55.

great a drain of population relatively as did the district of Ponta Delgada from 1913-1917, she would lose more than two million people annually. It is unfortunate that we do not have more recent data on Portuguese emigration, to show the effect of post-war conditions and of American immigration legislation. More recent figures on Portuguese immigration into the United States, which is our chief interest, are presented later in this chapter.

Causes of Portuguese Emigration

Most of the causes of this loss of population were mentioned in the last chapter. Young summarizes the chief repellent forces in Portugal as follows:

The pressure of direct taxation disproportionately heavy on the peasant, the rise in prices due to the highest tariff in Europe and an inconvertible paper currency, the absence of capital for land development and the want of alternative employment in industry, has been driving abroad not only the surplus population, but even the necessary race stock. The close relationship between the increase of emigration and the increase both of food prices and of the inconvertible currency, can be traced with considerable precision." [1]

The fact that one great cause of Portuguese emigration is economic distress does not necessarily mean that Portugal is losing her very lowest economic class. In most population movements of modern times, while it is the laboring class which emigrate, it is at first the more energetic among that class who leave home. Later this selective effect of emigration is weakened because of assistance given by relatives and others to the weaker members of the community to enable them to emigrate. Moreover, after

[1] Young, *op. cit.*, p. 315.

many have gone before it is less and less of an adventure to follow. Nevertheless, it is seldom the very lowest grade laborers and their families who emigrate. It is probably not the very lowest of the Portuguese who leave home, even to-day.

At least up to the period of the Great War it was the more progressive districts of Northern Portugal which sent emigrants to South America.

The strength of Portugal in one respect and its weakness in another lies in the population being still mainly agricultural, and emigration is necessarily mainly from the northern provinces where the peasantry is the most prolific, the most progressive, and the most prosperous. The rate of emigration is the highest from the less fertile inland fringe of these provinces, and least from the center and south, and it began to take on disquieting proportions coincidently with the financial collapse in the early nineties.[1]

Mainland emigration to the United States, however, is said to have been more largely from the less progressive southern provinces.

Overpopulation, mentioned in the above quotation, has been a factor in emigration from the Islands as well as from the mainland. In Madeira, at least, it appeared as early as the seventeenth century, and Koebel says that people were sometimes transported to Brazil by royal order.[2] But apparently it was not overpopulation *per se* which caused the voluntary movements of population, but overpopulation when associated with a relative economic well-being and energy slightly higher than that of the most degraded class. Portugal is also overpopulated in the sense that, though

---

[1] Young, *op. cit.*, p. 315.

[2] Koebel, *Madeira*, *op. cit.*, p. 23. *Cf.* also Thomas-Stanford, *op. cit.*, p. 10.

an agricultural country, she does not raise sufficient food to support her population. This shortage of food would not in itself be a cause of emigration, if Portugal produced enough other commodities to exchange for food imports, but she does not. Says Young: " Taking the latest information we find that the deficit in the native supply of cereals is about one-third of the total consumption, and that in the supply of wheat the deficit is even more serious, averaging about one-half the consumption." The country does not manufacture enough to export a surplus to pay for imported grain and so it is compelled to export its laborers themselves.[1] That is to say, Portugal being relatively unproductive finds herself with a poverty-stricken population. The more progressive of the poorer class therefore emigrate to lands with a higher productivity—lands which pay higher wages or whose farms are more productive under the kind of cultivation they can give. Many of these emigrants being able to produce a surplus abroad, send it in the form of money (bills of exchange) back to Portugal. These money transactions create a demand in New York or elsewhere for bills of exchange to send to Lisbon or Ponta Delgada or other points in Portugal. These bills of exchange, in turn, are used by Portuguese importers to pay their foreign debts—that is, to pay for the excess of imports of food et cetera over exports. The money sent home by emigrants is the equivalent of the money needed to pay for these excess imports when sold at retail to consumers. This is what Young means when he says that Portugal " is dependent upon foreign supplies for its food, and pays for this by exporting its own national labour, and by exploiting the labour of its imperial possessions." [2]

[1] Young, *op. cit.*, p. 314.
[2] *Ibid.*, p. 313.

The expellent forces back of Portuguese emigration seem to be primarily economic. They are not entirely such, however. Portuguese men have emigrated to avoid military service as well.[1] Low as is the economic status of the Portuguese peasant he has not looked upon three years of service at eight cents a day less the price of his uniform, as an attractive substitute for toil. He has therefore sought to evade the laws and escape service by emigration. At one time the government required a deposit of forty pounds from each emigrant to be used to pay a substitute should he not return for military duty.[2] It has been such requirements as this which have led to the considerable amount of clandestine emigration.

In addition to these expellent forces, there are, of course, the attractive forces in America. It is not because incomes in Portugal or the Islands are low, but because they are relatively low as compared with incomes in America, that the Portuguese leave home. We have elsewhere estimated the approximate economic gain which an unskilled Portuguese emigrant to the United States could expect.[3] In not a few cases this hoped-for gain has no doubt proven illusory. Unemployment, unexpectedly high costs of living, exploitation at the hands of native Americans or of fellow countrymen, or other misfortunes have frequently cheated the emigrant of expected gains. But there can be little doubt that for the great mass of emigrants to the United States, at least, there has been a genuine gain in real income. The continuance of emigration itself argues for this conclusion. A comparison between living conditions in the homeland and in New England supports it, while increased savings, improved standards with longer resi-

---

[1] Henriques, *op. cit.*, p. 103.

[2] Walker, *op. cit.*, p. 107; Roundell, *op. cit.*, p. 50.

[3] *Cf. supra*, p. 61.

dence in the United States, and the success of many who return home puts it almost beyond question.[1] To avoid possible misunderstanding it must be added, however, that by improved economic rewards is not meant necessarily just rewards. The Portuguese may be receiving more or less than they earn in the United States. The present study is not concerned primarily with that difficult question.

The forces attracting the Portuguese to the United States seem to the present writer to be chiefly economic. The glamor of America no doubt attracts somewhat; but the non-economic advantages of America do not seem to loom large in the minds of the Portuguese. They do not seek religious freedom, political liberty or educational opportunity.[2] Eventually, if they are successful, America offers them a much more complex environment and wider experience but these can hardly appear as important parts of the immediate prospect held out to the Portuguese peasant. Moreover, it is debatable whether they are not the losers by the change in certain respects. The immigrant quarter of a mill city is less picturesque than the rural surroundings of a hamlet in San Miguel, and the village gatherings and religious *festas* either are not held or are less frequent and less intimate. The Portuguese are not immediately "at home" in the United States. At any rate not a few elect to spend their old age in the old country.

No doubt there is something of the lure of the city for some of them, but it seems to be a relatively weak force. More important to-day are such seemingly minor factors as letters from America and the influence of the returned emigrant which is a composite of economic and other factors. It has become almost a habit, in the Azores, to emigrate to the United States. "Almost all of the inhabi-

---

[1] *Cf. supra*, pp. 65-72 and *infra*, pp. 275-282.

[2] *Cf.* the discussion of these matters in chapter vi, pp. 306 ff.

tants of some of the islands have been in the United States ", says Haeberle.[1] The Portuguese emigrate, then, partly because it is the style to do so.

The emigration of the Portuguese is thus essentially an economic phenomenon, but is stimulated also by non-economic causes. The Portuguese seek the United States because they can earn more here and perhaps satisfy their ambition to own land either in America or in the Islands. Though as mill hands or small farmers in this country they may remain poor, they are *relatively* well-to-do. Economic inefficiency, overpopulation and mistaken politico-economic governmental policies at home drive them from behind, and opportunity for industrial employment or more independent farming beckon them from abroad. In addition, they may be experiencing to some slight extent the same lure to the city which our own farm population feels, only as there is practically no industrial opportunity at home, their city is located abroad. It must be admitted, nevertheless, that a fair minority seek rural life in America, that many of the cotton mills are located in small villages, and that some leave the city to take up farm land after reaching the United States. In addition to the economic factors the desire to avoid military service and the love of a change in line with the fashion of the day, influence the peasant of the Islands. Whether his choice is ultimately wise from his own point of view, or beneficial to his adopted land, we can judge somewhat better after we have examined his life in New England.[2]

[1] Haeberle, *op. cit.*, p. 521.

[2] Much of this analysis of causes of emigration is confessedly based upon à priori reasoning. To get at the real motives of the emigrants some such method as that used by Thomas in " The Polish Peasant in Europe and America," where correspondence is studied, would be necessary.

History of Portuguese Immigration Into the United States

Turning from causes to the history of Portuguese immigration to the United States, we find that for the most part the movement has been very recent and has been directed either to California or to New England. Isolated cases of Portuguese settlers are reported as early as the seventeenth century, but it was not until the thirties and forties of the nineteenth century that they began coming in any numbers, and the great rush has been since 1890. Probably the first groups came as sailors aboard the whaling ships which used to land at Fayal and bring back natives as part of their crews, to New Bedford and Cape Cod. In 1765, we are told, restrictions were put on fishing by the Governor of Labrador and in the following year he decreed that any vessels in the Gulf of St. Lawrence coming from the Plantations and found to have any fish but whale aboard should be confiscated. " This action drove the fleet from these seas and they pursued their calling along the edge of the Gulf Stream, Western Islands, Cape de Verdes and Brazil Banks." Commercial intercourse between New Bedford and the Azores began about 1830 and immigration with it.[1] That a number may have come on the whaling ships is evident when we remember the size of the whaling industry in New Bedford. At its height in 1857 the New Bedford fleet numbered 329 ships and employed 10,000 seamen.[2] By 1867 the Portuguese of New Bedford became sufficiently numerous to warrant the sending of a priest to care for them, and two years later they are said to have numbered eight hundred.[3] As late as 1889, however, they

---

[1] Ellis, *History of New Bedford* (Syracuse, 1892), pp. 411 and 578.

[2] U. S. House, 42nd Cong., 2nd Sess., *Miscellaneous Documents*, vol. xiii, pt. 18, " 10th Census of the United States," vol. xviii, pt. 1, 1880 (Washington, 1882-3), p. 256.

[3] Pease, *History of New Bedford* (New Bedford, 1918), p. 295.

are not specially mentioned as cotton mill hands along with
the English, Scotch, Irish and French Canadians, although
they doubtless are included under the caption " a few of other
nationalities."[1] They must have entered the cotton mills
not long after this, for in 1899 Mr. Borden wrote: "The
nationality of the operatives [of New Bedford] has un-
dergone radical changes . . . . Portuguese and French
Canadians predominating."[1] Today there are perhaps 30,-
000 Portuguese or people of Portuguese descent in New
Bedford.

The stream of Portuguese immigration to California may
have begun as early as that to Massachusetts. We know,
at least, that a considerable number of Portuguese partici-
pated in the gold rush of 1849, after which they continued
to come in increasing numbers to take up farming in that
state.[3]

The Portuguese immigration to Fall River, however, has
been much more recent, practically all having come within
the last thirty-five years. Despite their late arrival they
have increased rapidly in numbers until now they are only
less numerous there than in the New Bedford colony, and
make up about a fifth of the population. In Portsmouth,
Rhode Island a well-informed farmer told the writer that
he first saw a Portuguese in 1868 and that they began
coming in that neighborhood as early as 1872. As late as
1885, however, there was but one Portuguese landowner
in Portsmouth. The location of this property is marked
with a cross (x) on our map.

The first contacts of the Azores with America were, as
we have seen, through whaling ships which stopped at the

[1] New Bedford Board of Trade, *New Bedford, Mass., Its History*
(New Bedford, 1889), p. 151.

[3] Borden *et. al., Our County and Its People* (Boston, 1899), p. 414.

[3] *Literary Digest*, vol. lxiii, p. 40.

port of Horta in the island of Fayal. It is natural, therefore, that the early comers to New England and California as well were from that island and others of the more westerly group. The large immigration of recent years to Fall River and vicinity, at least, has been from the more easterly islands of St. Michael's and St. Mary's. We have already noted Hoffman's reference to the particular sources of early Portuguese immigration. "Fifty years ago," says Callender, writing in 1911, "Americans referring to the Azores thought only of Fayal." [1] Mrs. Caswell, writing in the seventies of work among the Portuguese of Boston, is apparently referring to the Fayalese women when she says that a Portuguese woman "abhors dirt and rags. Her home is tidy, however poor." [2] The Portuguese consul of Boston, writing in the same number of the same magazine, pictures the home life of these people in Fayal in different colors from those of our last chapter: "The poorer sort of houses contain but one floor of hard clay, not much unlike our cemented cellar floors. As you pass them you frequently observe through the open doors and windows the neatly made beds, with parti-colored spreads of their own manufacture over them, and which enhance the whiteness of the pillows and turned-down sheets." [3] Is this a bit more evidence that the people of Fayal are a different type of Portuguese from the rest, or must we make wide allowances for the words of a Portuguese official seeking favorable consideration for his people by the philanthropists of Boston, and who has perhaps seen Fayal peasant homes through the open door chiefly? At any rate we have al-

[1] Callender, *op. cit.*, p. 34.

[2] Caswell, "The Portuguese of Boston," in *The North End Mission Magazine*, vol. ii, p. 64, July, 1873.

[3] Henriques, "The Portuguese in Boston," in *The North End Mission Magazine*, vol. ii, p. 74, July, 1873.

ready suggested that the Fayalese may differ somewhat racially from other Portuguese; have found them living somewhat better than others in their homeland; and now possibly, we find evidence that their early homes in Boston were in contrast to some Portuguese homes of to-day. We do find such homes, however, in Fall River and Portsmouth to-day. At any rate it is worth noting that the Fayalese were the early comers to New England. This fact by itself, quite apart from any possible natural difference, would lead one to expect them to be more advanced to-day. To-day, as table 10 shows, nearly half of the Portuguese immigrants from the Islands come from the single district of Ponta Delgada, which means the island of San Miguel for the most part.

Statistics of Immigration to the United States

Table 12 below shows the number and sex of Portuguese immigrants to the United States since 1899, of emigrants since 1908, and the net gain or loss since the latter date. This is as far back as record was made of these facts.

This table shows 9,457 more immigrants recorded as entering the United States than the Portuguese statistics record as leaving Portugal for North America during the period 1913-1917. The difference is presumably accounted for by a difference in the enumeration year (in the United States it is from June 15 to June 15), and by clandestine emigration which escaped record in Portugal.

The total immigration of 143,653 shown by this table for a period of 21 years is an average of a little less than seven thousand per year. The number varies from 1574 in 1919 to 13,566 in 1913. The combined effects of war conditions and of the literacy test are shown in the marked falling off in immigration during the year 1918 and 1919.

TABLE 12

UNITED STATES. IMMIGRATION AND EMIGRATION OF PORTUGUESE [1]

| | *Immigration* | | | *Emigration* | | | *Net Gain or Loss* |
	Male	*Female*	*Total*	*Male*	*Female*	*Total*	*Total*
1899	1101	995	2096				
1900	2386	1855	4241				
1901	2240	1936	4176				
1902	3117	2192	5309				
1903	4999	3434	8433				
1904	3867	2471	6338				
1905	2992	1863	4855				
1906	5096	3833	8729				
1907	5812	3836	9648				
1908	4019	2790	6809	633	265	898	Gain 5911
1909	2886	1720	4606	563	253	816	" 3790
1910	4887	2770	7657	591	315	906	" 6751
1911	4843	2626	7469	927	461	1388	" 6081
1912	5938	3465	9403	1275	472	1747	" 7656
1913	8696	4870	13566	1128	455	1583	" 11983
1914	6260	3387	9647	1397	451	1848	" 7799
1915	2853	1523	4376	1962	564	2526	" 1850
1916	8010	4198	12208	1552	633	2185	" 10023
1917	4878	5316	10194	946	367	1313	" 8881
1918	1349	970	2319	1689	327	2016	" 303
1919	1089	485	1574	3008	517	3525	Loss 1951
Totals	87318	56335	143653	15671	5080	20751	Gain 69077

Emigration has also steadily increased and did not fall
off with war conditions in 1918 and 1919, the latter year
showing the greatest return movement on record. The returning emigration averaged about 1700 a year for the
twelve years on record but with wide variations from a
minimum of 816 in 1909 to a maximum of 3525 in 1919.
The net gain in twelve years was no less than 69,077 or
between five and six thousand a year on the average. In
1919 there was a net loss of 1951. Since this table was
made emigration has continued to exceed immigration

[1] Computed from Reports of the U. S. Commissioner General of
Immigration, 1899-1919. These reports do not give data on emigration
prior to 1908. The totals for "Emigration" and for "Net Gain or Loss"
should not, therefore, be compared with those for "Immigration."

partly because of the literacy test enacted into law in 1917, and partly, since May 19, 1921, because of the Three Per cent Law which restricts the quota of admissable Portuguese to 2520 or three per cent of Portuguese resident in the United States in 1910. For example, in the immigration year 1921-1922, 2,486 were admitted or as near the quota as the immigration could be stopped. It will readily be seen that this quota is far below the normal immigration before the literacy test was put into operation in 1917. Thousands are said to be waiting their turn to come to-day (July 1922). Unless the laws are modified the quota of 2520 bids fair to be the annual immigration from Portugal.

The table also shows that while the Portuguese immigration is more largely male than female the excess of males is not so great as for some other nationalities. About three out of five immigrants have been males, but as more men than women return, the actual disproportion of the sexes is slightly less than this ratio would indicate. Census data on the proportion of the sexes are given elsewhere.[1] In 1917, probably because of the War, more women than men came. The demand for female labor in the cotton mills and even on the farms in part accounts for the fairly high proportion of women among Portuguese immigrants. An approximate equality in the number of the sexes is, of course, a socially desirable situation. The Portuguese have some excess of males but not a great excess.

Table 13 gives estimates of the number of Bravas coming to the United States since 1903. They have been coming much longer than that, however, and the table merely shows the recent situation. It contains those classified as of " African Descent " but coming chiefly from the Cape Verde Islands. These " Bravas " are not treated elsewhere

_____
[1] *Cf. infra*, p. 200.

in this study. They form a distinct type and deserve separate study. They are numerous in the cranberry bogs of Cape Cod and also in New Bedford. They are rare in

TABLE 13

ESTIMATED IMMIGRATION AND EMIGRATION OF "BLACK PORTUGUESE"[1]

	Admitted	Departed
1903	934	
1904	439	
1905	347	
1906	301	
1907	349	
1908	705	243
1909	615	279
1910	778	246
1911	1101	155
1912	1103	268
1913	972	464
1914	1711	290
1915	838	224
1916	653	308
1917	940	168
1918	407	148
1919	329	11
Totals	12522	2804

[1] Compiled from the several Reports of the U. S. Commissioner General of Immigration, 1903-1919. These reports record immigration classified both by "country of last permanent residence" and by "races and peoples." For most of our purposes the latter classification which has only been made since 1899 is preferable. Under this heading the classification "Portuguese" includes only the so-called "white Portuguese" who are the subject of this study, and not the black Portuguese commonly known as "Bravas" because many of them come from the island of Brava in the Cape Verdes. These black Portuguese are classified in the Commissioner's reports as "African (black)." But no attempt is made to distinguish them from the true African Negroes except as their place of last permanent residence is also noted.

The above table may therefore include some true African negroes, but it is the best estimate we have of the number of Bravas who have come recently.

The reports do not give data on emigration prior to 1908. The totals for the two columns are therefore not comparable.

Fall River and there are none in Portsmouth, R. I. This is fortunate for our study as the fact that they are a different type and yet have Portuguese names would seriously com-

TABLE 14

STATE OF INTENDED FUTURE RESIDENCE OF PORTUGUESE IMMIGRANTS [1]

(GROUPS OF LESS THAN 100 OMITTED)

	Mass.	R.I.	Cal.	Hawaii	N.Y.	Conn.	N.J.	Pa.
1899	1405	216	325					
1900	3244	383	372		113			
1901	2968	421	483		108			
1902	3109	535	795		519	260		
1903	5691	1029	1057		475	114		
1904	3920	769	1028		276	109		
1905	2909	467	901		412			
1906	6042	1020	1018		433			
1907	5674	745	1198	1328	513			
1908	3379	534	1104	1115	524			
1909	2897	307	870		381			
1910	4228	614	1386	864	371			
1911	3862	493	1762	548	619			
1912	4967	780	1753	1114	576			
1913	9002	1333	1839	228	905			
1914	6052	960	1562		802			
1915	2173	441	1184		400			
1916	8469	1147	1131		910	109		154
1917	6652	1266	702		936			
1918	1088	257	230		347			
1919	466				576		133	

88197

plicate our work. They are reported as more literate than the white Portuguese in New Bedford, but opinions differ as to the relative worth of the two groups.

Tables 14 and 15 give an idea of the distribution of the Portuguese immigrants who have come since 1899 and who

[1] Computed from the Reports of the U. S. Commissioner General of Immigration, 1899-1919.

have emigrated since 1908. They thus show recent changes in the direction of the Portuguese movement of population in the United States, and should be compared with table 26 below, which shows the Census data on the actual distribution of the population in Census years. In tables 14 and 15 no entries have been made when, in a given year, fewer than one hundred Portuguese entered or departed from a given state.

TABLE 15
STATE OF LAST PERMANENT RESIDENCE OF PORTUGUESE EMIGRANTS [1]
(GROUPS OF LESS THAN 100 OMITTED)

	Mass.	*R. I.*	*Cal.*	*Hawaii*	*N. Y.*	*N. J.*	*Pa.*
1908	558		129		122		
1909	443		100		126		
1910	540				187		
1911	799	116	153		249		
1912	1019	216	183		241		
1913	943	211	158		213		
1914	895	359	186		246		
1915	1495	431	134		357		
1916	1308	181	324		220		
1917	692	141	139		202		
1918	1017	263	166		280		115
1919	1267	579			722	180	222
Totals	10976				3165		

It is interesting to note that in 21 years time 88,000 Portuguese planned to make their homes in Massachusetts. If the figures were complete California would stand second and Rhode Island third. It is curious also that the immigration to Hawaii during this 21 year period was concentrated in six years but was of fair dimensions while it lasted. In no year were as many as 100 Portuguese recorded as returning from Hawaii. On the other hand, nearly 11,000 have returned from Massachusetts during the twelve year

[1] Computed from the Reports of the U. S. Commissioner General of Immigration, 1908-1919.

TABLE 16.

OCCUPATIONS OF PORTUGUESE IMMIGRANTS [1]

	Professional	Skilled	Farmers	Unskilled	Misc.	None	Total
1899	3	76	5	1415	20	577	2096
1900	4	238	1	3139	34	825	4241
1901	9	343	54	2796	14	960	4176
1902	0	332	4	2960	20	1993	5309
1903	7	299	76	5225	157	2669	8433
1904	31	409	31	3571	113	2183	6338
1905	31	257	29	2841	55	1642	4855
1906	29	277	86	5348	75	2914	8729
1907	31	338	22	5358	44	3855	9648
1908	23	358	46	3557	50	2775	6809
1909	24	149	46	2825	34	1528	4606
1910	20	219	39	4805	56	2518	7657
1911	31	356	107	4601	115	2259	7469
1912	42	371	110	5588	91	3201	9403
1913	51	495	135	8606	76	4203	13566
1914	28	427	48	6301	99	2744	9647
1915	36	249	56	2632	80	1323	4376
1916	43	482	73	8331	111	3168	12208
1917	59	536	28	5646	132	3793	10194
1918	42	354	66	924	54	879	2319
1919	49	375	15	556	80	499	1574
Totals	593	6940	1077	87025	1510	46508	143653
Per cent of total occupied	.6	7.1	1.1	89.6	1.6		

period of record, which is about one-fifth of the number which came during the same time. Only a slightly smaller proportion of the Rhode Island Portuguese emigrated during the eight year period 1911-1918; while only about one-eighth as many emigrated from California as entered during this same period. This is probably due to the fact that the Portuguese of California have many of them been there a considerable time and because they are farmers rather than mill hands. The Portuguese of New York, on the other

[1] Computed from Reports of the U. S. Commissioner of Immigration.

TABLE 17

TYPES OF UNSKILLED AMONG PORTUGUESE IMMIGRANTS

	Farm Laborers	Fishermen	Laborers	Servants	Totals
1899	79	0	715	621	1415
1900	59	0	1592	1488	3139
1901	231	0	1140	1425	2796
1902	214	0	1857	889	2960
1903	598	9	2793	1825	5225
1904	534	67	1894	1076	3571
1905	97	246	1674	824	2841
1906	321	174	3109	1744	5348
1907	347	77	3566	1368	5358
1908	301	150	2163	943	3557
1909	242	57	1860	666	2825
1910	606	118	2980	1101	4805
1911	772	187	2647	995	4601
1912	1437	164	2809	1178	5588
1913	2898	120	3666	1922	8606
1914	2440	95	2357	1409	6301
1915	631	125	1299	577	2632
1916	2811	77	3541	1902	8331
1917	624	44	2136	2842	5646
1918	86	18	391	429	924
1919	53	38	298	167	556
Totals	15381	1766	44487	25391	87025

hand are a peculiarly mobile lot.[1] The possible beginning of an immigration stream to New Jersey and Pennsylvania is also to be noted.

Portuguese immigration has long consisted predominantly of unskilled laborers. Table 16 classifies these immigrants by occupation into five general groups; and table 17 subdivides the unskilled into " farm laborers ", " fishermen ", " laborers (unclassified) " and " servants ".[2]

[1] It should be noted that by comparing emigration and immigration only in years when both amounted to 100 or more we probably somewhat exaggerate the proportion emigrating.

[2] In the classification of occupations given in the Commissioner's Reports four general categories are used: "professional," "skilled,'

These tables show that the Portuguese immigrants of recent years have been nine-tenths unskilled, seven per cent skilled, one per cent farmers, and about two and a half per cent, or one in forty, professional or business men. This great predominance of the unskilled must not be forgotten when we evaluate these immigrants. Strictly speaking, they should be compared with the unskilled of other nationalities and not with those nationalities as a whole unless they chance also to consist of the same proportion of unskilled. Since such a comparison is impossible we must be cautious in characterizing the Portuguese as low grade as compared with other groups. Unskilled laborers are, of course, never a fair sample of a nationality. Possibly they may be a fairer sample of the Portuguese than of some other nationalities because the opportunity to be anything else than an unskilled laborer in Portugal or the Islands is perhaps less than elsewhere. Nevertheless, the very fact of being engaged in unskilled work itself determines many other social characteristics.

The next table should be used only with great caution as a measure of the economic status of the Portuguese. It gives the proportion who showed more or less than a given sum of money to the American inspectors. It is obvious that immigrants by no means always show all the money they have with them. If they are wise they show only enough to get them past the inspectors. How much they show will depend not only upon how much they have,

"miscellaneous" and "no occupation." We have retained these classifications unchanged in table 16 except that the miscellaneous group, which is not homogeneous, we have divided into "farmers," "unskilled" and "miscellaneous." In its original form this group contained such diverse classes as "laborers" and "bankers." Our miscellaneous group now contains chiefly business men with the slight exception of a small group of teamsters. They are too few to affect the general picture which the table affords.

but upon how well they have been coached, and upon whether they are afraid to show what they have or not. We are therefore justified in saying only that other things being equal, a people who habitually show little money are probably economically worse off than those who show more.

TABLE 18

PORTUGUESE IMMIGRANTS SHOWING MORE OR LESS THAN SPECIFIED [1] SUMS OF MONEY AT THE PORT OF ENTRY

	Number Showing Over $30 or $50 [2]	*Number Showing Less*
1899	159	1131
1900	269	2052
1901	310	2274
1902	365	2555
1903	695	5625
1904	473	3827
1905	537	2789
1906	598	4897
1907	721	5678
1908	451	4350
1909	395	2761
1910	539	4512
1911	934	4216
1912	814	5179
1913	953	8549
1914	771	6671
1915	457	2859
1916	662	8895
1917	864	6479
1918	365	1351
1919	612	585
	11944	87235

This table shows that 11,944 or 12 per cent of Portuguese immigrants who were asked to show money at the port of entry between 1899 and 1919 showed more than thirty

[1] Derived from the several annual Reports of the Commissioner General of Immigration.

[2] The basis of classification was changed in 1904 from $30 to $50.

TABLE 19

AGE OF PORTUGUESE IMMIGRANTS [1]

	Under 14	14–44	45 and over
1899	477	1487	132
1900	1105	2778	358
1901	1030	2774	372
1902	1439	3410	460
1903	2072	5665	696
1904	1426	4382	530
1905	1035	3381	439
1906	1821	6171	737
1907	2431	6581	636
1908	1697	4665	457
1909	908	3404	294
1910	1526	5691	440
1911	1238	5765	466
1912	1863	6939	601
1913	2301	10366	899
1914	1338	7769	540
1915	638	3427	311
1916	1563	9725	920
1917	2172	6738	1284
	Under 16	16–44	45 and over
1918	581	1518	220
1919	234	1232	108
Totals	27313 [2]	99593	10410
Per cents	19.9	72.5	7.6

dollars from 1899 to 1903, or more than fifty dollars from 1904 to 1919. The Immigration Commission found wide variations in the amounts shown by different nationalities. Between 1904 and 1910 fifteen nationalities out of forty showed a smaller sum of money than was shown by the Portuguese. [3] The change in basis of classification made in

[1] Computed from several Reports of the U. S. Commissioner of Immigration.

[2] The change in classification introduces a slight error, of course, into our per cent calculations, but it is not serious.

[3] *United States Immigration Commission Report*, 61st Cong., 3rd Sess., vol. i, p. 103.

1904 does not seem to have appreciably affected the proportions in either class. The marked increase in the proportion showing more than fifty dollars in 1918 and 1919 probably does reflect the effect of the literacy test in selecting a somewhat more prosperous as well as more literate group. Except for these and one or two other years there is little variation shown in the proportions in the two classes.

The economic and social status of a people depends in part upon their age distribution. Tables 19 and 20 show the age distribution of the Portuguese immigrants and emigrants respectively.

TABLE 20

AGE OF PORTUGUESE EMIGRANTS [1]

	Under 14	14–44	45 and over
1908	50	697	151
1909	62	605	149
1910	96	663	147
1911	?11	1064	213
1912	110	1435	202
1913	105	1308	170
1914	129	1603	116
1915	154	2123	249
1916	186	1662	337
1917	64	1002	247
	Under 16	16–44	45 and over
1918	78	1609	329
1919	112	2811	602
Totals	1257 [2]	16582	2912
Per cents	6.1	79.9	14.0

These tables show that for the United States in both the ingoing and outgoing streams of Portuguese migration,

[1] Computed from Reports of the U. S. Commissioner of Immigration, 1908-1919.

[2] As in table 19 a slight error is involved in our percentages because of the change in the basis of classification.

men and women in the prime of life predominate. Children, however, form a small part of the emigrants while they make up one in five of all immigrants. The proportion of persons 45 years of age and over is twice as great among' emigrants as among immigrants. The Portuguese then, though bringing not a few children with them, are no exception to the general rule that immigration consists chiefly of those in the prime of life, the cost of whose up-bringing has been incurred elsewhere. This is probably poor economy for the United States in the case of the Portuguese, because it would have paid us better to have trained a literate population even at some expense. The table also seems to show that to a degree the successful Portuguese return home to spend their earnings and their declining years in the Islands or on the Continent.

Similarly tables 21 and 22 show the conjugal condition of immigrant men and immigrant women respectively. Record has been kept of the conjugal condition of emigrants for too short a period to make the data worth duplicating.

TABLE 21

CONJUGAL CONDITION OF IMMIGRANT PORTUGUESE MEN [1]

	Age 14-44 (16-44 for 1918 and 1919)				Age 45 and over			
	Single	Married	Widowed	Divoreed	Single	Married	Wid.	Divorced
1910	2101	1722	32	0	6	209	22	0
1911	2191	1743	30	0	22	202	33	0
1912	2405	2203	35	1	16	276	32	0
1913	3612	3379	40	1	19	416	29	0
1914	2720	2525	28	1	15	259	23	0
1915	1410	983	9	1	11	121	16	2
1916	3690	2928	32	3	32	519	29	0
1917	1836	936	12	2	39	792	45	3
1918	530	343	7	1	20	104	8	0
1919	613	298	8	0	9	53	2	0
Totals ...	21108	17060	233	10	189	2951	239	5

[1] Compiled from the several Reports of the U. S. Commissioner General of Immigration, 1910-1919.

TABLE 22

CONJUGAL CONDITION OF IMMIGRANT PORTUGUESE WOMEN [1]

	Age 14-44 (16-44 for 1918 and 1919)				Age 45 and over			
	Single	Married	Widowed	Divorced	Single	Married	Wid.	Divorced
1910	944	838	54	0	12	92	99	0
1911	946	815	40	0	21	89	99	0
1912	1166	1078	50	1	26	130	121	0
1913	1849	1396	85	4	29	209	196	1
1914	1370	1063	60	2	23	91	129	0
1915	524	474	25	1	14	71	76	0
1916	1848	1129	93	2	23	172	144	1
1917	2665	1151	131	5	39	193	171	2
1918	343	276	16	2	7	36	44	1
1919	149	149	14	1	3	26	14	1
Totals ...	11804	8369	568	18	197	1109	1093	6

As might be expected these tables show a predominance
of married men and women among the older age group, and
of single among the younger. The proportion of single is
somewhat greater among women than among men; and
the number of single men is more than double that of
women. Where the actual proportions of the sexes in the
Portuguese population are such as is shown in this table, one
would expect early marriage of women and perhaps immorality on the part of men. Many of these young men,
however, return home to marry. The excess of married
men reflects the degree to which they leave their wives in
the old country. In this respect they are like most immigrant men of the " new immigration ". The figures for
widowed women show that emigration is a means of meet-
ing the problem of widowhood abroad. The number of
divorced is, as would be expected in a Catholic country,
very small.

One of the chief handicaps of the Portuguese immigrant,

[1] Compiled from the several Reports of the U. S. Commissioner
General of Immigration, 1910-1919.

and one of his characteristics which most complicate our social problems, is his illiteracy.   Table 23 shows the number and percentage of illiterates among emigrants from Portugal for the combined years 1909-1917.   For the political divisions of the Islands it was possible to get data for the period 1913-1917 only.

TABLE 23

LITERACY OF EMIGRANTS [1]

(FOREIGNERS INCLUDED) [2]

1909-1917

		Emigrants		Number Illiterate			Per cent Illiterate		
From	Total	Men	Women	Total	Men	Women	Total	Men	Wom
Portugal	393,589	268,858	124,731	246,747	147,489	99,258	62.69	54.86	79.5
Continent	324,019	231,040	92,979	196,926	119,796	77,130	60.78	51.75	82.9
Islands	69,570	37,818	31,752	49,821	27,693	22,128	71.61	73.23	69.6

1913-1917

Ponta Delgada.	13,489	6,273	7,216	9,541	4,644	4,897	70.73	74.03	67.8
Funchal	8,528	5,145	3,383	6,420	3,847	2,573	75.28	74.77	76.0
Angra	5,432	2,832	2,600	3,516	1,971	1,545	64.73	69.60	59.4
Horta	3,107	1,557	1,550	1,478	795	683	47.57	51.06	44.0

Literacy in the above table means " ability to read and write ".   The first point which one notes in examining it is the startlingly high proportions of illiterates among emigrants from Portugal.   We were prepared to find such illiteracy, however, when we saw the illiteracy of the general population.[3]   Emigrants from Portugal are more than three-fifths illiterate.   Emigrants from the Continent are more literate than those from the Islands, but this is because of the large proportion of men in the total group—the island women curiously enough being more literate than the Continental.   Among emigrants from the mainland the

---

[1] Derived from *Estatística Demográfica, op. cit.,* Table 8, pp. 102-3 and Table 23, pp. 84-102.

[2] Insignificant in number.

[3] *Cf. supra,* pp. 79-80.

illiteracy of women exceeds that of men by more than thirty points, reaching for the latter the enormous figure of 83 per cent. Even the Continental men, however, were more than half illiterate. The emigrants from the Islands, on the other hand, show much less difference between the literacy of the sexes. Such difference as there is is in favor of the women. Quite as notable as these comparisons are those between the different divisions in the Islands. The largest number of emigrants to-day go from Ponta Delgada, and we shall see that they make up the large majority of the Portuguese in the communities we have especially studied. It is therefore important to note that the emigrants from that district are more illiterate than those from Angra or Horta, and but slightly less so than those from Funchal. The greatest contrast in other respects is that with the Horta group. The Horta women are less illiterate by 23 points than those from Ponta Delgada, and the men by practically the same amount. Indeed the Horta men are slightly more literate than their Continental brothers, while the Horta women are but 44 per cent illiterate against 83 per cent for Continental women. Whether attributable to race or to opportunity these contrasts are very striking.

Comparing table 23 with table 8 [2] above for the general population of Portugal, we find that the emigrant men are less illiterate than men of the general population. Thus emigrant men were reported 55 per cent illiterate while in 1911 61 per cent of the total male population were set down as unable to read and write. Women in the general population, however, were practically as literate as those who emigrated. If we consider the general population over seven years of age the men are again more illiterate than emigrant men, but the women are more literate than emigrant women.

[1] *Supra*, p. 79.

Table 24 gives the number and proportion of adult illiterate Portuguese immigrants to the United States. Unfortunately the Commissioner's reports do not classify these data by sex until 1908 and even then it is impossible to compute illiteracy ratios by sex because the number of men and women over fourteen is unknown.

TABLE 24

ILLITERACY OF PORTUGUESE IMMIGRANTS TO THE UNITED STATES [1]

1899–1917

	Immigrants over 14	Number Illiterate	Per cent Illiterate
1899	1619	1059	65.4
1900	3136	1875	59.8
1901	3146	1884	59.9
1902	3870	2745	70.9
1903	6361	4645	73.0
1904	4912	3306	67.3
1905	3820	2543	66.6
1906	6908	4667	67.6
1907	7217	5524	76.5
1908	5112	3308	64.7
1909	3698	2406	65.1
1910	6131	4162	67.9
1911	6231	3732	59.9
1912	7540	4224	56.0
1913	11265	6960	61.8
1914	8309	4780	57.5
1915	3738	2027	54.2
1916	10645	6226	58.5
1917	8022	4580	57.1
Totals	111680	70653	63.3

This table shows the same excessive illiteracy. The percentage of illiterates varied from 54 per cent in 1915 to 76 per cent in 1907, with a slight tendency to improvement in the later periods. If we compare this table with table 23

[1] Reports of the United States Commissioner of Immigration.

using the same period of time (1909-1913) only, we find
that 59.6 per cent of immigrants to the United States were
recorded by our inspectors as unable to read and write,
against 62.9 for all emigrants from Portugal and 71.6 for
those from the Islands. The difference in favor of the relative literacy of immigrants to the United States may represent an actual selective process, or it may be due simply
to different standards in use in the two countries. In any
case the problem of illiteracy among our Portuguese immigrants is obvious.

Table 24 above showed about one-fourth of Portuguese
immigrants to be in the habit of returning home, though
a much larger proportion have been going back in recent
years. Table 25 below gives the length of time which
these returning immigrants have usually spent in the United
States.

TABLE 25

LENGTH OF RESIDENCE IN THE UNITED STATES OF PORTUGUESE
EMIGRANTS [1] (WHERE KNOWN)

	Not over 5 yrs.	5-10	10-15	15-20	Over 20	Totals
1909	573	190	15	15	22	815
1910	681	180	23	12	10	906
1911	911	320	81	26	47	1385
1912	1201	446	48	23	28	1746
1913	1067	416	67	16	14	1580
1914	1184	538	103	9	11	1845
1915	1915	459	99	43	9	2525
1916	1543	477	106	42	17	2185
1917	974	248	65	13	13	1313
1918	1573	380	50	8	5	2016
1919	2053	1295	151	23	3	3525
Totals	13675	4949	808	230	179	19841
Per cents	68.9	24.9	4.1	1.2	.9	100.0

[1] Computed from Reports of the U. S. Commissioner General of
Immigration.

This table shows that more than two-thirds of those returning did so after a stay of five years or less; that a quarter more had been in this country between five and ten years; one in twenty-five between ten and fifteen years, and that those who had lived here longer were almost a negligible quantity. Apparently, while a large proportion of the Portuguese make their permanent residence in the United States, a considerable minority return home after a brief stay.

Distribution of the Portuguese in the United States

Before summarizing the history and characteristics of Portuguese immigration it will be well to present a few tables showing the distribution and occupations of the foreign-born Portuguese in the United States as enumerated by successive Federal Censuses,[1] and by the Massachusetts Census of 1915.

[1] Unfortunately these Census data are unsatisfactory for this purpose because of the indefiniteness and probability of error in the two classifications used—"born in Portugal" and "born in the Atlantic Islands". In the first place many individuals recorded as from Portugal are undoubtedly from the Islands; and in the second place some, though probably not a great number, classed as from the Atlantic Islands are non-Portuguese. Even where Census enumerators are instructed to distinguish between those born on the mainland and those born in the Islands the results are open to great doubt. If one asks a Portuguese where he is from, an Azorean from St. Michael's may answer either "Portugal", "Açores", or "San Miguel". The last two answers will lead to a correct classification, but the first will place his record among those from the mainland unless the enumerator is careful enough to ask a more specific question. The writer's experience with classifications made by others in Fall River, his own difficulties in securing correct information on this point, and his knowledge of apparent errors in classification in the communities which he has studied more intensively, lead him to suspect that both federal and state figures which attempt to distinguish between these two sources of immigration are open to many errors and indeed may be worthless in this respect. Fortunately the Immigration Bureau's tables used above do not attempt to make this distinction. Where we use Census data below we shall give the figures

TABLE 26

RESIDENTS IN THE UNITED STATES BORN IN "PORTUGAL" AND THE [1]
"ATLANTIC ISLANDS"

(INCLUDING ONLY STATES WITH 100 OR MORE OF THESE NATIVITIES)

Res. in	Born in	1860	1870	1880	Census of 1890	1900	1910	1920 [3]
U. S. ...	Port. ...	4,116	4,540	8,138	15,996	37,144	59,360 [2]	67,453 [2]
	At. Is. ...	1,361	4,219	7,512	9,739	10,955	18,274	38,984
Cal. ...	Port. ...	1,459	2,507	4,705	9,859	12,068	22,539	24,517
	At. Is. ...	121	946	3,356	2,587	3,515	2,898	8,892
Conn. ...	Port. ...	265	49	165	230	568	707	1,200
	At. Is. ...		194	79	183	87	89	210
Fla. ...	Port. ...			41	35	37	30	222
	At. Is. ...			291	83	109	94	87
Hawaii [3]. ..	Port. ...					6,512	7,585	
	At. Is. ...					1,156	913	

as they stand for immigration both from the Islands and from the mainland. In communities where the Portuguese have settled in considerable numbers the sum of these two figures will probably give only a slightly exaggerated idea of the real number of Portuguese here. For other communities the figures for Portugal will be usable and those for the Islands will be of little value. The writer does not recommend the use of these figures to determine what proportion of our Portuguese come from the mainland—they probably very greatly exaggerate that proportion.

[1] Taken from successive reports of the Bureau of the Census. See footnote page 118, for cautions as to use of this table. All states or territories are included which had a total from both sources of one hundred or more individuals.

[2] Figures for 1910 and 1920 for both "Portugal" and "Atlantic Islands" are for continental United States only. To make them more comparable with earlier figures those for Hawaii should be added. In addition there were also probably a very few in other non-continental possessions of the United States. Figures for Hawaii in 1920 were not available at the time this table was constructed.

[3] The Fourteenth Census of 1920 showed that Maine, Texas and Virginia (not shown in this table) also had slightly over 100 individuals from these two sources.

Ill.	Port.	395	76	424	255		291	110
	At. Is.	453	782	431	272	362	194	195
Ind.	Port.					200		
	At. Is.					7		
Lou.	Port.	145	125	141	112	94		100
	At. Is.	34	7	11		7		13
Mass.	Port.	988	734	1,161	3,051	13,453	26,437	28,315
	At. Is.	433	1,944	2,421	4,973	4,432	12,816	25,230
Nev.	Port.		104	207	197	176	305	149
	At. Is.		45	12		30	42	104
N. H.	Port.						110	115
	At. Is.						21	40
N. J.	Port.					62	145	646
	At. Is.					89	192	179
N. Y.	Port.	353	237	295	284	362	660	1,404
	At. Is.	96	152	137	496	461	741	569
Ohio.	Port.			38		117	182	146
	At. Is.			203		18	31	42
Ore.	Port.				115	142	174	125
	At. Is.				19	11	22	48
Pa.	Port.	90	89	175	131	124	225	798
	At. Is.	27	45	35	78	67	129	87
R. I.	Port.	86	146	210	833	2,545	6,501	8,624
	At. Is.	24	81	185	547	320	716	2,991
Wash.	Port.				110	137	179	156
	At. Is.				17	22	23	44

Table 26 shows the high degree of concentration of the Portuguese in south-eastern New England, California and Hawaii. In addition to the 8,498 Portuguese in Hawaii who were born in Portugal or the Islands, there were in 1910 13,766 native-born of Portuguese descent and 37 others of Portuguese " race ", presumably born elsewhere, making a total of Portuguese " race " of 22,301. They made up in that year the most important single group of so-called Caucasian peoples in the Hawaiian Islands. As we shall not refer to this group in detail again we may note in passing that only about a third of the Hawaiian Portuguese were dwellers in cities; that the ratio of males to females was 107.8 (indicating a family migration); that considerably more than half of the foreign-born Portuguese had been in Hawaii since 1890 or longer; and that only about a third of the adults among these foreign-born Portuguese were illiterate. Undoubtedly a special study of the Hawaiian Portuguese is needed.

Like the Hawaiian Portuguese those of California differ from their New England brothers in being chiefly a rural people, only 36 per cent being recorded as urban among those of the Pacific Coast states while nearly 93 per cent of the New England Portuguese are urban. In the Pacific coast states the Portuguese made up in 1910 proportionately a slightly more important element (2.4 per cent) in the foreign population than they did in New England, (1.9 per cent).

The Portuguese settlements in other regions besides Hawaii, California and New England call for little comment as they are very few in number and some settlements have grown up and disappeared between Census decades while others, with the exception of those in New York, have remained unimportant. The partial disappearance of the few hundred in Illinois is perhaps worth noting. The variation between the proportions recorded as born in Portugal or in the Islands probably is merely evidence of different classification of the same groups in different years. From 1880 to 1910 the foreign-born Portuguese increased in the country as a whole nearly one hundred per cent a decade. There was something of a falling off in the last decade and as noted elsewhere this falling off will probably continue for some time.

It is also possible to trace the coming of the Portuguese to the larger cities through the Census reports, but in most of them their numbers are so few that it is hardly worth while to do more than mention a few cities at different periods. In 1860 Boston reported nearly 300 Portuguese[1] and New Orleans 140. Ten years later Boston had added about two hundred more, and San Francisco, Providence and Fall River [2] had been added to the list,[3] the last named city reporting but 20 however. The Tenth Census of 1880 found these people in appreciable numbers also in Brooklyn and Cambridge, and the Eleventh in Lowell, Oakland, New Bedford, Sacramento, Somerville and Taunton. New Bedford at that time had 1,967 and was first in the list while Taunton reported scarcely 100, and Fall River 705. In 1900 Gloucester, Honolulu and Lawrence showed Portuguese settlements, those in the first two cities being of considerable size with no less than 2,406 in Honolulu and nearly 600 in Gloucester. To-day (1920) the most important Portuguese settlements in the larger cities are the following:

TABLE 27

FOREIGN-BORN PORTUGUESE IN SELECTED CITIES, 1920

	Born in Portugal	Atlantic Islands
New Bedford	7,457	9,772
Fall River	5,663	6,401
Oakland, Cal.	4,281	346
Providence	1,661	927
Lowell	1,666	402
Cambridge	1,946	346
New York	1,026	414
Boston	957	294

[1] The term " Portuguese" will be used in these paragraphs as referring to all reported as born in Portugal or the Atlantic Islands. The possible error in this procedure has already been noted.

[2] New Bedford undoubtedly had more Portuguese than Fall River at all periods but was not included in the list of cities reporting until 1890.

[3] With the exception of Fall River we are mentioning only cities with at least a hundred Portuguese.

Taunton Mass, though not belonging in the above group of large cities, has 1,542 reported as born in Portugal and 1,662 as born in the Atlantic Islands. We have not secured data on Portuguese urban population in small cities outside of New England. Turning to the region of our special interest we find the Portuguese of New England very largely in south-eastern Massachusetts and in Rhode Island. In 1870 the early comers were found distributed chiefly in the following counties of Massachusetts listed in order of importance: Bristol, Suffolk, Barnstable, Essex, Middlesex and Norfolk. This shows the importance of the early settlements in and near New Bedford, Boston and on the Cape. To-day the order of importance is: Bristol, Middlesex, Plymouth, Essex, Barnstable, Suffolk, Hampden, with less than 500 each in any of the other counties. The relative importance of Bristol County has increased due to continued growth of the settlement in New Bedford and the rise of the only less important group in Fall River. Despite many Portuguese on the farms this growth has followed the development of industrial cities and has been especially marked in the cotton mill centers. The following table shows the " Portuguese " population in cities and towns of Massachusetts having 10,000 or more population in 1920.

No other cities of this size reported so many as 100 Portuguese in 1920, and the population of smaller places was not classified by country of birth at the date of writing (1922). The Massachusetts Census of 1915 shows, however, that the Portuguese are an important element in many smaller towns. These state figures are for those

TABLE 28

FOREIGN-BORN PORTUGUESE POPULATION IN MASSACHUSETTS CITIES AND
TOWNS [1] HAVING 10,000 OR MORE TOTAL POPULATION IN 1920

	Born in	
	Portugal	*Atlantic Islands*
New Bedford	7,457	9,772
Fall River	5,663	6,401
Taunton	1,542	1,662
Lowell	1,666	402
Cambridge	1,946	346
Boston	957	294
Somerville	686	239
Gloucester	341	516
Peabody	318	200
Lawrence	491	11
Attleboro	172	77
Holyoke	194	2
Brockton	162	25
Chicopee	164	0

"born in Portugal, including island possessions". Only
towns not included above are given below:

TABLE 29

PORTUGUESE IN OTHER MASSACHUSETTS CITIES AND TOWNS, 1915

Provincetown	962	Bridgewater	204
Plymouth	959	Westport	188
Dartmouth	928	Middleborough	179
Fairhaven	700	Hudson	175
Falmouth	658	Freetown	170
Wareham	634	Tisbury	161
Dighton	403	Mattapoisett	153
Somerset	393	Harwich	151
Ludlow	377	W. Bridgewater	149
Seekonk	276	Raynham	141
Nantucket	229	Easton	133
Rehoboth	229	Edgartown	129
Carver	220	Acushnet	127
Oak Bluffs	216	Holyoke	117
Swansea	212	Bourne	114
Marion	211	Cohasset	114
Barnstable	210	Brockton	106
		Milford	101

[1] From the 14th Census of the United States.

Reference to a map of Massachusetts will show that these smaller towns are for the most part in the eastern and especially south-eastern part of the State. In Rhode Island the Portuguese population of to-day are found in all five counties although there are practically none (18) in Washington County. The largest number are in Providence County, with more than 2800 in Bristol County. The County of Newport where our rural study was made reports 778 as born in Portugal and 1,081 as born in the Atlantic Islands. The State as a whole records 8,624 of the former and 2,991 of the latter. The probable inaccuracy of this distinction has already been noted.[1] The Rhode Island cities with over 10,000 population reported foreign-born Portuguese as shown in the following table:

TABLE 30

FOREIGN-BORN PORTUGUESE POPULATION IN RHODE ISLAND CITIES AND TOWNS [2] HAVING 10,000 OR MORE TOTAL POPULATION IN 1920

| | Born in | |
	Portugal	Atlantic Islands
Providence	1,661	927
Bristol	2,228	67
East Providence	989	516
Pawtucket	1,102	61
West Warwick	542	10
Newport	290	133
Cumberland	373	8
Cranston	165	23
Central Falls	152	0

In considering the occupations of the Portuguese of New England we shall confine our attention to those resident in

[1] *Cf. supra*, p. 118.
[2] From the advance sheets of the 14th Census of the United States. Cities and towns reporting less than a hundred are not included.

Massachusetts.[1] In the year 1915 of the 673,509 foreign-born 14 years of age and over, gainfully employed in the State, 29,606, or 4.4 per cent were born either in Portugal or in the Atlantic Islands, and practically all of the latter were from the Azores. The difference between the Portuguese and other foreign-born with respect to employment of women and girls is slight, 5.0 per cent of gainfully employed women being Portuguese and 4.2 per cent of gainfully employed men.

The following table gives the proportion of all foreign-born Portuguese gainfully employed in each of the nine major divisions of occupations used in the Census, and similarly the proportion of all foreign-born in each division.

TABLE 31

DISTRIBUTION OF FOREIGN-BORN PORTUGUESE AND OF OTHER FOREIGN-BORN
IN MAJOR OCCUPATIONAL GROUPS, MASSACHUSETTS, 1915 [2]

	Agriculture Forestry and Animal Husbandry	*Extraction of Minerals*	*Manufacturing and Mechanical*	*Transportation*
Portuguese	9.8%	(less than) .1%	74.7%	3.5%
All foreign-born .	4.5%	.2%	57.8%	6.5%

	Trade	*Public Service*	*Professional*	*Personal and Domestic Service*	*Clerical*	*Total*
Portuguese	4.5%	1.2%	.4%	5.4%	.5%	100.1%
All foreign-born ..	9.5%	2.3%	2.5%	14.2%	2.5%	100.0%

It must be remembered that this and the following comparisons are all with other foreign-born and not with the total of gainfully employed in the State. Moreover, un-

---

[1] The following description of the occupational distribution of the Portuguese of Massachusetts is derived and the percentages computed from the *Decennial Census of the Commonwealth*, 1915, pp. 497 and 536-631.

[2] Computed from *Census of the Population of the Commonwealth of Massachusetts*, 1915, part iv.

like some of the tables in the next chapter, we are here comparing the Portuguese with a group of which they themselves form a part. A comparison between the Portuguese and the non-Portuguese, including in the latter the nativeborn as well as other foreign-born, would doubtless make still more striking many of the contrasts we are noting here. Table 32, beyond, shows that the Portuguese are more frequently found on the farm than are the foreignborn in general, that they are negligible in mining, and that three-fourths of them are in manufacturing pursuits as against less than three-fifths of the foreign-born in general. In every other group of occupations except agricultural and manufacturing the Portuguese are considerably less conspicuous than the general group. Especially notable is the fact that but .4 per cent of them have attained professional positions while six times that proportion of the general group have been thus advanced; and the fact that only onefifth the proportion of Portuguese are in clerical positions as of the foreign-born of the State. On the other hand, it is perhaps a point in their favor that but 5.4 per cent are in domestic and personal service as against 14.2 per cent of all foreign-born.

The significance of these contrasts will become more clear in the discussion below where the composition of these groups is examined. It is to be noted, however, that the percentages given below, unlike those in Table 31, represent the proportion of the foreign-born in each occupational group who are Portuguese. The following list gives these proportions in all the important major divisions of occupations and most of the subdivisions. It omits, however, a number of smaller groups of less importance numerically or of less significance for our present study.

TABLE 32

OCCUPATIONS OF FOREIGN-BORN PORTUGUESE IN MASSACHUSETTS, 1915 [1]

	Total Foreign-born	Portuguese Foreign-born	Per cent Portuguese
Agriculture, Forestry, Animal Husbandry	30,200	2,893	9.6
Farmers	6,199	561	9.0
Farm laborers	11,450	931	8.1
Fishermen and Oystermen	3,304	974	29.5
Fruit-growers and Nurserymen	153	71	46.4
Laborers in Gardens, etc.	4,109	122	3.0
Lumbermen, etc	758	5	.7
Manufacturing and Mechanical	389,286	22,118	5.7
Apprentices	1,244	23	1.8
Bakers	3,883	77	2.0
Blacksmiths, etc.	212	22	10.4
Boilermakers	728	2	.3
Masons	4,698	103	2.2
Builders and Contractors	2,863	31	1.1
Cabinet-makers	1,268	63	5.0
Carpenters	21,778	457	2.1
Compositors and Type-setters	2,001	20	1.0
Coopers	492	23	4.7
Dressmakers, etc.	5,440	111	2.0
Dyers	1,518	45	3.0
Electricians, etc.	1,954	12	.6
Mechanical Engineers	317	3	.9
Stationary Engineers	3,983	34	.9
Engravers	314	2	.6
Filers, grinders, etc.	1,863	53	2.8
Firemen (n. o. c.)	4,380	387	8.9
Foremen and Overseers	6,513	108	1.7
Glassblowers	89	6	6.7
Jewelers, etc.	732	11	1.5
Manufacturing Laborers (n. o. c.)	57,636	3,927	6.8
Building and Hand Trades	21,792	849	3.9
Chemical	1,042	12	1.2
Clay, glass and stone	1,254	66	5.3
Iron and steel	7,941	286	3.6

[1] Computed from *The Decennial Census of the Commonwealth of Massachusetts*, part iv, table 29.

Other metal	688	115	16.7
Lumber and Furniture	1,464	57	3.9
Textiles	11,286	2,231	19.8
Other Industries	12,169	311	2.6
Loomfixers	3,018	70	2.3
Machinists, etc.	16,833	105	.6
Managers, superintendents	1,347	8	.6
Manufacturers	5,316	44	.8
Officials	179	0	.0
Mechanics (n. o. c.)	811	6	.7
Milliners, etc.	1,017	6	.6
Molders, etc.	3,454	59	1.7
Oilers of machinery	549	150	26.8
Paper-hangers	407	4	1.0
Pattern-makers, etc.	554	1	.2
Plasterers	1,068	15	1.4
Plumbers, etc.	2,998	18	.6
Printing Pressmen	270	1	.3
Rollers (Metal), etc.	57	2	3.5
Roofers ~~~ ¹ ~~	564	4	.7
Sawyers	280	10	3.6
Semi-skilled (n. o. c.)	186,851	15,460	8.3
Chemical	1,183	28	2.4
Clay, glass and stone	965	39	4.0
Clothing	2,907	109	3.8
Food	3,597	142	3.9
Harness and saddle	626	5	.8
Iron and steel	12,126	161	2.3
Other metal	2,960	30	1.0
Liquor and beverage	896	10	1.1
Lumber and furniture	5,790	184	3.2
Printing and publishing	1,604	13	.8
Paper and pulp	4,688	52	1.1
Shoe factories	27,475	246	.9
Tanneries	5,830	185	3.2
Textiles	99,543	13,785	15.8
Beamers, warpers and slashers	1,900	128	6.8
Doffers, etc.	3,215	1,189	37.0
Carders, combers and lappers	5,910	1,225	20.7
Drawers, rovers and twisters	6,661	1,904	27.1
Spinners	14,493	2,710	18.7
Weavers	34,090	2,321	6.8
Winders, reelers and spoolers	7,010	1,663	24.1

Other textile occupations ...	26,264	2,745	10.5
Electrical supply	1,940	9	.5
Paper box	971	11	1.1
Rubber	5,661	268	4.7
Other factories	5,716	71	1.2
Sewing machine operatives, etc.	9,384	257	2.7
Shoe-makers and cobblers (not factory)	3,233	63	1.9
Skilled (n. o. c.)	436	3	.7
Stone cutters	2,262	10	.4
Structural ironworkers	390	1	.3
Tailors and tailoresses	8,122	113	1.4
Tinsmiths and coppersmiths	1,200	5	.4
Upholsterers	562	2	.4
Transportation (Water)	43,877	1,031	2.3
Captains and other officers	501	42	8.4
Longshoremen	1,870	156	8.4
Transportation (road and street)	15,027	343	2.3
Cab and hack drivers	403	7	1.7
Chauffeurs	3,472	45	1.3
Teamsters, etc. (n. o. c.)	8,427	244	2.9
Livery foremen	159	0	.0
Garage keepers and managers .	173	1	.6
Hostlers and stable hands	1,646	28	1.7
Stable keepers and managers ..	183	5	2.7
Transportation (Railroad)	15,910	279	1.7
Laborers	6,590	235	3.6
Locomotive engineers	366	1	.3
Locomotive firemen	289	5	1.7
Motormen	2,480	8	.3
Officials	105	0	.0
Overseers and foremen	830	4	.5
Street-car conductors	1,381	9	.7
Switchmen and yardmen	985	9	.9
Other transportation	8,140	127	1.6
Express, post, etc.	1,628	12	.7
Trade	63,798	1,427	2.1
Bankers, etc.	399	1	.3
Clerks (not sales)	690	5	.7
Commercial travelers	1,737	3	.2
Deliverymen	6,378	177	2.8
Floor-walkers, foremen, etc. ..	452	7	1.5

Inspectors, etc.	147	1	.7
Insurance agents and officials .	1,366	25	1.8
Laborers in coal yards, etc. ...	2,270	220	9.7
Laborers, etc. in stores	1,422	47	3.3
Newsboys	192	0	.0
Real estate agents	1,578	20	1.3
Retail dealers	26,740	421	1.6
Salesmen and saleswomen	17,492	352	2.0
Undertakers	153	6	3.9
Wholesalers, etc.	552	1	.2
Public Service (n. o. c.)	15,402	364	2.4
Laborers	8,955	260	2.9
Policemen	1,328	6	.4
Professional Service	17,019	124	.7
Actors	207	1	.5
Architects	163	0	.0
Artists	410	5	1.2
Authors, editors and reporters	268	2	.4
Chemists	221	0	.0
Civil and mining engineers	203	0	.0
College professors	177	0	.0
Clergymen	1,202	27	2.2
Dentists	404	10	2.5
Draftsmen	468	3	.6
Lawyers	415	1	.2
Musicians	1,423	8	.6
Photographers	462	7	1.5
Physicians and surgeons	993	8	.8
Showmen	224	8	3.6
Teachers	2,935	9	.3
Trained nurses	4,480	5	.1
Veterinary surgeons	37	0	.0
Semi-professional	1,399	21	1.5
Domestic and personal service...	95,855	1,576	1.7
Barbers	6,036	392	6.5
Bartenders	2,059	52	2.5
Boarding-house keepers	5,209	163	3.1
Midwives and nurses	3,000	26	.9
Saloon keepers	442	5	1.1
Servants	46,608	440	.9
Waiters	7,100	25	.4

Clerical	16,562	135	.8
Agents, canvassers, etc.	1,026	13	1.3
Book-keepers, cashiers, ac-			
countants	4,721	21	.4
Clerks (not store)	8,133	68	.8
Shipping clerks	2,736	26	1.0
Other clerks	5,397	42	.8
Stenographers and typewriters	1,752	0	.0

Since, as we noted above, 4.4 per cent of the adult foreign-born gainfully employed are Portuguese, in the above table the Portuguese have their expected proportion of representatives when they show a percentage of 4.4. If now we consider some of the more interesting groups, we may divide our data arbitararily into five divisions of unequal intervals as follows:

1. Portuguese extremely rare or not found—those showing under 1% in the table
2. Portuguese relatively few in numbers —those showing 1–3.3%
3. Portuguese in about normal proportions—those showing 3.4–5.3%
4. Portuguese somewhat conspicuous —those showing 5.4–10.0%
5. Portuguese very conspicuous —those showing over 10%.

Group 1. Using this classification we find that the Portuguese are extremely rare in the general groups of professional service and clerical occupations and in most of the more skilled subdivisions of these and the other groups. To mention a few examples, we find very few Portuguese engineers, mechanics, manufacturers, pattern makers, plumbers, structural iron workers, railroad officials (none), conductors, bankers, wholesale dealers, book-keepers, or stenographers (none). Of eighteen professional groups the foreign-born Portuguese are non-existent in five and make up less than one per cent in all but five.

Group 2. The Portuguese are also relatively few in numbers in the general fields of transportation, trade, public service. semi-professional service, and domestic and personal service. This last field is not, however, for the most part one requiring high grade intelligence. In the professions of artists, clergymen, dentists and photographers we find the Portuguese relatively few but slightly more numerous than in other professions except the small group of showmen. In group 2 we also find the majority of the skilled workers who were not included in group 1.

Group 3. This group contains a small number of occupations but none of the general divisions. We find about the proportion of Portuguese which we should expect among railroad laborers, undertakers, showmen, cabinet-makers, coopers, laborers in three of the manufacturing industries, metal rollers, sawyers, and among the semi-skilled of four industries.

Group 4. Turning to the groups of occupations where the Portuguese are somewhat conspicuous we find the two general groups of agricultural (and related) occupations and of manufacturing and mechanical pursuits included, and within the latter the intermediate group of the semi-skilled. As farmers and farm laborers among the agricultural group; as firemen (except locomotive or fire department), and as unclassified laborers in the manufacturing group, and in the two sub-groups of beamers etc., and weavers in the textile mills; as boat's officers, longshoremen and sailors in transportation; and as laborers in yards, in trade; the Portuguese are somewhat conspicuous. The group in water transportation is interesting as representing presumably the older type of immigrants from the Azores and as differing from the type we study particularly in the next chapter. With these possible exceptions and that of some of the farmers these occupations are not those requiring great skill.

Group 5. Finally we find among those occupations where the Portuguese are remarkably conspicuous the interme-

diate group of semi-skilled workers in textile mills, and the
sub-groups of fishermen and oystermen and fruit-growers
and nurserymen among the agricultural division; of blacksmiths, laborers in "other metal" industries, laborers in
textile mills, oilers of machinery, and in six sub-divisions of
the semi-skilled textile workers—bobbin boys, doffers and
carders, combers and lappers, drawers, rovers and twisters,
spinners, winders, reelers and spoolers, and "other textile
occupations". The only really skilled group among these
are the blacksmiths and there are but 22 of them.

Our table leaves no doubt that the Portuguese are
characteristically unskilled and semi-skilled workmen and
women in Massachusetts with five or six hundred classified
as farmers. If we had used the Rhode Island figures the
proportion of farmers would probably have been greater.
The Portuguese also are still prominent in fishing and
other sea-faring occupations but their total number in these
pursuits, though considerable, is not great when compared
with those in the textile mills. Indeed slightly more than
half of the gainfully occupied Portuguese of Massachusetts
were reported as working in unskilled or semi-skilled occupations in the textile mills in 1915. Even within the
textile mill occupations there is some evidence that the
Portuguese are employed in largest numbers in those occupations requiring least skill.

All this is only to be expected. An illiterate people are
attracted to the textile mills where there is a demand for
their labor. In the textile mills they are found in occupations for which they are adapted and can be easily trained.
In addition some continue the farming or fishing to which
they have been accustomed; a good many enter unskilled
or semi-skilled work in new fields, and a few of the abler
and of those who have been longest in the new country rise
to more attractive positions.

It is interesting to try to compare the occupational status of the Portuguese as reported at the time of immigration with that of Portuguese in the United States. It is impossible to do this accurately. Table 16 above, it will be remembered, showed that about nine-tenths of Portuguese immigrants had been unskilled laborers in their homeland. We have no comparable category in our table of occupations in Massachusetts, but by adding together the numbers in occupations obviously of this nature we find about 27 per cent [1] which we may estimate to be unskilled. But this leaves out all cotton mill operatives except laborers. Though such operatives are classed as semi-skilled a large majority of the Portuguese engaged in them would be considered by some to be little above unskilled laborers. If we add the semi-skilled in textile mills we find about 73 per cent in our group of relatively unskilled laborers. If, again, we add all Portuguese listed as in any semi-skilled occupations we find a total of something like 79 per cent, to compare with 90 per cent among immigrants. Even if we accept this largest percentage, then, we find some apparent improvement in occupational status of the Portuguese after settling in Massachusetts. The real question here is: Is the change from the work of a peasant or farm laborer in Portugal and the Islands, to work such as the Portuguese do in cotton mills, an advance in occupational status? The present writer would say that it is to some degree, but others might think differently. There is also, of course, the question whether the Portuguese who settle in Massachusetts are a fair sample either of Portuguese immigrants to the United States or of the economic success of Portuguese in the United States. While this question cannot be answered

---

[1] This and the following percentages were computed from *The Decennial Census of the Commonwealth of Massachusetts*, 1915, part iv, table 29, *passim*.

finally, it is probable that the cotton mills do not attract to Massachusetts the highest types of Portuguese, and also that the Portuguese of California have been somewhat more successful economically than those of Massachusetts. If this is so, then it would seem to follow that even considering the foreign-born alone, immigration to Massachusetts has improved somewhat the occupational status of these people. To say this is not to deny the obvious fact that they have remained as they came—characteristically unskilled or at best semi-skilled laborers.

We have discussed briefly the sources, causes and history of Portuguese emigration to the United States. We have shown some of the important characteristics of the Portuguese as immigrants, their distribution in the country, and their occupational status in Massachusetts. We can better evaluate the significance of the change, to them and to others, after we have studied some of them more intimately in the next chapters.

CHAPTER V

PORTUGUESE INFANT MORTALITY

A consideration of infant mortality among the Portuguese will be of interest in itself and also as an index of the social status of these people. As will appear below, the mortality of Portuguese infants is shockingly high. Whether such excessive infant mortality measures chiefly the inherent nature of a people or the advantages and disadvantages of their environment is in dispute. It probably measures both, and most readers will agree with Davis when he writes: " A high infant mortality rate . . . . reflects on clergy, physicians, nurses, school teachers and editors alike and gives a low rating for the intelligence of the people." [1] Differences of opinion arise, however, as soon as one attempts to apportion the responsibility between the families immediately concerned and the rest of the community.

Such differences of opinion are not lacking in our more serious studies of infant mortality. They appear as differences of emphasis upon one or the other of two groups of alleged causes for infant mortality. The first group includes the more impersonal factors such as insufficiency of family income, the employment of mothers both before and after childbirth, unsanitary and overcrowded living conditions, and lack of provision by the community for care of infants and for education of mothers. The second group of factors includes customs and beliefs of certain

[1] Davis, " Infant Mortality in the Registration Area for Births ", in the *American Journal of Public Health*, vol. x, pp. 338-341, April, 1920.

nationalities which are detrimental to the child, ignorance or indifference of mothers, improper feeding, illiteracy or inability to speak English, low-grade intelligence, too frequent pregnancies and sometimes alleged innate racial characteristics of certain groups.

No reputable student of infant mortality, of course, confines his attention to one group of these causes alone, but the difference in emphasis is undeniable. For example, Davis[1] and Hibbs[2] stress the more personal causes of infant mortality; while such writers as Dublin[3] and Miss Lathrop[4] emphasize the more impersonal factors. The tendency in the more recent studies has been to give weight to both groups of causes with perhaps an increasing emphasis upon personal characteristics.

The Racial Hypothesis

It is important to note, however, that even an extreme emphasis upon such a personal factor as ignorance, does not necessarily imply that the writer holds such ignorance to be a racial trait—an innate characteristic. Ignorance, though a personal characteristic, may obviously be the result either of low-grade innate capacity or of lack of opportunity to learn, or it may be a product of both these factors. Those, therefore, who stress personal characteristics as causes of infant mortality think of them either as essentially inborn and permanent or as subject to partial or complete modification under more favorable conditions.

Popularly, however, personal traits are thought of as in-

[1] *Ibid.*, p. 341.

[2] Hibbs, *Infant Mortality: Its Relation to Social and Industrial Conditions* (New York, 1916), p. 58.

[3] Dublin, "Infant Mortality in Fall River, Mass.," in *American Statistical Association Publications*, vol. xiv, p. 517.

[4] Lathrop, "Income and Infant Mortality," in *American Journal of Public Health*, vol. ix, p. 274, April, 1919.

herent in the individual or group. An explanation of infant mortality in terms of racial heredity is the easy explanation—it calls for no further investigation and for no community action. It is important therefore that we not only ask whether infant mortality is due to personal or impersonal causes but also whether such personal causes as exist are racial or acquired. It so happens that in Fall River some who think they can demonstrate that the causes are personal—ignorance, indifference of mothers et cetera—are concluding that they are innate and therefore ineradicable so long as the racial composition of the city remains as it is. A prominent business man of that city said to the writer: " It is the Portuguese who are responsible for our high infant mortality rate; but the Portuguese are half negroes anyhow." He may be right in his conclusion, but the mere fact that personal factors are prominent in the infant mortality of the Portuguese does not of itself prove his point.

We may get a little light upon this racial hypothesis by comparing the infant mortality among the Portuguese with that of other groups in some degree similar to them in racial characteristics, and with groups of different racial makeup. The Portuguese have some negro blood;[1] they are predominantly of Mediterranean stock; they are largely foreign-born with old world mores; and they may be racially and culturally contrasted with other European nationalities. We shall therefore consider four questions: (1) Is a high rate of infant mortality a characteristic which the Portuguese have in common with the negro? (2) Do immigrants of predominantly Mediterranean stock have similarly high rates in the United States? (3) Is excessive infant mortality characteristic of the foreign-born in gen-

---

[1] *Cf. supra*, ch. ii.

eral? (4) Have other nationalities shown infant mortality rates comparable with those of the Portuguese?

We cannot answer these questions finally because we do not possess statistics for each of the groups mentioned living under precisely the same conditions as the Portuguese and comparable with them in every respect. We must use such data as we have, therefore, with great caution.

The Mortality of Negro Infants

If the Portuguese infant death rate is due to an intermixture of negro blood we should expect to find that other things being equal negroes would have as high or higher rates. Every bit of evidence demonstrates that negro infants die in greater relative numbers than do white infants. We have at hand as evidence the general tables of the Federal Birth Statistics and special studies made in Baltimore and Detroit. In 1920 the white infant mortality rate for the Birth Registration Area was 82 while the colored rate was 132.[1] For cities the corresponding figures were 87 and 158, and for rural districts 76 and 118. Thus, for the country as a whole the colored had a rate 61 per cent higher than the white, the contrast being somewhat greater in cities than in rural districts. In Massachusetts the white rate of 90 was somewhat higher than for the country as a whole and the colored rate of 128 considerably lower. For the six years 1915-1920 the excess of the colored rate over the white for the country as a whole varied from a minimum of 58 per cent in 1919 to a maximum of 87 per cent in 1916. The variation in Massachusetts was from a minimum of 34 per cent in 1917 to a maximum of 66 per cent in 1919. Rhode Island has been dropped from the Registration Area since 1918 but prior to that the excess of the

[1] These and the following data are taken from U. S. Bureau of the Census, *Birth Statistics for the Registration Area 1920* (Washington, 1922), pp. 26 *et seq.*

negro rate over the white rate varied from 68 per cent in 1918 to 75 per cent in 1917. This contrast between negro and white infant mortality rates is well-nigh universal though varying considerably in degree. In New York City the colored rate varied in 1920 from 144 in Brooklyn to 224 in the Bronx. Whatever the variation, however, the negro rate exceeds the general rate at every age period.[1]

An examination of the causes of death by color shows some striking contrasts. The negro infant mortality rate in 1920 was three times the white for influenza; six times for dysentery;[2] seven times for tetanus; four times for syphilis; and nearly eight times for unknown and ill-defined causes. One the other hand, the excess due to diarrhea and enteritis and to prematurity was inconsiderable, while the whites exceeded the negroes in their death rate from injuries at birth and from malformations.[3] Davis mentions the correlation between a high general infant mortality rate and a high death rate from diarrhea and enteritis.[4] This appears to be absolutely but not relatively true of the negro. In other words, the excessive infant mortality of the negro is not due primarily to abnormally high mortality from diseases due to improper feeding, although the rate from these causes is higher for negroes than for whites.

Special studies of infant mortality in Baltimore and Detroit show similar contrasts between white and negro rates. In Baltimore the negro rate was 159 against 96 for whites.[5]

---

[1] U. S. Bureau of the Census, *op. cit.*, pp. 35-36.

[2] It is possible, however, that the word "dysentery" may be loosely used in some communities to include what is elsewhere called "diarrhea and enteritis."

[3] *Ibid.*, pp. 37-38.

[4] Davis, *op. cit.*, p. 339.

[5] Woodbury, "Infant Mortality Studies of the Children's Bureau," *American Statistical Association, Publications*, vol. xvi, p. 38.

In Detroit the negro rate of 151 exceeded that for native whites by 56 points and was higher than that of any foreign-born group, although the Greeks, with a rate of 149, were barely below the negroes.[1] Palmer attributes the high negro rate from respiratory diseases to climatic change. In this respect the negro is similar to the Portuguese, but his low rate from prematurity is in contrast with a high one for the Portuguese.[2]

There is no question, then, that negroes have higher rates of infant mortality than do whites in the United States. How far, if to any degree, this characteristic is a purely racial trait is less easy to determine. Mangold writing in 1910 says of this matter:

The negro possesses certain constitutional disqualifications on account of which he suffers from a uniformly high death rate in every age period of life. . . . The mortality of negro infants is more than twice as high as that of whites. The wide disparity between the rural and urban ratio is evidence that his high mortality is not entirely dependent upon heredity, but is attributable in large measure to other causes.[3]

It may be added that to-day the negro infant mortality rate is considerably less than "twice as high" as that of the whites, and that that fact is added evidence that it is not entirely due to racial constitution; unless, indeed, it be maintained that in a very short time a process of selection has greatly improved the negro stock in this respect.

At this point it will be well to compare negro and Portuguese infant mortality rates. We shall discuss below [4]

---

[1] Palmer, "Infant Mortality in Detroit," *American Journal of Public Health*, vol. xi, pp. 502-506, June, 1921.

[2] The Woman's Club of Fall River, *Report on Infant Mortality* (Fall River, 1915), p. 14.

[3] Mangold, *Child Problems* (New York, 1910), p. 39.

[4] *Cf. infra*, p. 150 ff.

several studies of the Portuguese showing infant mortality rates varying from a minimum of 188 for certain rural Portuguese and for native-born of Portuguese descent in Fall River, to 299 for a group of foreign-born Portuguese in Fall River. These rates are higher than those quoted above for the negro except that for the Bronx. In other words, there is a greater contrast between the rates of the Portuguese in certain communities and the general rates for whites for either the Registration Area, Massachusetts and Boston, than between the colored and white rates for these latter areas. Unfortunately, we have to use rates for smaller localities for the Portuguese and in these areas the number of infant deaths among the negroes is too few for comparison.

A high infant mortality rate is, then, a characteristic which the Portuguese have in common with the negro, but in the communities we are studying their rate is higher than the usual rates for negroes. In view of the great variability of the rates for both Portuguese and negroes, and in view of the paucity of our data, the writer does not feel that the racial hypothesis is proven. Neither is it proven that negro blood is not a factor in Portuguese mortality.

Infant Mortality and General Nativity of Mothers

General comparisons between infant mortality among children of native and of foreign-born mothers are of little value for our study. For the Registration Area the statistics show for 1920 a rate of 75.8 for native-born whites and of 96.9 for foreign-born.[1]

In the more careful studies of the Children's Bureau, also, the infants born to foreign-born mothers were usually found to have a higher mortality rate than those born to native-born mothers. For example in Akron, Ohio the rate for

[1] U. S. Bureau of the Census, *op. cit.*, p. 35.

children of native mothers was 70.1 against 109.3 for foreign-born; in New Bedford the corresponding rates were 108.4 and 138.9 respectively; in Saginaw, Michigan 70.5 and 127.6; in Waterbury, Connecticut 97.9 and 134.8; in Manchester, N. H. 128.1 and 183.5; in Johnstown, Pa. 104.3 and 171.3; in Montclair, N. J. 49.0 and 88.1.[1]

On the other hand, in Baltimore, Md. the rates for children of native and foreign-born mothers were the same,[2] and in Brockton the foreign-born rate was only 92.0 while the native was 101.5.[3] But perhaps the situation in New York City is the most important exception to the general rule that foreign-born mothers lose their children more frequently than native-born. In studying the statistics for 1915 Guilfoy found that while the general rate was 98.2, the rate for children of native-born mothers was 106.3.[4] A computation from Guilfoy's table gives a rate of 95.3 for children of foreign-born mothers—eleven points below that for children of native-born mothers. Guilfoy's explanation is as follows: " The foreign stock of recent acquisition, i.e. the Italian and Jewish mothers, seem to be of sturdier mould than those of native origin." [5]

[1] See U. S. Department of Labor, Children's Bureau, *Infant Mortality Series*, as follows: no. 11, Haley, " Infant Mortality in Akron, Ohio," p. 17; no. 10, Whitney, " Infant Mortality in New Bedford, Mass.," p. 18; no. 9, Allen, " Infant Mortality in Saginaw, Mich.," pp. 22-23; no. 7, Hunter, " Infant Mortality in Waterbury, Conn.," p. 70; no. 6, Duncan and Duke, " Infant Mortality in Manchester, N. H., p. 58; no. 3, Duke, " Infant Mortality in Johnstown, Pa., p. 27; no. 4, " Infant Mortality in Montclair, N. J.," p. 16.

[2] Woodbury, *op. cit.*, p. 38.

[3] U. S. Department of Labor, Children's Bureau, *op. cit.*, no. 8, Dempsey, " Infant Mortality in Brockton, Mass.," p. 24.

[4] See reference to Guilfoy's study in Meyer, *Infant Mortality in New York City* (New York, 1921), pp. 32-39. See also Guilfoy, *The Influence of Nationality upon the Mortality of a Community*, in Department of Health, New York City, *Monograph Series*, no. 18 (New York, 1917).

[5] Guilfoy, *op. cit.*, p. 12.

Obviously, in view of such discepancies as the above data disclose, we cannot say that the mere circumstance of foreign birth of mothers in itself is always a factor in excessive infant mortality. We must use more refined data and compare the mortality of infants of different nationalities separately. We may also ask in passing whether some of the discrepancies in the relative mortality rates of children of native and of foreign-born mothers may not be explained by the varying composition of the group " native-born ". For example, a Sicilian mother born the year after her parents arrived from Sicily is, of course, native-born. She has been subjected to some of the influences of the American environment, including perhaps that of the American school. Her children dying under one year of age go to swell the infant mortality rate of the children of native-born mothers. Yet in many American communities such a mother is racially very different from the Teutonic types of mothers with whom she is classed. Moreover, she has very likely lived in an Italian colony and she may be culturally also more Italian than American. Our category " native-born " is far from representing a homogeneous group. Moreover, that group varies greatly in different communities. Therefore it is not strange if the infant mortality rates of the native-born differ in different communities. To stress this point is not, of course, in the least to deny the validity of Guilfoy's contention that the presence of many Italians and Jews in New York City is a chief cause for the relatively low infant mortality rates of the foreign-born.

We conclude, therefore, that a high rate of infant mortality is a characteristic which the Portuguese share with some, but by no means with all, the foreign-born. We shall see that the Portuguese rates are among the highest.

Infant Mortality of South Europeans

As representatives to some degree of the Mediterranean race the Portuguese may share with them some inherent traits which may conceivably account in part for their excessive infant mortality. But where shall we find examples of pure Mediterranean stock with which to compare them? The best that we can do will be to consider the mortality of other South Europeans in the United States. Obviously, such a comparison is open to serious objection. South Europeans are not uniformly of Mediterranean stock. South Italians may be fairly good examples of that race, but our statistics do not distinguish between north and south Italians, although we know that the latter outnumber the former as immigrants to this country. It is only with the greatest caution, therefore, that we may use the following data.

In the Birth Registration Area of the United States the infant mortality rate for children of Italian mothers in 1920 was 94.1 as compared with a general rate for the foreign-born of 96.9.[1] This is the only group for which we have figures for the whole Registration Area which we are in any degree warranted in assuming to be predominantly of Mediterranean stock. Since the Italian rate is lower than the general rate for foreign-born we find so far no confirmation of the suggestion that South Europeans are characterized by a high infant mortality rate. Indeed the Italians are one of the two nationalities whose presence, according to Guilfoy, tends to depress the infant mortality rate for New York City.

By referring to the following table we may compare the mortality of the Italians with that of other nationalities.[2]

---

[1] U. S. Bureau of the Census, *op. cit.*, p. 35.

[2] The figures for Johnstown, Montclair, Manchester, Waterbury,

TABLE 33

INFANT MORTALITY RATES IN SPECIFIED CITIES CLASSIFIED BY NATIVITY OF MOTHERS

	Johnstown, Pa.	Montclair, N. J.	Manchester, N. H.	Waterbury, Conn.	Brockton, Mass.	Saginaw, Mich.	New Bedford, Mass.	Akron, Ohio.	Pittsburgh, Pa.	Detroit, Mich.	New York, N. Y.	Baltimore, Md.
Bohemians											135	
English								101				138
French Canadians				225			83	115				
Germans							135		105			116
Greeks											149	
Hebrews												51
Irish					185					129	119	
Italians	183	89			110	72	128		116	92	103	
Lithuanians					208							
Lithuanians and Poles						116						
Magyars									103			
Poles					189		180	120			111	163
Portuguese								201				
Scotch												79
Serbo-Croatians	264											
Swedes												65

This table indicates that the Italian rates varied all the way from 72 in Brockton to 183 in Johnstown. Surely no conclusions as to the mortality of the Mediterranean stock in the United States can be drawn from figures so diverse.

Brockton, Saginaw, New Bedford, Akron and Pittsburgh are from the published studies of the Children's Bureau, *Infant Mortality Series,* Nos. 3, 4, 6, 7, 8, 9, 10, 11 and 12 respectively, published 1915-1920. Those for Detroit are from Palmer and Blakeslee, "Infant Mortality in Detroit," *American Journal of Public Health,* vol. xi, pp. 502-507. Those for New York are from Meyer, *op. cit.,* p. 34. Those for Detroit are from Woodbury, *op. cit.,* p. 38.

The figures for New York and Detroit are not quite comparable with the rest since they refer to country of birth rather than to nationality. Where this fact made the figures without value they have been omitted for these two cities.

The Infant Mortality of Different Nationalities

But can we say that a certain approximate rate of infant mortality is a characteristic of any nationality? Disregarding the Portuguese for the moment, let us examine table 33, page 147 above, to see what degree of uniformity we find for given nationalities. For many nationalities the number of studies is too few to permit our drawing conclusions. Quite possibly this is true of all of them. As they stand, however, the variation in rates among different studies is as follows: for the English 39 points in two studies; French Canadians 142 points in three studies; Germans 30 points in three studies; Irish 76 points in two studies; Polish 78 points in five studies; and Italians 121 points in seven studies.

We see that the variability among different communities is considerable. We cannot say that a given nationality shows, regardless of other conditions, approximately the same infant mortality rate. Neither can we say that a given nationality is always characterized by a relatively high or low rate as compared with another. It is true that the Poles show in all communities studied a uniformly high rate; but in New Bedford their rate exceeds slightly that of the French Canadians, while in Manchester it falls considerably below theirs. This variability does not, of course, prove that the characteristics of nationalities are not factors in determining their rate of infant mortality. Presumably each nationality may contain different types, different social classes, perhaps even different racial stocks in different communities. Or, the nationality may find itself exposed to environmental conditions so different in different places that no uniformity in its infant mortality rates appears. In other words, it seems that the causes of infant mortality are too complex to be explained in terms of nationality alone; or else that each nationality is too heterogeneous in its composition to be treated as a unit. In a community demanding skilled labor a different type of immigrants will be attracted than in a community requiring unskilled, though the nationality may be the same in each case. A community of north Italians is not comparable with a community of south Italians. We stress this point here because below [1] we do explain Portuguese infant mortality largely in terms of national traits. We also note below [2] the existence of different types of Portuguese. Since our data are now so meager we must confine our generalizations to communities studied instead of attempting to characterize whole nationalities.

The susceptibility of particular nationalites to certain diseases has sometimes been noted. Whether such susceptibility will result in a high infant mortality rate or not will depend, of course, upon the influence of other counteracting factors. Guilfoy finds Italian mothers remarkably free from premature births with resulting infant deaths.[3] Meyer commenting on Guilfoy's study concludes : " It would seem that the influence of the racial factor was most marked in the groups of diarrheal and congenital diseases." [4] Palmer and Blakeslee [5] and Meyer [6] note the abnormally high death rates from respiratory diseases among Italian infants, Meyer attributing it to climatic change. Those inclined towards the racial hypothesis for infant mortality will note that Italian, Portuguese and negro infants all show high rates from respiratory diseases. Thus a single disease

[1] *Cf. infra*, pp. 192-3.
[2] *Cf. infra*, pp. 343-4.
[3] Guilfoy, *op. cit.*, p. 12.
[4] Meyer, *op. cit.*, p. 36.
[5] Palmer and Blakeslee, *op. cit.*, p. 506.
[6] Meyer, *op. cit.*, p. 36.

seems to be characteristic of these nationalities; but we cannot say that a high infant mortality rate is also characteristic of them regardless of differing conditions.

The Infant Mortality of the Portuguese Urban and Rural

Our information as to the infant mortality of the Portuguese is confined to four localities and four sources. We have an excellent Children's Bureau study of infant mortality in New Bedford; a Bureau of Labor Statistics study of the effects of the employment of women on infant mortality in Fall River in 1908; an unusual study of all infants born in Fall River during three summer months of 1913 undertaken by the Fall River Woman's Club with the assistance of Dr. Louis I. Dublin; and such additional data as the writer has been able to gather for 1920 in Fall River, for a number of years in Porstmouth, R. I., and just a hint of the situation in Provincetown, Mass. Unfortunately, the Bureau of the Census does not present separately births and deaths for the Portuguese in the Birth Registration Area, although in a few cities this means losing sight of the most important single group. In none of the Children's Bureau studies except New Bedford were the Portuguese of sufficient importance to warrant their separate considertion.

What, then, are the facts as shown by these studies? The Bureau of Labor Statistics study was concerned with the factor of employment of women as related to infant mortality and will be referred to later under that head. As it was a study of deaths only no infant mortality rates by nationality were figured.

The Woman's Club investigators adopted a method new at that time. They traced all births registered, and such others as could be found, which had occurred during the summer period of three months. They followed these children throughout a year of life recording the conditions surrounding them and noting the mortality for that year. As noted above, the infant mortality rates obtained in that way are not exactly comparable with other rates, because the mortality may be affected by the fact that these infants passed their earliest months of life during the heat of summer. After making allowance for the infants who were lost sight of during the year Dr. Dublin finds a general infant mortality rate for the city of 202.4; for infants born to native mothers of 152.9; for infants born to mothers born in Portugal and the Azores of 298.9; for infants born to mothers born in Canada of 172.4; and for infants born to mothers born in other countries of 200.0. Needless to say, these rates are shockingly high, although, as noted above, they probably exaggerate the true rates somewhat. As for the Portuguese, practically thirty per cent of their infants died before they reached their first birthday anniversary.[1]

For New Bedford the Children's Bureau study found a general infant mortality rate of 130.3. Classifying the foreign-born mothers by nationality the Portuguese showed much the highest rate (200.9) of any group. The Poles, the next group, had a rate of only 119.8 with the French Canadians slightly lower with 115.5.[2] Thus on the face of the figures the infant mortality problem of New Bedford appears to be pretty largely a problem of the Portuguese nationality. To quote from that study: " If the Portuguese group with its high birth and high mortality rate were omitted from New Bedford, the rate would have been only 103.7 or much more like that of Brockton." [3] The

---

[1] Dublin, "Infant Mortality in Fall River, Mass.," reprinted from the *Quarterly Publications of the American Statistical Association,* June, 1915, p. 12.

[2] Whitney, *op. cit.,* p. 18.

[3] *Ibid.,* p. 69.

Portuguese are said to make up roughly a quarter of the total population of New Bedford to-day, yet each year since 1918 at least, more than half the infant deaths have been in Portuguese families.[1] Except for the year of Miss Whitney's study we do not have information as to what proportion of the births in New Bedford are in Portuguese families. Consideration of the above startling figures helps one to understand the significance of the advertisement of an enterprising photographer in one of the Portuguese districts: " Photos live after death—Bring the old folks, bring the babies."

The writer has also analyzed the birth and death statistics for Fall River using the records in the office of the City Clerk. The method here was slightly different, however, for by including births and deaths of infants born to native mothers of Portuguese descent with those of infants of foreign-born Portuguese a comparison between Portuguese and non-Portuguese stock was possible. Thus this table refers to descent rather than to nativity.

TABLE 34

INFANT MORTALITY IN FALL RIVER, MASS., 1920

(STILLBORN EXCLUDED)

NON-PORTUGUESE COMPARED WITH PORTUGUESE [2]

Descent of Mothers	Births	Deaths under one year	I. M. Rate
Non-Portuguese	2483	271	109.1
Portuguese	1054	228	216.3

[1] New Bedford, Mass., Board of Health, *Annual Report for 1920*, proof sheets shown the writer. Also computed from other material furnished by the Board.

[2] Births and deaths to Portuguese mothers married to non-Portuguese included as "Portuguese". Births and deaths to mothers who were non-Portuguese but who were married to Portuguese included as "non-Portuguese". In the few cases where it was necessary to determine nationality by names a slight error may be involved. The writer believes it to be very slight. If such errors occur they operate to understate by so much the number of Portuguese births and deaths. The employment of Portuguese midwives or physicians was of some help in doubtful cases.

The contrast shown by this table is interesting. It becomes still more so when we reflect that among the non-Portuguese we include foreign-born French-Canadians, Poles, Italians, Syrians, English and Irish. That despite this the Portuguese rate is practically double that of the non-Portuguese is indeed remarkable.

The following table divides our Portuguese into two groups of mothers, "native-born of Portuguese descent", and "foreign-born."

TABLE 35

INFANT MORTALITY OF PORTUGUESE

(STILLBORN EXCLUDED)

FALL RIVER, MASS., 1920

Mothers	Births	Deaths under one year	I. M. Rate
Native-born Portuguese descent	90	17	188.9
Foreign-born Portuguese	964	211	218.9

The above table will perhaps be disappointing to those who expect to see the problem of infant mortality disappear after the immigrant has become adjusted to American conditions. A difference of but thirty points in favor of the native-born mothers of Portuguese descent is not very great. In view of the importance we have attached elsewhere [1] to the effects of residence in this country upon the standard of living of the Portuguese, the writer is somewhat surprised at the smallness of the difference in these rates. The New Bedford study showed a much greater influence of residence here.[2] Perhaps the numbers concerned are too small to be significant, and at any rate the difference is in the right direction.

Our infant mortality rates for the rural community of Portsmouth are not strictly comparable with those given

[1] *Cf. infra*, pp. 275-282.

[2] *Cf. infra*, p. 159.

above. Since Portsmouth records only about a dozen infant deaths a year no significant rates for any one year can be figured. Therefore our data are for a period of eleven years beginning in 1910. A longer period was not used because prior to 1910 there was no assurance that births had been registered with even their present degree of completeness. Since 1910, however, under the direction of the present town clerk, the reports of physicians, midwives or other witnesses of births have been checked up by sending a messenger from the Town Clerk's office to report unregistered births. Physicians have been at times very tardy in reporting births in Portsmouth, but despite the fact that Rhode Island has been dropped from the Birth Registration Area, it is believed that registration has been reasonably complete in Portsmouth since 1910.

The Portsmouth data also classify as Portuguese all mothers whether foreign-born or native-born of Portuguese descent. In this respect they are comparable with the data given in Table 35 above for Fall River. Since the two groups of mothers have not been separated, however, the rates are not quite comparable with those of the other studies quoted above. In Portsmouth, however, the number of women of Portuguese descent born in this country is so small that their inclusion can have but little effect upon the infant mortality rate. Thus table 62 [1] shows but thirteen mothers of families resident in Portsmouth who were born in this country. This fact may possibly account in part for the difference in the mortality rate of the Portuguese in Portsmouth and in Fall River, but the writer does not believe this is the true explanation. Table 36 below gives the record of births and infant deaths in Portsmouth for the eleven year period 1910-1920 inclusive.

[1] *Cf. infra,* p. 274.

TABLE 36

PORTSMOUTH, R. I., BIRTHS AND DEATHS UNDER ONE YEAR 1910-1920 CLASSIFIED BY DESCENT

	Native [2]		Portuguese [3]		Other Foreign		Unknown		Totals	
	Births	Deaths	Births	Deaths	Births	Deaths	Births	Deaths	Births	Deaths
0	19	2	31	14	6	1	0	0	56	17
1	12	1	42	5	13	5	0	0	67	11
2	14	0	44	8	12	1	0	0	70	9
3	17	2	54	7	7	0	0	0	78	9
4	15	1	60	14	5	0	0	2	80	17
5	14	5	48	15	2	0	0	1	64	21
6	30	4	51	12	5	0	1	0	87	16
7	19	0	61	9	4	0	0	0	84	9
8	20	1	73	11	5	0	0	0	98	12
9	25	5	61	6	10	0	0	0	96	11
10	29	3	49	7	1	0	0	0	79	10
Totals	214	24	574	108	70	7	1	3	859	142

PORTSMOUTH, R. I., COMBINED INFANT MORTALITY, 1910-1920 (STILLBORN EXCLUDED)

General infant mortality rate 165
Rate for children of native mothers (those of Portuguese descent omitted) 112
Portuguese (including native-born of Portuguese descent) 188
Other foreign rate .... 100 [4]

The above table is instructive. While the rate for the non-Portuguese native-born is abnormally high as it is, the presence of the Portuguese raises the general rate for the town from 112 to 165, or fifty-three points. That the Portuguese of Portsmouth should lose nearly two out of every

[1] Computed from birth and death registers in Town Clerk's office.

[2] Omitting those where either parent was of Portuguese nationality—these were few in number.

[3] Including births and deaths of infants whose parents were born in the United States but who were of Portuguese descent.

[4] This rate is probably too low because of the mobility of the population after the closing of the coal mines.

ten babies born, before they are a year old, is mute testimony to the conditions among these people. It is not to minimize the importance of the economic factors in infant mortality that we call attention to the fact that these babies die without any of the handicaps of city and industrial life to which high infant mortality is frequently attributed.

In three communities and four studies the Portuguese have shown an extremely high mortality of infants. In New Bedford they had a rate of 201; in Fall River of 218.9 for foreign-born and of 216.3 when natives of Portuguese descent are included; in Portsmouth of 188 when natives of Portuguese descent are added; while Dr. Dublin found a still higher rate for summer-born babies in 1913. Even if we grant the entire contention of those who stress nonpersonal causes of infant mortality we must admit that the Portuguese do largely account for the excessively high infant mortality rates of these communities. Whatever the cause it is the Portuguese babies that die. Perhaps future study will discover Portuguese communities, say in California or elsewhere, without this extraordinary mortality of infants; but to date we must characterize these people as afflicted with this curse wherever they have been studied.[1]

The Portuguese lose somewhat fewer babies in rural Portsmouth than in urban Fall River. This is in spite of

---

[1] Since this paragraph was written the writer has figured the Portuguese and non-Portuguese infant mortality rates for Provincetown for the five year period from 1916-1920. During this period there were 519 births and 48 deaths under one year recorded. 383 births and 32 infant deaths were of children of Portuguese parents. Thus the Portuguese infant mortality rate is 84 and the non-Portuguese 118 for the five years combined. This is in contrast to our other data. The lower rate for the Portuguese may be due to longer residence here or it may be due to the presence in Provincetown of a different type of Portuguese. The earlier settlers there were fishermen largely from the Horta District, but we have no recent data on the present composition of the population.

practically entire lack of community aid in Portsmouth. In Fall River and New Bedford a great deal of most excellent work is being done for babies of all nationalities. In Fall River a splendidly organized District Nursing Association is the chief educational and remedial force. In New Bedford a similar though smaller Instructive Nurses Association co-operates with the City Board of Health. In Portsmouth, except that recently the Child Welfare Bureau of the State has sent a nurse to look up new-born babies, and except for a year's experiment with a Red Cross nurse, the babies are left to survive or perish without community aid.

In Portsmouth the extremes of poverty were quite as evident as in Fall River if one may judge by living conditions. It must be confessed, however, that Fall River was seen under favorable economic conditions and that many a Portuguese farmer who lives in dirt and squalor is saving money to purchase a farm.

Women are employed in Portsmouth quite as much as in Fall River, but they work in the fields, an employment which is harder than mill work but which does not take the mother away from home and so perhaps is somewhat less important in interfering with breast feeding. In the absence of an intensive infant mortality study in Portsmouth we have no information as to methods of feeding nor as to other matters of similar importance. If the work of the city nurses counts for anything breast feeding should be more common there than in the country. Perhaps birth returns are more complete in the city but this would operate to exaggerate the rural rate so that the true rate would be lower still as compared with that in Fall River.

The factors which may in part account for the higher city rate are: somewhat greater congestion in living quarters, employment of mothers away from the home, the healthful out-door life in the rural community, and the better adaptation of the Azorean peasant to the simple life of the farm. Yet however we explain the lower rural rate of 188, it cannot be city life alone which causes the high mortality among Portuguese infants.

Length of Residence in the United States

The Portuguese do have an abnormal rate of infant mortality. We hesitate, however, to conclude that the presence of the Portuguese must always mean this curse because of the paucity of our data, the great variation shown by other nationalities in different communities, and because of the variation among the Portuguese themselves. Anyone confining his attention to the Children's Bureau study of Manchester, might easily come to the conclusion that the presence of French Canadians will always mean a high infant mortality rate, for in that city they showed a shocking rate of 225.[1] Yet in New Bedford, also a cotton mill city, the same nationality had a rate scarcely half that they showed in Manchester. Speaking of this difference the report on New Bedford comments: " The difference in these figures is the more difficult to explain since both cities are textile centers and in both a large proportion of the French Canadian mothers worked in the mills. The New Bedford group represented an earlier immigration and therefore many have already adopted American customs." [2]

In view of the correlation shown elsewhere between length of residence and standard of living the writer is inclined to accept this explanation. To accept it is, of course, to emphasize ignorance and national characteristics as causes of the immigrant's ills. It is at the same time a conclusion which permits one to be somewhat hopeful of improved

---

[1] *Cf.* table 33, *supra.*

[2] Whitney, *op. cit.,* p. 19.

conditions even for a very ignorant people. This tentative conclusion is also in harmony with the explanation offered in the Manchester study. " In their method of feeding and in the size of their families the French Canadians show distinctive conditions which may account partly for the difference between their infant mortality rate and the rates of other groups of foreign-born." [1] Thus at the end of three months 75.9 per cent of other foreign, 60.9 per cent of native, and only 52.6 per cent of French Canadian mothers were feeding their babies exclusively at the breast.[2] The French Canadians also had unusually large families.[3]

Neither the studies of infant mortality in Fall River nor our own investigations permit us to correlate infant mortality with length of residence in this country. But Miss Whitney's study in New Bedford gives data on this subject. There for the Portuguese white group the infant mortality rate decreased in a striking manner as the length of residence increased. Portuguese mothers who had been here less than three years had a rate of 283, while those resident here from twelve to fifteen years had a normal rate of only 95.[4] Moreover, our comparison between mothers in Fall River of Portuguese descent and those born abroad confirms this impression though in a less striking way.[5] Still more, in the writer's judgment, do the findings of this study with reference to standard of living and length of residence confirm this conclusion.

[1] Duncan and Duke, *op. cit.*, p. 63.
[2] *Ibid.*, p. 68.
[3] *Ibid.*, p. 118.
[4] Whitney, *op. cit.*, p. 20.
[5] *Cf. supra*, p. 153.

Inability to speak English

Common sense would assure us that ability to speak English must be an asset to a mother in caring for her children. Yet evidence is strangely confused on this point. Among Italians in Waterbury [1] and among French Canadians in New Bedford [2] the reverse was found to be true. The weight of evidence is, however, with common sense; among non-English speaking nationalities of Saginaw and of New Bedford considerably higher rates were found for those who had not mastered the English language; [3] and among the Portuguese of New Bedford, the children of 571 mothers who were unable to speak English died at a rate of 224.8, as against only 82.9 for children of mothers who could speak it. [4] The large number of Portuguese mothers who are ignorant of English is thus probably a fairly important characteristic which makes for high infant mortality.

Illiteracy of Mothers

The New Bedford study does not show how large a proportion of Portuguese mothers were unable to read or write in their own language, but we have shown elsewhere [5] that the Portuguese are among the least literate of our immigrant nationalities with an illiteracy of about two-thirds that in their homeland. For all nationalities in New Bedford the rate for children of literate mothers was 107.1, and for those of illiterate it was 188.0. Too great emphasis can scarcely be laid upon this matter of illiteracy.

[1] Hunter, *op. cit.*, p. 74.
[2] Whitney, *op. cit.*, p. 20.
[3] Allen, *op. cit.*, p. 25 and Whitney, *op. cit.*, p. 20.
[4] Whitney, *op. cit.*, pp. 20-21.
[5] *Cf. supra*, p. 116.

It is not so much that illiteracy causes infant mortality, although it no doubt is a real factor. It is rather that illiteracy is such a good index of the ignorance of a people. No one can visit the Portuguese homes of the poorer type without being impressed with the intellectual barrenness of their lives. It is not surprising that people so ignorant are unable to keep their babies alive.

Attendance at Childbirth

The habit of employing midwives to deliver infants sometimes, though not always, implies less expert care at childbirth and by some has been associated with a high infant mortality rate. Statistics, however, have sometimes seemed to prove the opposite where physicians, who doubtless attend the more serious cases, have been seen actually to lose more infants than have the midwives. It is therefore unsafe to draw dogmatic conclusions as to the influence of attendance by midwives. We shall nevertheless simply note the facts: In New Bedford " The racial group which had the largest percentage of births attended by midwives was the Portuguese white with 56.8 per cent." [1] A little over half the Portuguese colored (Bravas), somewhat under half the Poles, only 11 per cent of the English and a " negligible " proportion of French Canadians and other nationalities employed midwives. The infant mortality rate for all mothers employing midwives was 169.1 against 115.5 for those employing physicians. In Fall River the writer has found on investigation that 65.7 per cent [2] of all Portuguese births occuring in 1920 were attended by midwives. As this percentage is based upon a consideration of native-born of Portuguese descent as well as foreign-born Portuguese it seems to show that the employment of

[1] Whitney, *op. cit.*, pp. 31-33.
[2] *Cf.* table 37, p. 162.

midwives was somewhat more common among the Portuguese of Fall River than among those of New Bedford. For the reasons given above, however, we can hardly list the employment of midwives among the characteristics of the Portuguese which make for a high infant mortality rate.

TABLE 37

ATTENDANCE AT CHILDBIRTH,[1] FALL RIVER, MASS., 1920

Birth Reported by Mother born in	*Physician*	*Midwife*	*Father*	*Nurse*	*Unknown*	*No one*[3]	*Neighbor*	
St. Michael's	73	459	7					5:
Terceira		5						
St. George		1						
Azores (not specified)	118	116	13	1		1	1	25
Lisbon	2	17						1
Portugal (not specified)	51	64	17	4		2	1	13
United States	65	37	3					10
Bermuda	3	4	1					
Brazil	3	3						
Hawaii	2	2			1			
Cape Verde	1							
Canada[2]	5	1						
France[2]	1							
England[2]	1	2						
Mexico		1						
Ireland[2]	1	1						
Scotland[2]		1						
Madeira	1	12						1
Totals	327	726	41	5	1	3	2	11
Per cents	29.6%	65.7%	4.0%	.4%	.1%	.3%	.2%	100

Preventable Causes of Death

The standards of care given babies are largely reflected in the death rates from gastric and intestinal diseases. Respiratory diseases are also, according to the Children's

[1] Computed from the Birth Register of Fall River, Mass. for 1920.

[2] Father Portuguese but mother non-Portuguese.

[3] That is no attendant.

Bureau, an index of child care. In New Bedford the death rates from gastric and intestinal diseases were 31.6 for the native-born, 54.9 for the foreign-born and 101.9 for the Portuguese, showing that this nationality is almost entirely responsible for the excessive rate for the foreign-born from these causes.[1] For respiratory diseases the rate among children of native mothers was 17.8, of foreign-born 31.8 and of the Portuguese 51.0. To quote the study:

The causes of these unfavorable conditions resulting in a high rate of infant mortality from intestinal and respiratory diseases, must be sought in the kind of care given the infants, in the kind of feeding, and also in part in the customs of the mothers and in the surroundings in which they live.[2]

While the Woman's Club study of infant mortality in Fall River gives no tables showing causes of death by nationality, those responsible for this study have informed the present writer that the Portuguese who made up 39 per cent of all infant deaths studied, made up about 50 per cent of deaths from diarrhea and enteritis, 53 per cent of deaths from diseases of the lungs but only 27 per cent of deaths from diseases of early infancy. The study also makes the following comment:

The death rate of the Portuguese infants is unfortunately large, 298.9 per thousand. . . . It may be seen by reference to the record cards that a great many of these fifty-two Portuguese infants who died, were born in poor condition, and that the majority had mothers who were themselves in poor condition if not actually sick. The most notable excess of deaths was from diseases of the respiratory organs, though the Portuguese infants have also far more than their proportion of deaths following premature birth.[3]

[1] Whitney, *op. cit.*, p. 23.

[2] *Ibid.*, pp. 24-5.

[3] The Woman's Club of Fall River, *Report on Infant Mortality* (Fall River, 1915), p. 14.

Dr. Dublin, who throughout stresses economic rather than personal causes of infant mortality, says in this connection:

The foreign-born mother in Fall River, for example, is more likely to work in the mills during pregnancy, to have many children, and to live in crowded and unhygienic quarters. She, more than the native mother, reflects the injurious influences of an unfavorable industrial and economic environment. We find accordingly that the excessive deaths of infants of foreign-born mothers are due especially to pneumonia, to diarrhea and enteritis, and to premature birth and congenital debility. We may illustrate the above with reference to infants of Portuguese mothers who showed the highest death rate. Of the 182 mothers 72, or 39 per cent, were engaged in work outside the household during pregnancy, while only 17 per cent of the mothers of other nationalities were so engaged. Of the fifty-two deaths of Portuguese children 20 were due to diarrhea and enteritis, 17 to pneumonia and bronchitis, and 13 to prematurity, congenital debility and other causes peculiar to early infancy.[1]

Thus one interpreter emphasizes the poor physical condition of the Portuguese; the other the great amount of outside work on their part. We shall discuss this economic factor later.[2]

Artificial Feeding of Infants

Artificial feeding is universally recognized as a factor in infant mortality. When it is combined with uncleanliness and ignorance on the part of mothers its effects are most pronounced. Woodbury, for example, found the rate for the breast-fed to be only 21.3 per cent of that for the artificially fed.[3] While often due to physiological causes

---

[1] Dublin, "Infant Mortality of Fall River, Mass.," reprinted from the *Quarterly Publications of the American Statistical Association*, June, 1915, p. 13.

[2] *Cf. infra*, p. 171.

[3] Woodbury, *op. cit.*, p. 40.

beyond control, artificial feeding seems often to be traceable either to employment of mothers away from home, lack of adequate provision on the part of the community for the instruction and aid of mothers, ignorance of mothers or too frequent pregnancies. These various more fundamental factors are considered elsewhere.

In neither account of the 1913 study of infant mortality in Fall River do we find data on the method of feeding classified by nationalities. Both accounts show the usual relationship between artificial feeding and a high infant mortality. In the study of infant mortality in Fall River for the year 1908, however, we learn that only among Irish mothers was breast feeding less common than among the Portuguese. The percentages of breast-fed infants by nationalities were: Polish 55.6 per cent, French Canadians 33.6 per cent, Portuguese 27.4 per cent and Irish 16.7 per cent.[1]

In the New Bedford study we read: " A much smaller percentage of the infants of Portuguese-white mothers than of other foreign nationalities was breast-fed, smaller even than that of the infants of native mothers. The Portuguese contributed the largest proportion of mixed-fed infants." In the third month 39.9 per cent of Portuguese infants, 37.7 per cent of infants of native-born mothers, and 28.5 per cent of infants of other foreign-born mothers were fed artificially.[2] That other factors may nevertheless be quite as important as the method of feeding is indicated by the fact that the infants of native-born mothers who fed their babies artificially had a mortality rate of 153.2, while those of foreign-born mothers had a rate of 247.1.[3] Im-

[1] U. S. Bureau of Labor Statistics, *Bulletin no. 175, Summary of the Report on the Condition of Women and Child Wage-earners in the United States*, p. 356.

[2] Whitney, *op. cit.*, p. 33.

[3] *Ibid.*, p. 35.

proper feeding does nevertheless probably account for the high death rate from gastric and intestinal causes among Portuguese infants.[1]   Thus we find that improper feeding is common among the Portuguese mothers and helps to explain the high mortality of their infants.

Inadequate Income

Perhaps no other alleged cause of infant mortality has been more emphasized than the low incomes of fathers. This is, of course, the fundamental *economic* factor to which other factors such as employment of mothers, overcrowding in the home, et cetera, are largely though not entirely secondary.

Most studies have shown that the infant death rate drops as the father's wage or income rises.   Miss Lathrop, who lays great stress upon this economic factor, summarizes the results of the Children's Bureau studies thus:

The fathers of 88 per cent of the babies included in the Bureau's studies earned less than $1250 a year; 27 per cent earned less than $550.   As the income doubled the mortality rate was more than halved.   Which is the more safe and sane conclusion: that 88 per cent of all these fathers were incorrigibly indolent or below normal mentally, or that sound public economy demands an irreducible minimum living standard be sustained by a minimum wage and such other expedients as may be developed in a determined effort to give every child a fair chance? [2]

In support of her argument Miss Lathrop quotes figures from the Bureau's studies in Johnstown, Manchester, Brockton, Saginaw, New Bedford, Waterbury, Akron and Baltimore.   In all cases the infant mortality rate was seen

[1] *Ibid.*, p. 36.

[2] Lathrop, "Income and Infant Mortality," in *The American Journal of Public Health*, vol. ix, p. 274, April, 1919.

to vary markedly with income of fathers except in Brockton where the rate for those with incomes of over $1250 was 73.5 as against 67.1 for those with incomes under $550. For all cities combined the rate for the high income group was but 64.3 while that for the low income group was 151.4. In New Bedford as elsewhere the infant mortality rates were thus found to vary with the father's income. There one-fifth of all fathers had incomes of less than $450.[1] and their infants had a mortality rate of 201.9; while those infants whose fathers received over $1250 a year had the remarkably low rate of 59.9.[2]

Neither account of the Woman's Club study of Fall River, as published, gives figures as to income. We present herewith a more recent tabulation of data obtained in that study covering this factor though very inadequately. Except for the appearance of some government data on wages in Fall River this table could have been constructed in 1915 when the study was published. This was not done because of the incompleteness of the data. The matter of income is so important that it seemed best to include this table in the present study despite its incompleteness.[3]

[1] Care must be taken not to compare incomes in different cities for these studies were made at different times and radical changes in incomes have taken place since this study in New Bedford was made. This fact does not, however, invalidate comparisons between income groups in the same study.

[2] Whitney, *op. cit.*, pp. 39 *et seq.*

[3] This table is a revision by the writer of a table furnished by the authorities in Fall River who were active in the earlier investigation. For the facts therein contained, therefore, they are responsible. The revision and the comments are those of the present writer. The table was constructed as follows. Most of the original schedules gave the occupation of the father. In some cases information was obtained after the first study was made. In not a few cases the actual weekly wages of fathers were recorded. Where these were not recorded the occupation was used as a guide where possible. Had the income groups used been narrower this course would have been impossible. In all doubtful cases fathers' incomes were classified as unknown.

TABLE 38

WEEKLY WAGES OF FATHERS AT THE TIME OF THE BIRTHS OF THEIR CHILDREN

FALL RIVER, 1913

(THOSE OF MIXED DESCENT AND "AMERICANS"[1] OMITTED)

	Under $12 a week		Over $12 a week		Wage unknown		Totals
	No.	Per cent	No.	Per cent	No.	Per cent	
French Canadian ...	52	25%	47	22%	111	53%	210
Portuguese	125	61%	11	5%	68	34%	204
Polish	59	74%	1	1%	20	25%	80
English	21	30%	15	21%	35	49%	71
Irish	13	25%	12	23%	26	50%	51
Italians	12		4		7		23
Jewish	1		3		12		16
Syrians	5		0		4		9
Totals	288	43%	93	14%	288	43%	669

Nothing more than a general impression is warranted from this very imperfect table. Its significance depends much upon the composition of the group " wage unknown ". The list of occupations under this heading is too long to print here but it may be said that it includes in about equal proportions occupations such as " storekeepers " where one would expect the income to be over $12 a week, and " farm laborers " where it may have been less. The writer gets the impression from a study of this table that the Portuguese do belong to a low income group in Fall River but that it is no lower and probably not so low as that of the Poles. In other words, this table confirms the usual discovery that a low income group also has a high infant mortality rate; except that the Poles seem to be a still lower income group. We have no data as to the infant mortality of the Poles in Fall River except the information that only 13 per cent of

---

[1] In this table those only are included both of whose parents and all of whose grandparents were of the nationality under consideration. Similarly, "Americans" who are omitted consist of only 37 children whose parents and grandparents were native-born.

the 80 Polish babies studied by the Woman's Club in 1913, died. We noted that they had shown uniformly high rates in other studies. In table 40 below [1] we show that while 50.9 per cent of Portuguese children died before they were five years old, only 35.2 per cent of Polish children died before that age. Our above table is too incomplete to make comparisons between income and infant mortality of other descent groups possible. If our Poles were a little more numerous and our data more complete the comparison between Poles and Portuguese would be very significant. As it is, they seem to indicate that the inferior non-economic characteristics of the Portuguese outweigh in their influence upon infant deaths, their somewhat superior economic position. The writer does not assert that this is true. Many more comparisons of this kind will be necessary, and comparisons based upon more accurate and complete data, before we can assert or deny that national characteristics are more important in their effects upon infant mortality than is income.

Of course the most obvious objection to attributing a high infant mortality to low wages because the two are often correlated, is the danger that both high infant mortality and low wages may be due to a common cause or group of causes. The Portuguese are relatively recent immigrants, they are relatively ignorant of American ways as compared, let us say, with the French Canadians, and they are relatively illiterate. These characteristics among others all make for a high infant mortality rate, and they also make for relative economic inefficiency. Relative economic inefficiency means relatively low incomes, other things being equal. This is undoubtedly one of the reasons why so large a proportion of Portuguese are in unskilled work in the cotton mills or elsewhere. Even though the Portu-

[1] *Infra*, p. 185.

guese should prove to be peculiarly efficient in these unskilled ocupations, it would still remain true that they have
as yet largely failed to reach the better paid occupations
where we find other nationalities in larger numbers. It
is true that Fall River does not offer so many opportunities
for more skilled work outside of the cotton mills as do
some other communities; yet other nationalities have found
such better-paid occupations in larger numbers than have
the Portuguese.

It is conceivable that this is only a temporary situation.
It is conceivable that with the removal of illiteracy.and other
changes the Portuguese may enter better paid occupations.
The writer's study in Portsmouth makes him somewhat
optimistic of this ultimate result. It is conceivable, too, that
the Portuguese may be somewhat more exploited than other
peoples because of their ignorance. We have gathered no
data on this subject. But granting all this, the danger mentioned above still remains and there is some evidence that
it is real. When we correlate low wages and high infant
mortality, to repeat, there is a danger that we may be
largely measuring the results of a common cause—the ignorance of the people under consideration. There is abundant
evidence in this study and elsewhere that ignorance is a
reality among the Portuguese.

On the other hand, the writer would not be understood as
implying that there is no causal relationship between low
income and high infant mortality. Undoubtedly higher incomes would mean better food, better housing, and better
surroundings in general. In the long run, despite much
ignorance, a rise in income raises the standard of living.
That such an effect is not immediate, however, the war experience with higher real wages in some occupations abund-
antly proves. There is no evidence of which the writer is
aware that the higher real wages in the cotton mills saved
the lives of Portuguese babies in 1919 and 1920.

The Portuguese then are a low income group and low incomes are correlated with high infant mortality. It is not proven that these low incomes are or are not important causes of the high infant mortality. To the writer, while both ignorance and low income doubtless have their influence, the former seems the more fundamental among the Portuguese.

Employment of Mothers Before and After Childbirth

The evidence as to the importance of the employment of mothers in the problem of infant mortality is somewhat conflicting. Mothers who have been employed outside the home have usually lost their babies more frequently than those not so employed. Thus for the combined figures of the Children's Bureau for Brockton, Manchester, Saginaw and New Bedford, the mortality rate for children whose mothers were not gainfully employed was 105.5, for children whose mothers were gainfully employed 158.4, and for those whose mothers were gainfully employed away from home it was 179.1.[1] The greatest contrast was for Saginaw where the rate for children of unemployed mothers was only 78.3, while where they were employed it was 132.7. On the other hand, Brockton was an exception to this general rule with a rate for the former of 105.5 as against only 85.5 for the latter. The type of employment, the type of employee and the degree of skill is very different in Brockton from what it is in the cotton mill cities.

So far as insufficiency of income is a cause of infant mortality the employment of mothers may tend to prevent death. As Ashby says:[2] " There is the question whether the baby is not worse off, if the family is in great poverty with the mother at home than if she is employed and thereby

---

[1] Dempsey, *op. cit.*, p. 38.

[2] Ashby, *Infant Mortality* (Cambridge, 1915), p. 38.

assisting to augment the family income." As Hibbs says, the fundamental economic and industrial factor in infant mortality is low wages. Employment of mothers is merely a means of remedying low income. Moreover, it does not prove employment of women to be the chief cause to correlate the proportion of women employed and the mortality rates, for along with this factor go usually a high proportion of foreign-born, a high female illiteracy and a high birth rate.[1] The same author writing in 1916 concluded on this point: " Little accurate information is available on this point, yet enough to show that the proportion of mothers employed in gainful occupations does not account for the excessive mortality in industrial cities." [2]

We have already noted above [3] Dr. Dublin's comment for Fall River that about twice as large a proportion of Portuguese mothers as mothers of other nationalities were engaged in work outside the household during pregnancy. From this fact and the fact of the high infant mortality of the Portuguese he assumes a causal relationship between employment of Portuguese mothers and the early deaths of their infants. He himself says, however: " It has been impossible to determine from the schedules . . . . how long before childbirth the employed mothers quit work, or how soon after childbirth work was resumed." In view of this lack of information in his data and of the results of other studies where this information was available, his assumption of causal relationship does not seem to be established, despite a fairly strong presumption. Moreover, he does not present information showing just how employment affected the welfare of the children.

[1] Hibbs, *op. cit.*, pp. 126-127.

[2] *Ibid.*, p. 105.

[3] *Cf. supra*, p. 164.

The earlier Fall Fiver study of 1908 made a special investigation of the effect of the employment of mothers upon infant mortality. Unfortunately infant deaths alone were studied so no comparative mortality rates for children of employed and of unemployed mothers could be figured. It was found that 45.9 per cent of the 580 mothers studied were employed outside the home during pregnancy.[1] But while 271 mothers continued work at home up to within four days of childbirth, only fourteen remained so long at work away from home. The investigators conclude: " It would appear then that the conditions which were found existing do not indicate that the work of the mother in the cotton mill before childbirth was producing results notably different from the work of mothers at home." [2]

Of the effect of work after childbirth the authors say: " Artificial feeding . . . . was much more general among the children of mothers at work than among the children of mothers at home." [3] But they found that only 83 or 14.4 per cent of all children dying under one year had been deprived of the mother's care because of her going to work. " This per cent represented the extent of the possible effect of the mother's absence from home." But in only 42 cases or 7.9 per cent of all was the mother's nursing in any way affected by her absence from home. Nevertheless, among this small number, diarrhea, enteritis and gastritis killed an 80 per cent larger proportion (62.7 per cent) than where mothers remained at home (34.6 per cent). They concluded: " The high infant mortality rate of Fall River as a whole clearly is not due, except in very small part, to the excessive rate among the children of mothers at work outside the home. . . . The mother's ignorance of proper

[1] Bureau of Labor Statistics, *op. cit.*, p. 340.

[2] *Ibid.*, pp. 350-351.

[3] *Ibid.*, p. 353.

feeding, of proper care, and of the simplest requirements of hygiene " was considered the chief cause. " To this all other causes must be regarded as secondary." [1]

On the other hand, comparison of the bare figures for the infant mortality of children of mothers gainfully employed with those for children of housekeepers certainly indicates a high correlation between employment of mothers and excessive infant mortality. Dublin presents such a comparison for Fall River and shows a rate for children of housekeepers of 160.5 and for children of mothers gainfully employed of 303.6.[2] The account of the same study published by the Fall River Woman's Club divides the group " gainfully employed " into 107 who were also housekeepers whose infants showed the shockingly high rate of 592.0, and " gainfully employed not housekeepers " whose rate was only 118.8.[3] It adds, " Therefore gainful employment seems not in itself a factor in the infant mortality of the births here considered." [4] Whether one agrees with this interpretation of the data or not, it is a striking enough fact that 107 women in Fall River should have tried to raise a baby, work away from home and keep house at the same time, and that the price they paid for the attempt was the loss among them of nearly six out of every ten children born, before they reached their first birthday anniversary. This is a terrible state of affairs whether it was poverty chiefly or ignorance chiefly which led them to go to work or to lose their babies. In the face of such facts one cannot avoid giving some weight to employment of mothers in accounting for infant mortality.

[1] Bureau of Labor Statistics, *op. cit.*, p. 358.

[2] Dublin, *op. cit.*, p. 14.

[3] Fall River Woman's Club, *op. cit.*, p. 15.

[4] It is interesting to note what different interpretations are made of the same data by different students.

In the New Bedford study data are given showing the higher rates for children of employed mothers, but this study emphasizes still more, if anything, the effect of the ignorance of the Portuguese and their national habits. 47 per cent of the births studied there were to mothers gainfully employed during the year preceding the baby's birth.[1] The mortality of children whose mothers were gainfully employed was 154.1, but where they were not so employed the rate was 108.8. A slightly higher rate (167.8) was found where the mother was employed away from home.[2] With reference to employment after childbirth the same study shows that of 578 live-born infants whose mothers worked outside the home 146 died during the first year giving a rate of 252.6. But 103 of these deaths occurred before the mother went to work and so cannot have been affected by her employment.[3] To quote:

The effect upon infant mortality of the mother's employment away from home during the year after the infant's birth may be shown by the following calculation. There were 475 infants who were alive when their mothers commenced or resumed work. If the average infant mortality rate for the city for the remainder of the year had prevailed among them a total of 29 deaths would have occurred; but actually 43 of their infants died. The ratio of 43 to 29 expresses the extra mortality among these infants of gainfully employed mothers.[4]

This is equivalent to a ratio of 148 to 100. We may note in passing that the ratio between the Portuguese infant mortality rate and the general rate was 155 to 100. Of course the former rate cannot be accepted as measuring the

---

[1] Whitney, *op. cit.*, p. 41.
[2] *Ibid.*, p. 42.
[3] *Ibid.*, p. 43.
[4] *Ibid.*, p. 44.

real effects of employment of mothers because we do not know how comparable the mothers or the infants were in other respects. The comparison is also an understatement of the effects of employment in that the rate which is taken as normal includes children of employed as well as unemployed mothers. Moreover the children of mothers who went to work were presumably somewhat older than those of mothers in general as it is in the later months of the child's life that mothers are more liable to leave their children to go to the mill. Since the older children may have had a lower death rate this fact also tends to an understatement of the effects of employment.

With such diversity of evidence it is very difficult to come to any conclusion at all. The writer feels that the Fall River data are too striking to permit us to dismiss employment as a rather unimportant factor among a fair number of children in that city. Nevertheless, the evidence from other sources is much less striking. Moreover, some information from England where the problem is not so complicated by the presence of foreign nationalities tends to contradict the Fall River evidence. Thus in a study in Birmingham England it was found that of 3777 mothers visited in three years, 1908-1910, 1657 were employed in gainful occupations, 1441 being employed in factories and 675 elsewhere. The infant mortality rate was 173 among children whose mothers were gainfully employed and 179 among children whose mothers were not so employed.[1] Such data and the results of the other studies quoted above make one hesitate to give full credence to the apparently fatal effect of employment shown by the 1913 study in Fall River. We are handicapped in coming to a conclusion also by the lack of information in the Fall River study for

[1] Hibbs, *op. cit.*, p. 110.

1913, as to the time when mothers went to or quit work with reference to the birth of the child, and as to the effect of employment on the welfare of the child. In the earlier investigation of 1910 where these matters were more carefully studied the number of infants actually adversely affected by the mother's employment was found to be much less than appeared at first consideration. Nevertheless, the ill effects of employment where it was at a time and under circumstances which affected the child, were all the more striking. Whether a similar analysis of the Fall River study of 1913 would have disclosed similar explanations for the high mortality cannot be said.

Summarizing then, we can say that the Portuguese mothers are employed in Fall River to a larger degree than other nationalities; that children of mothers employed away from home died in that city at a much higher rate than those not so employed, especially where house-work was combined with work elsewhere; that information is lacking as to the extent to which this employment actually affected the lives of the children; that an earlier study showed that the numbers affected were not sufficient to make employment a chief cause in determining the general rate; that some effect (but much less striking) of the employment of mothers was found in New Bedford; that very high rates are found in Portsmouth without employment of mothers away from home; that evidence as to the effect of employment of mothers in other cities and in Birmingham, England is conflicting; and that therefore we can come to no scientific conclusion on this important matter. After some study the writer's opinion is that employment of mothers is a contributing cause but not the fundamental cause of the high mortality of Portuguese infants. Another student might come to the opposite conclusion, however.

Size of Families and Frequency of Pregnancies

In the writer's judgment insufficient attention has been paid to the relationship between frequency of pregnancies and the number of dependent children, and the mortality rates of infants. The two factors are not the same, as will be shown. This relationship has usually been shown by means of comparing the infant mortality rates of children born to mothers of different ages. The age of the mother should be an approximate index of the size of the family but is not a perfect one. The Fall River study of 1913 showed the usual relationship between age of mother and infant mortality—the rate rising as the age increased.[1] A more accurate method is to find the number of dependent children alive in each home at the time of the recorded birth. This, of course, does not measure the effect of frequent pregnancies. Table 39 below is a recent tabulation from the same schedules which were used in the 1913 Fall

TABLE 39

DEPENDENT CHILDREN AND DESCENT, FALL RIVER, 1913

(NO MIXED DESCENT CONSIDERED)

	1 child.	2 children.	3 children.	4 children.	5 children.	6 children.	7 children.	8 children.	9 children.	10 children.	11 children.	None.	Totals.	Average.
French Homes	32	24	25	26	11	20	3	4	1	..	1	62	209	2.4
Portuguese Homes	51	33	23	19	9	3	1	..	..	..	..	64	203	1.4
Polish Homes	18	9	13	4	5	..	1	..	..	..	..	27	77	1.5
English Homes	20	8	4	6	2	..	2	1	..	..	..	27	70	1.5
Irish Homes	16	7	7	..	2	2	1	..	..	..	..	14	49	1.6
Italian Homes	1	2	4	3	3	2	..	1	..	..	..	7	23	2.7
Jewish Homes	3	3	..	4	1	..	..	..	..	..	..	5	16	1.7
Syrian Homes	1	3	..	..	..	..	..	..	..	..	..	4	8	.7
Totals	142	89	76	62	33	27	8	6	1	..	1	210	655	1.8

[1] Woman's Club, *op. cit.*, p. 13.

River study. It will be noted that the Portuguese were born into homes with but 1.4 dependent children on the average. This was the smallest family shown by any nationality except the Syrians who were few in number. The Italians had the largest number of dependent children in their homes but they too were too few to be of significance and no infant mortality rates were figured for them in Dr. Dublin's report. The French Canadians had on the average one child more than the Portuguese, and they had an infant mortality rate of 172.4 as against 298.9 for the Portuguese.

The relatively small number of dependent children in Portuguese homes is probably accounted for in part by the fact that they are a newer immigration than the French Canadians who were probably composed of a larger number of women who had been married a number of years. This, however, cannot be proven. It also must be due in part to the fact that Portuguese children die at a higher rate than do the French Canadians. We show in a later table [1] that at the end of the fifth year about half of the Portuguese children have died whereas only about three tenths of the French Canadian children fail to survive the fifth year. In any event in view of the very high birth rate among the Portuguese [2] their relatively small families cannot be due to fewer pregnancies.

The size of the Portuguese families does not differ greatly from those of other nationalities. Such difference as exists, however, is of course a factor in the economic status of these people. Adequacy of income is largely dependent upon the number to be supported in the family. While the high death-rate among Portuguese children doubt-

[1] *Cf. infra*, p. 185.
[2] *Cf. infra*, p. 288 ff.

less involves considerable expense for funerals and for medical attention due to miscarriages, it is safe to say that the smaller size of the family makes the economic burden less for the Portuguese than for most other nationalities. All this does not mean that the Portuguese do not often have too large families which are a real burden to them. They do. It simply tends to modify to this extent the economic causes of their ills.

The question of the number of pregnancies seems to be a much more important one. Hibbs shows that the effects of many pregnancies are both prenatal and postnatal. The postnatal are seen in the overcrowding of the home and a lower per capita income while the children are young. This effect we have already discussed. But he also maintains that frequent pregnancies are correlated with improvidence and low grade intelligence of the mother.[1]

Woodbury, in an article in which he has in view most of the studies of the Children's Bureau, lays especial stress upon this factor. He concludes that the rate increases as the number of successive births following one another by intervals of less than two years, increases. "One might fairly conclude that an important cause of high infant mortality is the lack of proper spacing of births."[2] We have shown elsewhere[3] that Portuguese women had a refined birth rate in 1920 or 199.3 as compared with a rate of 103.1 for non-Portuguese. We have also shown the frequency of their pregnancies.[4] This wide discrepancy is in spite of the fact that the non-Portuguese included large numbers of other foreign-born with high birth rates and also in spite

[1] Hibbs, *op. cit.*, p. 58.
[2] Woodbury, *op. cit.*, pp. 43 and 46.
[3] *Cf. infra*, p. 292.
[4] *Cf. infra*, p. 296.

of the fact that the Portuguese included the native-born of Portuguese descent. If we consider foreign-born Portuguese only we get a refined birth rate of 217.1. In the writer's opinion this excessive birth rate goes far to explain the high infant mortality of the Portuguese despite their smaller number of dependent children.

Other Characteristics of the Portuguese as Related to Infant Mortality

The frequency of pregnancies is apparently closely connected with another characteristic of some of the lower grade Portuguese,—a certain apparent indifference to the welfare of their children. I say " apparent " indifference advisedly for it may be more apparent than real. The writer visited many homes of Portuguese in Fall River in company with district nurses. In one of the poorest homes the mother was cooking in a kitchen full of young children —her own and those of neighbors. The youngest was ill and the nurse told the mother that the baby would die if it did not get better care. " Oh well ", she replied as she stirred the stew, " one more in heaven then." This is merely a single incident. It is not typical of the attitude of most Portuguese mothers visited, but it is an extreme example of the feeling of the lowest grade Portuguese when babies are so numerous as to be a bit in the way in the kitchen. On returning to Portsmouth a second summer the writer expressed sympathy to an unusually bright young mother on the death of her baby the year previous. " I got another now," was her only reply. Such incidents do not prove Portuguese mothers lacking in maternal love; they express in the writer's judgment, the effect upon women of mediocre education of the habit of experiencing a pregnancy almost every year.

The fatalistic beliefs of any people tend toward indifference toward the efforts to help them or their families. Unfortunate or unhealthy conditions resulting from their own ignorance or inertia are attributed to the will of God and therefore accepted as unalterable.

In common with the more ignorant of other nationalities there is an almost universal use of the blind rubber nipples known as pacifiers, comforts or bluffs. These are supposed to stop the crying but so confirmed is the habit of popping them into the mouths that they are often thrust back when the babies have voluntarily expelled them and are laughing or perfectly happy. These are sometimes moistened in the mouths of the mothers before giving them to the babies. They are dropped on the floor or used by the other children and returned to their owners without washing. Some of the mothers have reached the point of hiding them when the nurse is heard coming up the stairs, and are even ready to apologize for not getting them out of sight sooner.

More serious in its results is the not uncommon custom of feeding bread and milk or bread and water to the babies of a few days or a few hours of age. This is rubbed into a more or less moist paste and carried to the mouth on a spoon or the unwashed finger of the grandmother and not infrequently that same finger will be used to assist the process of swallowing by pushing the substance part way down the throat.

Some of the homes are as well kept as could be expected considering the lack of conveniences, but too many are overcrowded and unsanitary with toilets in the cellar or in the corner of the pantry,—often without even a partition to screen them. The flies are numerous and no attempt is made to keep them out or to cover the food on the pantry shelves.

The physician is often at a loss to know what prognosis to give the parents regarding the sick children. If he says the child is not very ill, then they feel he is not required for a second visit; if he feels it more serious then they conclude it may die anyway and there is no necessity of wasting money for his services or for medicine. These examples illustrate Portuguese characteristics nearly all of which may be resolved into the one major trait of ignorance. Whether this ignorance can itself be traced back to low grade native intelligence or whether it is the product of illiteracy and other handicaps is more difficult to say. We have compared elsewhere [1] the school records of Portuguese and non-Portuguese children. We found the comparison unfavorable to the Portuguese, but whether their backwardness could be explained chiefly in terms of home backgrounds of illiteracy and ignorance, or was due to innate mental weaknesses we could not determine. It is unfortunate that we have not records of mental tests applied to Portuguese. The army tests given to immigrants, however, have raised the question whether such tests really do measure innate mentality apart from opportunity. The fact that immigrant soldiers long resident in this country did very much better than those who had recently arrived, raises a strong suspicion that the tests do not altogether eliminate the factor of opportunity. Still it would be well if we could add the Portuguese I. Q. to our list of traits.

In the absence of direct proof we may suggest the likelihood that emigration from the Islands is not selecting the abler from among the Portuguese people. So long as the cotton mills employ relatively unskilled labor, so long will they attract relatively ignorant elements from among our immigrant throng. To say this is not to suggest that the Portuguese as a whole are naturally inferior. This point is far from being established though it may be true. It is simply to point out that these simple-minded people are

[1] *Cf. infra*, p. 316 ff.

attracted here because, with all their illiteracy and low-grade intelligence, they can do the simple things which the cotton mills need to have done.[1]

Mortality of Children under Five Years of Age in Fall River

Before we ,summarize the above discussion of infant mortality we shall present the results of a study of the mortality of children under five. These children are the same which were the subject of investigation in the 1913 study of infant mortality in Fall River. They were followed for four additional years and the writer is able to show the results through the kindness of the authors of the original study. They should have both the credit and the responsibility for the data presented. The comments thereon and some revision in the table have been made by the writer.

Table 40 below shows for the 802 infants born during the summer months of 1913 the number of children emigrating or lost sight of, the number dying, and the proportion dying before they were five years of age, all classified by nationalities. The percentages have been figured on two bases: total births including those which emigrated or were lost sight of; and those remaining after deducting those emigrating or lost sight of. Somewhere between these two, rates lie the true figures. In the present writer's judgment it is more nearly accurate to deduct the emigrants before figuring the rates. But since these children emigrated or were lost to view at different ages, this procedure somewhat exaggerates the mortality. On the other hand, it is obvious that to assume that all who were lost to view are now living outside of Fall River must be to understate considerably the number and proportion dying.

---

[1] Compare, however, what was said above on the racial characteristics of the Portuguese, *supra*, pp. 22-50.

Children of all types of descent, except those of mixed descent, have been listed by name even where the numbers were few. The groups are listed in order of descending rates, but no rates are set down where the number of births considered was under 50. It must be carefully noted that this table refers to descent and not to nationality. That is to say, under each category are included native-born with native parents whose grandparents were born

TABLE 40

MORTALITY UNDER FIVE YEARS BY DESCENT, FALL RIVER, 1913–1918

Descent	Total Births Considered	Emigrated or lost from view	Deaths in 5 years	Per cent [1] Dying	Per cent [2] Dying
Syrians	9	3	5		
Portuguese	204	37	85	41.7	50.9
Poles	80	26	19	23.7	35.2
Irish	51	4	15	29.4	31.9
French Canadians	210	47	51	24.3	31.3
"Americans"	37	9	8		
English	71	18	9	12.7	17.0
Jews	16	7	1		
Italians	23	3	2		
Mixed descent	100	23	19	19.0	24.7
Total	801 [3]	177	214	26.6	34.2

abroad. This method leaves classified under " Americans " only those all of whose grandparents were born in this country. Those of mixed descent are omitted from each group and themselves grouped together under " Mixed descent ". Unfortunately this table does not permit us also to distinguish those who are techincally native-born of

[1] Based upon total births.

[2] Based upon children remaining in Fall River until end of study or until death, and who were not lost from view.

[3] One unknown omitted.

native parentage from those whose parents were foreign-born.

It is interesting to note from the above table that the Portuguese retain much of their excessive mortality through the fifth year. Their mortality for the five year period is, as compared with that of the French Canadians, somewhat less excessive than it was at the end of the first year of life. The French Canadians are probably favored, however, by the fact that they presumably include a larger proportion of children of native parentage than do the Portuguese, who are a much more recent immigration. That more than half the Portuguese who could be followed through the five year period had died, is a striking evidence of their excessive mortality in Fall River. The only group whose mortality exceeded theirs, the Syrians, were too few in number to permit of any conclusion as to their characteristic mortality.

As these children were visited periodically by a district nurse, some interesting records are available as to other social handicaps under which some of these children lived. These social handicaps were only such as were brought to the attention of those who made the study either as a result of a personal visit or through the records of some other social organization. No one of these handicaps taken by itself is of great significance for our study. The fact, for example, that four French Canadian children had parents who were chronic drunkards and that no Portuguese were so noted, may or may not be indicative of a national characteristic; the numbers are too few to permit a conclusion. If all social handicaps noted could be reduced to a common denominator and summated we might compare the relative handicaps of the different groups. Since this is impossible we shall simply enumerate a number of the more important handicaps noted, indicating with respect to which the Portuguese children seemed peculiarly unfortunate, and which were least noticeable among them. We shall most frequently make comparisons between the Portuguese and the French Canadians who made up the largest groups, with occasional reference to the Poles.

The following social handicaps seem to have been fairly evenly distributed among the different descent groups: illegitimacy (21 cases) although the Poles had none; tuberculosis in the home (39 cases); home supported by overseers of the poor (11 cases but Poles had none); father died without leaving support (Poles no cases, Portuguese 4, French 2); brutal parents (9 cases); born twins (26 cases); Society for the Prevention of Cruelty to Children in charge of family (5 cases).

The only handicaps from which the Portuguese seemed especially to suffer (though none of these are to be thought of as typical of the Portuguese) were: immigration from abroad during pregnancy (13 cases of which 9 were Portuguese); and no attendant at birth (3 cases, two of which were Portuguese).

On the other hand the Portuguese seemed unusually free from the following handicaps: desertion of family by father (17 cases, none Portuguese); both parents chronic drunkards (9 cases, none Portuguese); mother dying at childbirth or soon after (18 cases, of which 2 were Portuguese). The general impression which one receives from examining the data upon which the above list is based, keeping in mind the proportion of the different descent groups in the total of births, is that the Portuguese have as many but hardly more of these social handicaps than other groups. The more general and more important social handicaps such as illiteracy, inability to speak English et cetera are treated elsewhere in this study.

Summary and Tentative Conclusions

We are now in a position to summarize our information on infant mortality among the Portuguese. We have found their infant mortality rates to be extraordinarily high both in one rural and two urban communities, though highest in the cities. Remembering that our conclusions apply only to the communities studied, and that even there many of them are purely tentative, let us review briefly the relationship of the Portuguese to each of the more important alleged factors in infant mortality.

1. *Race.* We have insisted that the Portuguese are a nationality and not a race: that racially they are made up of a number of strains on the mainland though remarkably homogeneous with respect to the chief physical criteria of race. We have shown evidence for the belief that they are somewhat less homogeneous in the Islands and have queried whether a strictly scientific study should not recognize the difference between different types predominating in different islands. We have seen that they contain an intermixture of negro blood varying in degree in different places but probably more prominent on the Islands than on the mainland. We have suggested the possibility, but have not proven it true, that emigration selects stock with a larger intermixture of negro blood than is characteristic of their group as a whole.

Pursuing the racial clue we have inquired whether a high infant mortality is a characteristic which the Portuguese have in common with the negroes in the United States. We found this to be true but noted that the Portuguese have rates higher than those for negroes in the same sections of the country. Because of this, because other nationalities have shown rates higher than those of the negro, because negro rates vary so much from time to time and from district to district, we concluded that the intermixture of negro blood could not be proven to be the cause of the high infant mortality of the Portuguese. We also examined the suggestion that a high mortality of infants may be a characteristic of the Mediterranean race. We found our data very limited but because of the low mortality of the Italians we rejected this suggestion as at least an inadequate explanation. We found, however, that many South Europeans have a high death rate from respiratory diseases among their infants.

2. *Nationality.* We found that rates of infant mortality are far from constant within a given nationality; nor are high rates without exceptions characteristic of the foreign-born as a whole. We also found cases where the same nationality had a high rate in one community and a low one in another. Nevertheless, we found that the Portuguese have shown a uniformly high and an excessively high rate in all communities studied to date, except Provincetown.

3. *Length of Residence in the United States.* We found that for all nationalities for which we have information the infant death rate drops as the length of residence increases, and that the Portuguese are no exception to this rule. We were disappointed, however, that the native-born of Portuguese descent did not show a more marked improvement in this respect over the foreign-born Portuguese.

4. *Illiteracy.* We found a very high degree of illiteracy among the Portuguese, and that all studies have shown that the illiterate have a higher infant death rate than the literate.

5. *Ability to speak English.* We found a large proportion of Portuguese mothers unable to speak English and found that this trait also is associated, as a rule, with high infant mortality.

6. *Employment of midwives.* We saw that the Portu-

guese prefer to employ midwives at childbirth, but we were unable to attribute infant deaths to this practice with confidence. Portuguese babies do not as a rule die from diseases of early infancy.

7. *Deaths from preventable Causes.* We found that Portuguese babies are especially liable to die from diseases which are most easily prevented with ordinary care on the part of the mother.

8. *Feeding.* We found some evidence that Portuguese mothers are less likely to nurse their babies at the breast than are the mothers of some other nationalities; and we saw that lack of breast feeding is recognized as one of the chief immediate causes of infant mortality.

9. *Income.* Although our data were incomplete, we found the Portuguese a low income group. We found a single nationality showing an apparently lower income than the Portuguese, but with a lower infant mortality rate. As compared with all other nationalities, however, the Portuguese seemed to have both a lower average income and a higher infant mortality rate. We found nearly, but not quite, universal testimony that infant mortality increases as the father's wages decrease; but we also found many competent authorities doubting the importance of this correlation. We concluded that there probably is some causal relationship between income and infant mortality, but inclined to the belief that for the most part low wages and high infant mortality are effects of a common cause, namely ignorance and inefficiency.

10. *Employment of mothers.* We found Portuguese mothers rather frequently employed both on the farms and in the city. We found a high proportion of employment of Portuguese women associated with a high infant death rate for the nationality as a whole. We saw, however, that study has shown that the number of employed women who

neglect their children because of employment is not as great as has sometimes been asserted. We felt, therefore, that employment of mothers could not account for all the excess of mortality found among children of Portuguese women. So extremely high, nevertheless, are some of the death rates reported for employed women, especially where they combine housework and employment outside the home, that we could scarcely escape the conclusion that this is a real cause of the evil. But since rates almost as high were found among Portuguese in rural districts, and since in New Bedford the evil effects of employment were less evident than in Fall River, we prefer to list this cause as a minor factor, though an important one, accounting in part, perhaps, for the higher death rates for urban than for rural Portuguese. We admit, however, that a conclusion on this point is peculiarly difficult to reach.

11. *Number of pregnancies.* We gave evidence that the Portuguese are a very prolific people but not a people with larger families of dependent children than other nationalities. This fact led us to minimize the economic effects of the large family among the Portuguese, but to stress all the more the importance of a lack of proper spacing of pregnancies—a further evidence of improvidence and ignorance.

12. *Other social handicaps.* By listing a number of special handicaps by nationality we found that most of them were present among the Portuguese in about the same proportions as among other nationalities.

13. *Other characteristics.* We discussed a number of minor characteristics of the Portuguese which would seem to effect the mortality of their infants, and found that most of them were secondary effects of the general factor of low-grade understanding. We found it impossible to determine, however, whether this low-grade understanding was due

to low innate intelligence or lack of opportunity especially in the Islands. We nevertheless expressed the belief that the process of emigration was presumably not selecting the superior intellectual classes of Portuguese, because such are not attracted to a cotton mill community. We have hope, however, that longer residence in this country and perhaps a greater effort to help these people may raise their standards of living and that with their improvement the infant death rate for the Portuguese may fall.

14. We found that excessive mortality continued to be a characteristic of the Portuguese at least until the end of their fifth year.

15. *Climate.* We noted in another chapter the contrasts between the climate of the Islands and that of the communities studied. The effects of such a climatic change seem to be still too little known to warrant a conclusion, although some have attributed high infant death rates from respiratory diseases to this cause.

General Conclusion

We do not yet know enough about the Portuguese to formulate dogmatic conclusions as to the causes of their admittedly excessive infant mortality. Communities may yet be found where this characteristic is not present. Such facts as have been gathered lead the writer to recognize the importance of both types of causes distinguished at the beginning of this chapter.[1] Starting with a considerable prejudice in favor of the economic and non-personal causes of infant mortality, he finds his emphasis changed at the close of this study. While there can be little doubt that a better income would benefit the Portuguese and eventually would raise their standard of living and to some extent

---

[1] *Cf. supra*, p. 137.

reduce their infant mortality, it could hardly do so unless it could also remove the personal causes of the infant deaths. The latter seem to be the immediate and probably the more important factors. If the writer were compelled to list the most important causes of infant mortality among the Portuguese, he would say that ignorance on the part of mothers, improper spacing of pregnancies which accompanies ignorance, and certain other characteristics of the nationality were the primary causes, with low incomes and employment of mothers as important secondary factors. What the infant mortality of the Portuguese will be in the future time only can tell.

CHAPTER VI

THE PORTUGUESE OF PORTSMOUTH, R. I. AND FALL RIVER, MASS.

FOR a more intensive study of the Portuguese in New England we have selected two communities—Portsmouth, Rhode Island and Fall River, Massachusetts. In Fall River our house to house study has been confined to fifteen city blocks, the choice of which will be explained later, but statistics for the entire city have also been analyzed. In Portsmouth very nearly 100 per cent of the Portuguese families were interviewed.

The United States Immigration Commission which made its report in 1911 studied a number of Portuguese including a few of those then living in Portsmouth, Rhode Island. Only 20 families were personally interviewed in this community, however. In addition, the Commission included a less detailed study of 55 Portuguese households in California, and of 232 Portuguese households in manufacturing and mining, chiefly in New England. 6319 Portuguese individuals were also included in its study of employees in manufacturing and mining. We shall refer to the results of this study at appropriate points. But with the exception of the study of the 20 families of Portsmouth no community of these people was investigated intensively.[1]

[1] United States Immigration Commission Report, 61st Cong., 3rd Sess., Washington, 1911. We may note here that the Commission found little which is not in harmony with the present study. Their study, though necessarily less intensive, has the advantage of comparing certain char-

194

When these communities were first selected it was thought that they would prove fairly representative, at least of the white Portuguese of New England. As the study progressed, however, it became apparent that there are several types of white Portuguese. Those from the mainland are in some respects unlike those from the Azores or Madeira; and differences appear even between immigrants from different islands of the Azores. It is also quite possible that the cotton mills attract a somewhat distinctive type and that therefore the Portuguese of Fall River and vicinity may not be entirely representative. For this reason it will be necessary to confine any conclusions we may reach to the two communities studied. Nevertheless, there is little doubt that the types we are studying make up a very large element in the total of Portuguese immigrants.

The reasons for the selection of Fall River and Portsmouth were the following:

1. Fall River is the second largest Portuguese center in America. There are probably 10,000 fewer people of Portuguese descent there than in New Bedford and the latter city is the older settlement. For several reasons, however, New Bedford would have been a less satisfactory city to study:

a. The very age of the settlement makes it more difficult to separate the Portuguese from the other inhabitants because the longer immigrants are resident in America the more likely are they to anglicize their names and conceal their nationality in other ways.

b. A greater difficulty in New Bedford is the presence

acteristics of the Portuguese with those of other nationalities. Their study of 20 families gives possibly a slightly more favorable impression of Portuguese rural homes than will be found below. See especially vol. i, pp. 316-328, 552-557 and 639. Also vol. xxii, pp. 443-461.

there of a large number of Bravas or black Portuguese. These people are a distinct type but having Portuguese names they cannot be distinguished in written records. Fall River has but few Bravas.

2. Fall River is also more distinctly a cotton mill city than is New Bedford where there are somewhat more varied industries. This fact simplifies the industrial factor in our study.

3. Fall River, somewhat more frequently than New Bedford, has been the subject of previous studies. There are thus available for comparison two studies of infant mortality in Fall River, various wage and cost of living studies, a housing survey and a recent survey of public schools.

4. The original choice of Portsmouth was more nearly a matter of chance but it proved a wise choice. Like Fall River this rural community was largely a one occupation town. Moreover, the problem of analysis was simplified there because the Portuguese make up practically the only foreign element. Besides the relative simplicity thus secured the contrast between the two communities in this respect was of interest.

5. Portsmouth is also a good town to study because it gives us a picture of Portuguese life when these people are left largely to their own devices without much help from the native population.

Composition of the Population

Portsmouth, Rhode Island is a small town of 2,590 inhabitants situated at the northern end of the Island of Rhode Island which it shares with the town of Middletown and the city of Newport. The Federal Census of 1920 divides the population of Portsmouth into 1300 male and 1290 female; and by nativity into 1072 native white of native parentage, 915 native white of foreign or mixed parentage; 584 foreign-born and 19 negro. The Census does not tabulate the age distribution of the population by nationality, and the present writer has therefore prepared the following tables direct from the original Census schedules in Washington.

TABLE 41

AGE DISTRIBUTION OF THE POPULATION OF PORTSMOUTH, R. I.,[1] 1920

Age Groups	*Portuguese*[2] *Descent* Male	Female	*Non-Portuguese Native-born* Male	Female	*Non-Portuguese Foreign-born* Male	Female	*Colored* Male	Female
Under 1	18	21	9	13				
1–4	70	75	56	38			1	
5–9	92	125	65	56	1	1		
10–14	89	78	56	55	2	3		2
15–19	55	43	51	49	4	2		2
20–24	30	24	49	58	1	1		
25–29	25	31	57	39	6	4		
30–34	30	40	42	46	7	8		1
35–39	43	41	38	33	7	6		
40–44	30	14	37	38	8	18	1	
45–49	33	17	39	42	9	12		
50–54	16	3	43	29	10	10		
55–59	6	6	28	40	5	10		
60–64	1	4	41	39	5	4		
65–69	4	1	33	24	3	2		
70–74	4	1	22	29	4	2		
75–79	2	1	19	13	1	2		
80–84		1	10	7				
85–89			1					
Unknown				3				
Totals	549	528	696	651	74	85	2	5

[1] This table was made possible through the kindness of the Director of the Census who put the schedules at the writer's disposal. It no doubt contains some minor errors as it was not feasible to recheck the figures. The total population agrees with that given in the advance sheets of the Census which have since appeared, but there is a small and unimportant discrepancy between the totals for the sexes.

[2] The term "Portuguese descent" is used to include both foreign-

TABLE 42

PERCENTAGE DISTRIBUTION IN GENERAL AGE GROUPS

	Portuguese Descent	Non-Portuguese Descent
Under 5	17.1%	7.7%
5–9	20.2	8.1
10–14	15.5	7.8
15-19	9.2	7.2
20–44	28.6	33.5
45 and over	9.5	35.6
Totals	100.1	99.9

Fall River, Massachusetts is a city of 120,458 inhabitants situated near the mouth of the Taunton river about twelve miles north-east of Portsmouth. According to the advance sheets of the 14th Census 57,918 are male and 62,567 female. By nativity 19,168 are native white of native parentage, 45,235 native white of foreign parentage, 42,331 foreign-born white and 371 negro or other colored. Thus more than a third of the population of Fall River were born abroad making her one of the most foreign of the large cities of the country. Tables 43 and 44 below give the age distribution of the total population of Fall River and of those of Portuguese descent.

born and the descendants of foreign-born. The latter are chiefly children. Our house-to-house study found out of 333 fathers and mothers whose birthplace was known but 6 fathers and 13 mothers who were born in America. A few children of these native-born mothers of Portuguese descent are included in our " Portuguese " group.

TABLE 43

AGE DISTRIBUTION OF THE TOTAL POPULATION OF FALL RIVER [1] AND OF THOSE
OF PORTUGUESE DESCENT,[2] 1920

| | Total Population | | | | Portuguese Descent | | | | | |
| | Male | | Female | | Male | | | Female | | |
groups	No.	%	No.	%	No.	%	%Total Pop.	No.	%	%Total Pop.
der 1 ..	1482	2.6	1402	2.2	502	4.5	33.9	465	4.2	33.2
der 5 ..	6788	11.7	6852	11.0	1857	16.5	27.4	1895	16.9	27.7
......	6676	11.5	6613	10.6	1507	13.4	22.6	1616	14.4	24.4
14	6024	10.4	6100	9.8	1193	10.6	19.8	1192	10.7	19.5
19	5215	9.0	5820	9.3	1006	8.9	19.3	1126	10.1	19.3
44	21129	36.5	23998	38.4	4278	38.0	20.2	4202	37.6	17.5
or over .	12073	20.8	13170	21.1	1403	12.5	11.6	1156	10.3	8.8
als	57905	99.9	—	—	—	—	—	—	—	—
	—	—	62553	100.2	11244	99.9	19.4	11187	100.0	17.9

[1] This table, like Table 41, was obtained from the original Census schedules through the kindness of the Director of the Census. Like it also this table may contain minor errors as the labor involved in re-checking the figures was prohibitive. The total in the table falls 23 short of the total subsequently published by the Bureau, but this error is insignificant in a total of more than 120,000 inhabitants.

[2] This group includes all of Portuguese descent wherever born. Table 44 below separates these into native-born of Portuguese or mixed parentage, native-born of native parentage but of Portuguese descent, and foreign-born. It is impossible more than to guess at possible errors in our Portuguese group. The Census gives data on the foreign-born Portuguese only and these are divided into those born in the Atlantic Islands and those born in Portugal. The total given for these two nativities is 12,064 which is 401 less than our total for foreign-born Portuguese. The difference is presumably made up of Portuguese born neither in Continental Portugal, the Azores nor the Cape Verde Islands, but largely in South America, Hawaii and Madeira. We have included the few Portuguese born in Hawaii as foreign-born. Any native-born of Portuguese descent whose parents were also native-born and who have anglicized their names were indistinguishable from the native-born and are included with them. These last are unquestionably exceedingly few in number, however.

TABLE 44

AGE DISTRIBUTION OF THE POPULATION OF PORTUGUESE DESCENT, FALL RIVER, MASS., 19⸱

Age Groups	Foreign-born Male	Foreign-born Female	Native-born of Foreign or mixed Parentage Male	Native-born of Foreign or mixed Parentage Female	Native-born of Native Parentage Male	Native-born of Native Parentage Female	Total Portuguese Descent Male	Total Portuguese Descent Fem
Under 1	2	0	490	460	10	5	502	4€
1–4	21	18	1318	1393	16	19	1355	143
5–9	140	146	1353	1460	14	10	1507	16⸱
10–14	264	273	924	913	5	6	1193	11⸱
15–19	572	652	429	472	5	2	1006	112
20–24	814	1102	178	199	2		994	130
25–29	969	996	82	70	1	1	1052	106
30–34	859	660	30	28			889	68
35–39	764	632	14	18			778	65
40–44	555	481	10	15			565	49
45–49	531	422	2	4		1	533	42
50–54	355	269	2	3			357	27
55–59	235	190	2				237	19⸱
60–64	146	134		1			146	13.
65–69	62	66		2			62	6⸱
70–74	44	39					44	3⸱
75–79	14	10					14	1⸱
80–84	5	8					5	⸱
85–89	5	5					5	⸱
90–94		1						⸱
95–99		1						⸱
Totals	6360	6105	4834	5038	53	44	11244	1118⸱

We may now compare our urban and rural communities with respect to their composition. In Portsmouth we find a little over half the population to be native-born and non-Portuguese, a little over two-fifths to be of Portuguese descent, only one in sixteen to be foreigners other than Portuguese, while a single family is colored. More careful examination of the foreign non-Portuguese group would show these to be made up pretty largely of English, Irish and

[1] From the orginal Census schedules. *Cf.* footnote to Table 41.

Scotch. To the popular mind, at least, the Portuguese are the only foreign nationality in this rural community. Very different is the situation in Fall River. There the Portuguese make up a large element but are only one of a number of foreign groups. They are, it is true, the largest single element among the foreign-born, exceeding in numbers even the French Canadians. But the Federal Census of 1920 shows more than 10,000 of the latter besides nearly 8000 English, 3200 Irish, 2500 Poles, 1600 Russians (presumably mostly Jews), and smaller groups of Italians, Syrians and Scotch. Despite their large numbers, then, the Portuguese make up but 18.6 per cent of the total population of Fall River. The Portuguese in Portsmouth have as neighbors American farmers of " the old stock " or other Portuguese. In Fall River they are more likely to rub shoulders with French Canadian, Jew, Pole or Syrian than with the Anglo-Saxon.[1]

In Portsmouth the contrast between the age distribution of the Portuguese and of the native-born non-Portuguese is striking. The former show relatively many more children and much fewer elderly people. This contrast is most striking between Portuguese and non-Portuguese women over 45. Among the Portuguese such women make up but 6.7 per cent of the total Portuguese female population, while among the non-Portuguese they make up no less than 34.3 per cent. This situation reflects not only the relative youth of the Portuguese immigration, but also the emigration from the rural township of the younger native women. The situation is only less striking in the case of men.

The contrast between the age distribution of the Portuguese and non-Portuguese is brought out also by comparing the proportions of the total population which the former

---

[1] The English are numerous, it is true, but they are not very frequently neighbors of the Portuguese.

constitute at different age periods. With a single exception the proportion of Portuguese decreases as the age rises. The proportion of Portuguese among the population under one year of age is four times the proportion among men and women over 45 years of age.

Turning to the data from Fall River we find contrasts less striking but roughly similar. There, too, the Portuguese make up nearly four times as large a proportion of the infants under 1 as they do of men and women over 45. They have not far from twice their normal proportion of infants under 1 and about half their proportion of people past the prime of life. The fact that our non-Portuguese in Fall River are composed of large numbers of other foreigners as well as of native-born make these contrasts the more worthy of note. The difference between the two communities in this respect is also due, no doubt, to the fact that in Fall River we do not see the exodus of young men and women among the native stock. The significance of these differences in age distribution will appear as we discuss different social phenomena where age is an important factor.

The Portuguese have been coming to these two communities for approximately the same period of time.[1] The coming of the Portuguese to the little town of Portsmouth is strikingly illustrated on our map. Whereas in 1885, thirty-five years before the date of our study, there was but a single Portuguese landowner in Portsmouth, to-day 194 different families own or rent land there and 84 are taxed for land. We cannot say how many were renters at the earlier date but the number was very small, the great influx having come since 1890. In another place

---

[1] *Cf.* tables and discussion, pp. 98 and 104 ff.

we show [1] that 139 out of 155 Portuguese fathers and 151 out of 155 Portuguese mothers who were born abroad came to Portsmouth after 1890; and 113 fathers and 130 mothers came after 1900. In Fall River likewise these people have come chiefly since 1890.

Opportunity in Porstmouth and Fall River

Such being the relative numbers of these recent immigrants in our two communities, into what sort of an environment do they enter? What are the opportunities offered such a people in Portsmouth and in Fall River?

Climate

The climate of New England is not such as to make the Portuguese feel at home. The average annual mean temperature at Fall River from 1886-1903 was reported as 49 degrees Fahrenheit, with a winter mean of 29, spring 48, summer 68 and fall 54.[2] The extremes of temperature are, however, much greater than these figures would indicate. At Narragansett, R. I., the highest temperature recorded for a 23 year period was 94 degrees and the lowest 12 below zero; while at Boston for a 34 year period the corresponding figures were 102 and 13 below respectively. The Portuguese from the Azores, then, come from a warmer and more even climate. We have seen [3] that at Ponta Delgada the mean annual temperature is some 13 degrees warmer than that reported above and that the range of temperature is only about 42 degrees. While the above figures which give extremes somewhat exaggerate the dif-

---

[1] Cf. infra, tables 63 and 64, pp. 275-6.

[2] U. S. Dep't of Agriculture, Weather Bureau, Bulletin Q, *Climatology of the United States* (Washington, 1906), p. 158; and Bulletin O, *Temperature and Relative Humidity* (Washington, 1905), pp. 5, 7 and 27.

[3] Cf. supra, p. 57.

ference in the variability of temperature there is a very wide difference between New England and the Azores in this respect. The Portuguese have never before experienced such cold as that of our New England winters for freezing temperature has been almost unknown to them, and they have seldom felt such heat as July can bring in this region. The winters are undoubtedly the most trying time for them here, and sometimes tempt them to the sunnier clime which their brothers in California enjoy. This climatic change may conceivably account for not a few of the ills which the Portuguese experience before they become adjusted to changed conditions.

The mean annual rainfall at Fall River is reported as 49.5 inches or about 14 more than that at Ponta Delgada. Without the distinct rainy season of the Azores, and with fewer rainy days, more rain falls in southern Massachusetts than in the Islands. The weather reports for Massachusetts report a total of 80 rainy days a year with a precipitation in the wettest year on record of 63.6 inches and of 40.0 in the driest.

As for other natural advantages, the Portuguese farmer finds in Portsmouth a fertile soil as good as the state can offer with a ready market for all that he can raise of the chief crops—potatoes, peas, beans and some strawberries, together with other miscellaneous vegetables and milk and live stock. He can buy land for from $100 to $300 an acre and rent it for from $10 to $15 a year. The Portuguese mill hand in Fall River shares only indirectly in the natural advantages of the city which include a good climate for textile manufacture, a favorable location for marketing products and excellent water-power. Distance from the source of supply of raw material is, of course, the great handicap.

Nature gives the Portuguese an opportunity to make a

living on the farm or in the cotton mill, but she is not so
kindly in her effect upon his physical comfort.

Contacts with Americans

When the peasant from St. Michael's arrives either in
Portsmouth or in Fall River, he finds himself in America
but not of America. The innumerable differences between
himself and the native-born American isolate him; and this
isolation is also promoted by peculiar conditions of the environment in which he finds himself.

In Portsmouth the Portuguese immigrant is fortunate if
he begins as a farm laborer for one of the more progressive
American farmers or for a fellow-countryman who knows
the farming and marketing methods of the community.
The Portuguese bring with them patient industry and some
knowledge of cultivation, but there is much to learn under
new conditions.

Work as a laborer is only an apprenticeship, however,
for every true Portuguese is ambitious to farm for himself, and his next step is to rent a farm from a native family
where the man has either died or moved to the city. Then
the Portuguese immigrant sends for his wife, if she has
not already come, and a life of real isolation begins. This
isolation is especially pronounced if he has chosen a farm
off from the main highway as is frequently the case. Even
then he has some contacts, of course, when he takes his
vegetables to market, purchases seed or supplies, or goes
to the town hall to procure a license for the inevitable dog.
But these contacts are for the new-comer very transitory
and he has no share in such active community life as there
is. For his wife the isolation is well-nigh complete for
she toils all day in the fields, bends over the wash-tub in the
yard, or minds or neglects the rapidly accumulating brood
of children. About every year she gets a very few days

vacation from these occupations to bear another child. Her life is altogether at home and she seldom talks with a native woman and never on the same social plane. As for the children, they run wild until the school age is reached when the mother is only too glad to get them out from under foot until they are strong enough to work in the fields, when their attendance becomes less regular. If a visitor drives up to such a secluded farm house these younger children may be seen peeking out from behind the curtains or from around corners. On the visitor's nearer approach they scurry away like rabbits, to return, perhaps, when the conversation with the mother reassures them. In school, of course, they do learn American ways and see some American children, but there is some evidence that they tend to form separate play groups. In one school, as we shall see, there are but two non-Portuguese children; but this is unusual and to some " Ports " school opens a new world. In general, however, life for the new-comer in Portsmouth is one of isolation. His illiteracy, foreign ways, and inability to speak English would create this isolation even if he were welcomed by the old stock. As compared with some other foreign communities Portsmouth evidences remarkably little open hostility to the Portuguese, but they certainly are not " of " the community which, though fast going to seed, is nevertheless Yankee, Protestant, relatively clean and just a little self-satisfied.

The isolation we have just described applies to new-comers. After considerable time has elapsed and the Portuguese have become semi-" Americanized " the isolation decreases. Not a few Portuguese farmers are respected, some even admired, by the older native stock. One resident of long standing delights in telling of kindly neighborly acts by the Portuguese nearby. On the occasion of illness one of them did all the farm chores for a considerable period and refused to accept payment for his work. The fact, also, that there is but one Catholic church in the town brings the few non-Portuguese Catholics into contact with the Azoreans and these contacts reach even the women. At least two minor efforts have been made to help the Portuguese of Portsmouth to adapt themselves to the new conditions. The teacher of the Coal Mines School has taken an especial interest in these people and has attempted to establish a class for adults; and near Bristol Ferry two cultured women have done what they could to cheer and uplift a few of the children through the establishment of a kindergarten and through a Christmas dinner given to children of the community regardless of nationality. Praiseworthy as have been these efforts, however, they have been either too transitory or too localized to have an extended influence. There is no evident lack of goodwill towards the Portuguese in Portsmouth. For the most part they are left alone, appreciated as good industrious workmen by most of the people, and vaguely feared as the coming " race " by the more thoughtful. The Americanizing influence of school, church et cetera, can best be appraised after we have described these various aspects of the social life of the Portuguese in Portsmouth.

For the moment we may summarize the situation in Portsmouth as one of isolation for the Portuguese newcomer, but with slowly increasing contacts which reach the children most intimately in school, the father less so in his business relations, and the wife at home least of all.

Despite this isolation in Portsmouth, it is questionable whether the Portuguese are not more nearly of the community there than in the city. It is true that their contacts were few for a number of years, but such contacts as they have are with the native-born " of the old stock " Moreover, class lines are much less rigid in the country than in the city. The most successful Portuguese farmer may live very much like his Anglo-Saxon neighbors, and his neighbor is as likely to be a native of the same occupation as himself, as a fellow-countryman. In Fall River, on the other hand, his neighbor is a mill-hand of either Portuguese or some other foreign nationality. The " upper-class," whether native or foreign-born, live " up on the hill " and there are but few Portuguese among them. The Portuguese of Fall River, it is true, associate much more intimately with non-Portuguese of their class, than they do in Portsmouth. There can hardly be said to be Portuguese colonies in Fall River, although there is a slight tendency, by no means universal, for Portuguese to occupy the same block or group of tenements. But the Portuguese belong to the great group of mill-hands, and between them and the controlling Anglo-Saxon element there is a great gulf fixed. As we shall see the crossing of this gulf is by no means an easy task. The Portuguese may save money and own property, but he may not manufacture cotton goods. If it be argued that this gulf is of the Portuguese's own making or is due to his own personal weaknesses, the reply is that we are not trying to explain the gulf or to determine responsibility for its existence. The gulf exists as a fact and it is a cause of real isolation to the newcomer.

If assimilation progresses most satisfactorily where there are contacts with other elements in the same social class, then Fall River is the place for such contacts. But if it is favored by life in a relatively simple environment where economic success comparable with that of the remnants of the old stock is within the bounds of possibility, then Portsmouth is to be preferred.

Economic Opportunity

Economic opportunity in Portsmouth consists principally in the opportunity to do farm work for others and when financially able to rent or purchase land at rents and prices indicated above. At the peak of the rise in prices and wages farm laborers were said to be asking $75 a month and board, a sum which farmers complained was prohibitive for them. Since 1920 the wages of farm laborers have undoubtedly fallen.

In addition to farming Portsmouth offers employment to a few laborers and a few skilled men at the Government Coaling Station and on the railroads. The coal mines operated about ten years ago proved a failure, and the laborers' cottages erected at that time are now occupied by Government and railroad employees chiefly.

No attempt has been made to measure the cost of living in Portsmouth and so to estimate real incomes. There is no reason to doubt that it is similar to that in other rural communities of Rhode Island and that it is lower than costs in the city. For our purpose it is sufficient to note that costs are low enough to enable the Portuguese to make good economically, as we shall see. It will be much more profitable for us to turn to Fall River where more accurate figures for real incomes may be determined. It must be remembered that the Portuguese have in good times the alternative of remaining on the farms or going to the city to the cotton mill. Indeed there seems to have been an approximately equal flow of population in each direction.

Fall River is " the foremost center of cotton manufacturing in the New World "[1] and boasts some 75,000 looms, 3,000,000 spindles, and 30,000 cotton mill employees.[2] It

[1] Fenner, *History of Fall River* (New York, 1906), p. 46.

[2] Howard, " The Fall River Sliding Scale Experiment," in the *American Economic Review*, vol. vii, p. 530, Sept., 1917.

is said to produce 2,000 miles of cotton cloth a day.[1] If we were to add to cotton mill employees those employed in occupations subsidiary to cotton manufacture and those who work to maintain the cotton mill employees, Fall River would appear almost as much a one-industry community as does the little town of Portsmouth. In reality, of course, the number of occupations is much greater in Fall River, but the fundamental industry is the manufacture and finishing of cotton goods, although there is also a large hat factory and smaller shops making braid, pianos et cetera. As compared with cities like Worcester, Mass. Fall River certainly offers very little variety of industrial opportunity.

It is maintained by some, however, that this one industry offers ample chance for advancement for an ambitious people, and that mill managers are constantly at a loss to find, locally, reliable well-trained men to take the more responsible positions which are frequently open in the mills. Nevertheless, the fact remains that the labor demand of the mills is chiefly for unskilled or semi-skilled workmen and women. Above these semi-skilled positions there is little opportunity for the skilled man. It is conceivable that much of the working class population of Fall River is incapable of performing more skilled work. But be that as it may, we have to record the fact that Fall River lacks a variety of industrial opportunity, and that her cotton mills do not offer a regular progression of increasingly exacting and correspondingly well-paid positions between those of the unskilled doffer or sweeper, and the executive positions for which the supply of able men is said to be below the demand. Therefore Fall River attracts low-grade workers, and therefore, perhaps, the more able among those who do come find less chance for advancement than they would elsewhere—in a shoe city for example.

[1] Dwight, "First Aid to 30,000 Children," in the *Child Labor Bulletin*, vol. v, p. 213, Feb., 1917.

But most immigrants who come to Fall River are presumably thinking of immediate income rather than of ultimate opportunity. In common with most cotton manufacturing centers, Fall River can use labor of low grade and pays correspondingly low wages. The wages have been much higher than those in the southern mills, however, and somewhat higher apparently than those in the mills of New Hampshire and Rhode Island. In New Bedford a somewhat finer grade of cloth is made and a somewhat higher grade of employees is found.

Residents of Fall River say, however, that while individual wages may be low, the mills supplement the family income by offering employment to women and children as well as to men. That such employment is a boon from the standpoint of immediate need and immediate economic welfare, there can be no doubt. From the long-time point of view the benefit is perhaps more questionable. In defense of the mills it must be said, however, that employment of women and children is not a new experience to these immigrants; that among the Portuguese at least it is quite as prevalent among the independent farming population as in the industrial city; that it is less prevalent in the north than in the south, and less in Fall River cotton mills than among the cotton mill employees of the country as a whole. About 1906, 6.1 per cent of all operatives in cotton mills of Fall River were children under 16 years of age, as against 12.8 per cent for the country as a whole.[1] More recent statistics would probably show somewhat less contrast between Fall River mills and those of the country as a whole because of the partial elimination of very young children from the mills of the South. Recent Massachu-

[1] *U. S. Senate Document No. 645*, vol. i, p. 217, in 61st Cong., 2nd Sess.; *Senate Documents*, vol. lxxxvi, 1919-20, "Women and Child Wage-earners in the United States."

setts legislation raising the requirements for working papers to an educational attainment of six instead of four years schooling, is also somewhat reducing the number of children between the ages of 14 and 16 in the mills. Nevertheless, Fall River has offered and does still offer employment to large numbers of women and children in the cotton mills. We show elsewhere [1] the types of occupations which children habitually enter in Fall River when they first leave school.

Fall River then, affords employment for unskilled or semi-skilled workers. What wages does Fall River offer? In answer to this question we have at hand wage data for certain cotton mill operatives of New England in 1905-6 contained in the study of Women and Child Wage-earners just referred to; data on wages in Massachusetts cotton mills for 1916, 1918 and 1920 from the studies of the United States Bureau of Labor Statistics; and a special tabulation of the wages of women in Fall River cotton mills in 1917 compiled for the writer by the Massachusetts Department of Labor and Industries. We have also information from the Cotton Manufacturers' Association of Fall River as to changes in the weaving rate from time to time. This weaving rate is the basis from which other rates are figured in Fall River. The following tables give certain data from these four sources.

TABLE 45

ACTUAL WEEKLY EARNINGS IN 44 NEW ENGLAND COTTON MILLS [2]

1905–6

	Male	Female
Doffers	$5.62	$4.85
Ring-spinners	5.63	6.17
Scrubbers and sweepers	5.32	4.74
Speeder tenders	8.44	7.67
Spoolers		5.79
Weavers	8.76	7.85

[1] *Cf. infra*, p. 232.

[2] *U. S. Senate Document No. 645, op. cit.*, p. 328.

The above table is interesting chiefly as showing wages paid at a time when the Portuguese were coming to Fall River in large numbers. It is faulty in that it refers to mills in different parts of New England although it is definitely stated that Fall River is included in the study. As we do not have data on the cost of living at this period it is impossible to discuss the adequacy of these wages. With all due allowance for the marked changes in costs and wages since 1906 there is no question but that the above wages are low.

Table 46 which follows gives the changes in the basic weaving rate in Fall River according to information furnished the writer by the Cotton Manufacturers' Association. " Changes in wages are based on the price for weaving 47½ yards of 28" 64/64".

TABLE 46

CHANGES IN WEAVING RATE, FALL RIVER, MASS.

FOR SOME YEARS PRIOR TO MARCH 25, 1912 THIS RATE WAS 19.66 CENTS

Advance 10% March 25, 1912 to 21.63 cents.
Advance 5% Jan. 24, 1916 to 22.71 cents.
Advance 10% Dec. 4, 1916 to 27.48 cents.
Advance 10% June 4, 1917 to 30.23 cents.
Advance 12½% Dec. 3, 1917 to 34.01 cents.
Advance 15% June 3, 1918 to 39.11 cents.
Advance 15% June 2, 1919 to 44.98 cents.
Advance 12½% Dec. 1, 1919 to 50.60 cents.
Advance 15% June 1, 1920 to 58.19 cents.
Reduction 22½% Dec. 30, 1920 to 45.10 cents.

TABLE 47

WEEKLY WAGES IN MASSACHUSETTS COTTON MILLS [1]

Occupations	Actual Wages 1916	Actual Wages 1918	Actual Wages 1920	Full-Time Wages 1920	Est. Actual Wages Oct., 1919	Index No. Actual Wages 1920 (1916 equals 100)
Card-strippers male $10.37	16.93	28.67	28.58	22.39	276
Drawing-frame tenders male .. 8.49	13.00	25.14	26.94	17.19	296
Drawing-frame tenders female 7.57	11.48	19.16	19.45	15.18	254
Slubber-tenders male 12.78	20.18	31.84	31.82	26.69	249
Speeder-tenders male 11.80	19.91	32.42	33.56	26.34	275
Speeder-tenders female 10.00	14.57	23.17	24.72	19.27	232
Mule spinners male 20.17	27.25	39.57	43.63	36.04	196
Frame spinners male 8.91	13.32	25.93	30.19	17.62	291
Frame spinners female 9.06	14.45	22.07	24.24	19.11	244
Doffers male 8.60	13.38	22.35	24.14	17.70	260
Doffers female 8.11	13.05	18.41	19.92	17.26	227
Spooler-tenders female 8.38	12.45	20.79	22.75	16.47	248
Warper-tenders female 10.02	14.29	22.75	24.58	18.89	227
Beamer-tenders male 15.24	25.23	36.46	37.30	33.36	239
Slasher-tenders male 15.49	22.63	32.45	33.89	29.92	209
Drawers-in female 10.69	15.40	23.82	25.39	20.37	223
Loomfixers male 16.32	24.03	37.20	37.92	31.77	228
Trimmers or inspectors female 7.45	10.30	16.74	17.59	13.63	225
Weavers male 10.52	15.99	26.13	28.70	21.15	248
Weavers female 9.88	14.83	24.00	26.30	19.61	243
Other employees male [2] 11.30	17.41	22.68	23.86	23.02	201
Other employees female [2] 7.66	10.92	15.92	17.48	14.44	208

[1] U. S. Bureau of Labor Statistics, *Wages and Hours of Labor in Cotton Goods Manufacturing*, in Bulletin No. 239, pp. 83ff., No. 262, pp. 88ff., No. 288, pp. 18ff. The estimated actual wages for October, 1919 were computed by the writer by adding to the wage data for 1918 15% plus 15% in accordance with table 46 which shows these increases made June 3, 1918, and June 2, 1919. The writer had ascertained from the Bureau that the wage data for 1918 were recorded as of a date prior to June 3, 1918.

[2] Wages for "other employees" are probably not comparable as between the different years because the occupations included in this category are not exactly the same, a few occupations not shown in this table having apparently been taken out of this category and listed separately in 1920.

TABLE 48

WEEKLY EARNINGS AND RATES OF WOMEN COTTON MILL [1]
EMPLOYEES, FALL RIVER, MASS.

	No.	Rate Jan.-June 1917	Earnings Jan.-June 1917	Est. Rate 1920	Est. Earnings Oct. 1919
Speeder tenders ...	117		$10.22		$16.73
Frame spinners ...	217–811 [2]	$12.17	8.65	$25.77	14.17
Weavers	421		10.35		16.94
Doffers	149	6.65		14.08	

For the purposes of our discussion we shall disregard table 45, simply noting that, like the more recent tables, it shows that cotton mill employees receive low wages. Table 47 is for cotton mill employees in Massachusetts and so raises the query as to how representative it is of wages in Fall River mills only. We may get a partial answer to this query by comparing the wage data for women workers in Fall River given in table 48 with corresponding data in

[1] Computed from unpublished tables furnished the writer by the Massachusetts Department of Labor and Industries. The rates and earnings given in the first two columns were taken from payrolls in the period January to June, 1917. June 4, 1917 there was an advance in wages in Fall River cotton mills of 10%. The figures in columns three and four in this table assume that the data were gathered before the wage advance in the last month of the period. Since the June payrolls were included in the actual computations of the Bureau it is probable that our estimates of rates and earnings for 1920 and 1919 respectively are very slightly too high since they were computed by adding the successive increases to a base which included the month of June. The maximum possible error which this procedure involves is about 2½% in the estimated rates for 1920 or the estimated earnings for 1919. If this error exists, as seems probable, then we should deduct about 65 cents from the estimated rate for frame spinners and 35 cents from that for doffers. Similarly the estimated earnings for speeder tenders would be 42 cents too high, those for frame spinners 35 cents too high, and those for weavers 42 cents too high. Estimated rates and earnings are obtained by adding the proper percentages given in table 46 to the rates and earnings given in the first two columns.

[2] 217 for earnings and 811 for rates.

table 47. Unfortunately, we have but four groups to compare, because the numbers in other occupations were too few to warrant the use of the data. For speeder tenders female, the estimated earnings for Oct. 1919 in table 47 is $19.27 as compared with $16.73 in table 48. For frame spinners the corresponding figures are $19.11 and $14.17; and for weavers $19.61 and $16.94. Thus we find that for these three occupations there is a difference of from two to nearly five dollars a week between the estimates for Massachusetts and those for Fall River. When we compare the full time wages for Massachusetts (Table 47) with the estimated rates for 1920 (Table 48) we find similarly that the Massachusetts figure for doffers is $19.92 as against $14.08 according to the figures for Fall River. On the other hand, the situation is reversed when we consider rates for frame spinners, although the difference is not so great. The Massachusetts figure for them is $24.24 while the Fall River figure is $25.77. Table 47 shows that there is in Fall River a great difference between the rate and the actual earnings of the spinners considered by the State Bureau. While the 1917 rate was $12.17 the actual earnings were only $8.65. It must be noted, however, that neither the mills nor the spinners considered are identical in the two cases. Whereas 217 female frame spinners in two cotton factories were considered in figuring the actual earnings, 811 in seven factories were used to find the figure for rates. Whether the difference between earnings and rates is due to differences between the mills considered, or the amount of voluntary or involuntary short-time, we cannot say. The possibility that such differences exist between mills in the same city, suggests that considerable differences may exist between mills in different communities in Massachusetts. It does not inspire much confidence in the representativeness of the wage data given in table 47, which we are compelled to use for what they are worth. Nevertheless, with the exception of wage rates for frame spinners the differences we have noted have all shown lower earnings or rates in Fall River than in the state as a whole. It is probable, though not certain, therefore, that by using the data for earnings in Massachusetts cotton mills we shall overstate, rather than understate, the actual earnings in Fall River.

Turning, then, to the data for Massachusetts mills given in table 47 we note that actual earnings and full-time wages did not differ very greatly in 1920 except for mule spinners and male frame spinners who actually earned about four dollars less on the average than their full-time wages would have brought them. 1920 was, it is true, a year of unusually full employment. An inspection of the actual and full-time wages given in tables for 1916 and 1918,[1] however, shows no absolute differences as great as the two mentioned for 1920. The relative difference appears to be about the same as in 1920. As our interest is chiefly in actual earnings rather than in rates we shall therefore use the former remembering that voluntary or involuntary unemployment reduces them to somewhat less than full-time wages.

Disregarding the group "other employees" we find weekly earnings varying in 1920 from $16.74 for female trimmers or inspectors to $39.57 for male mule spinners with the numerically more important groups of frame spinners, weavers et cetera occupying intermediate positions.

Data as to wages are of small importance, however, except as they are related to information as to the cost of living. Real and not monetary wages are the test of economic welfare and opportunity. Here we have available some studies of the Bureau of Labor Statistics for different com-

---

[1] Not shown here for lack of space.

munities in the United States, and a special study of living costs in Fall River made in October 1919 by the National Industrial Conference Board. Unfortunately the former studies too often do not show Fall River data separately and can only be used for certain details. The latter are of interest because made by a group of representatives of the manufacturers. It is no criticism of the National Industrial Conference Board to call attention to the fact that their data on the cost of living will not tend to exaggerate costs, nor to overestimate the amount needed for the maintenance of a " reasonable " or a " minimum " or an " American " standard of living.

According to this study in 1919

to maintain a family consisting of man, wife and three children under fourteen years of age at a minimum American standard of living but without any allowance for savings, $1,267.76 will be required, or a steady income of $24.38 per week. . . . To maintain a somewhat more comfortable standard, again without specific allowance for savings, $1,573.90 per year will be necessary or a steady income of $30.27 per week.[1]

The fifth column in table 47 gives estimated weekly earnings for 22 occupational groups in the cotton mills, 12 of which consist of males. If we use the lower standard set by this manufacturers' association we find among males that drawing-frame tenders, frame spinners, doffers and weavers all fell below it. That is to say, to the extent that our figures are acceptable, these four large groups earned less than sufficient to maintain themselves and a family of five at this minimum standard. If we adopt the higher of the

[1] National Industrial Conference Board, *The Cost of Living Among Wage-Earners, Fall River, Massachusetts,* October, 1919 (Boston, 1919), p. 17.

two standards we find that only mule spinners, beamer tenders and loomfixers were able to support familes without other financial assistance, even though they put aside no savings. How large a proportion of these workers were actually married men with families to support it is impossible to say. That wages of husbands fall below our minima in certain occupational groups is, however, well known. For example there are many married doffers, and their earnings were in 1919 far from sufficient to maintain a family of five on the Board's minimum. Many doffers are, on the other hand, mere boys just out of school. The large group of male weavers are set down as earning $21.15, or more than three dollars less than the lower family minimum.

Does it follow, then, that Fall River mill families were necessarily suffering in Ocotober 1919? No, except in individual cases. They were *relatively* well-to-do and *relatively* happy as we shall show. But it does follow that, if our statistics are true, children in many families must go to work as soon as they are fourteen, and mothers in many cases. Their earnings supplement those of the father of the family and enable the family to live at their standard and even to save considerable sums. It also probably follows that many Fall River families live at something below an " American standard of living ". Are these employees paid less than they earn, or is the lower grade cotton mill operative incapable by his own labor of supporting a family of five in Fall River, just as he was incapable in the old country? The present writer does not know.

In order to get an idea of the extent to which women and children supplement the family income we can examine data as to the sources of family incomes in Fall River. In 1919 the incomes of 158 families in Fall River were studied by the Bureau of Labor Statistics. Unfortunately some of these data are lumped in with those for other cities. If the proportion of families in the different income groups was the same for Fall River as for other cities studied, 88.5 per cent of the families had incomes between $900 and $2100, with 56 per cent between $1200 and $1800. The following table shows the relative proportions of Fall River families, as compared with all white families studied, having incomes from designated sources.

TABLE 49

PROPORTIONS OF FAMILIES HAVING INCOME FROM SPECIFIED SOURCES [1]

	U. S. *12,096 total* *white families* *studied*	*Fall River* *158 white* *families* *studied*
Income from wife	8.9%	15.8%
Income from children	18.6	27.2
Income from dependents	.7	.6
Income from lodgers	5.1	.6
Income from garden, etc.	44.3	22.2
Income from gifts	73.3	77.8
Income from rents and other investments	11.2	2.5
Income from other sources	28.4	26.6

This table shows that Fall River as compared with the other 91 localities studied had a high proportion of families with incomes from wives and from children and a low proportion with incomes from lodgers and from rents and other investments. The relatively low proportion with incomes from garden and poultry is due to the fact that many of the other communities are rural. The Portuguese, at least, keep poultry and have gardens whenever it is physically possible to do so. Of the 92 localities studied, Fall River stood last in proportion of families with incomes from lodgers, 89th from rents and other investments, but

[1] *Monthly Labor Review*, vol. ix, pp. 29-41, Dec., 1919.

8th from wives and 6th from children. Practically four-fifths of the total income of these Fall River families came from husbands, between two and three per cent from the twenty-five wives employed, 14 per cent from children, a little over 2 per cent from gifts and the balance from dependents, lodgers, rents and other investments and miscellaneous sources. The average total income among Fall River families was $1,365.03.

That Fall River mill families were relatively well off in 1920 is evident from a comparison between their wages in that year and those of 1916 and earlier; and from a comparison between the cost of living in each year. In table 46 we have shown the percentages of advances in wages in Fall River cotton mills. Between Jan. 24, 1916, and Dec. 29, 1920 these increases amounted to an advance of 156.2 per cent. Advances in actual earnings are shown for 23 occupational groups in table 47. The contrast between wages of 1916 and those of 1920 are shown in the column of index numbers. These index numbers vary from a low of 196 for mule spinners to a high of 296 for male drawing-frame tenders. Although all wages in Fall River are said to be based upon the weaving rate we see that actual increases in earnings in Massachusetts vary considerably among occupations. For all except mule spinners, however, money wages considerably more than doubled during this four year period.

According to the Bureau of Labor Statistics the index numbers for the total cost of living increased from 103.6 (Average 1913 equals 100) in Dec. 1915 to 216.5 in June 1920, or 104 per cent.[1] The National Industrial Conference Board found an increase in Fall River of 73 per cent from October 1914 to October 1919.[2] The rise between

[1] *Monthly Labor Review*, Oct., 1920, p. 689.
[2] *Op. cit.*, p. 15.

1914 and the beginning of 1916 was not great, but from that time on the increase was so rapid that it makes great difference in what month of the year statistics are gathered. All that we can say is that the rise between the date in 1916 when the wage data were gathered (mostly in May)[1] to the date of those gathered in 1920 (mostly in July) was certainly more than 77 per cent and probably not far short of 100 per cent. If we take 100 per cent as a high estimate of the increase in cost of living in 1920 over 1916 and refer to our wage table (47), we see that all cotton mill operatives with the possible exception of mule spinners were better off economically at the latter date than at the former, while some had received a very large increase in real wages. Since 1920 both costs and wages have dropped but we have not made calculations to determine which has fallen the more rapidly.

Summarizing our wage and cost of living information, we may say that according to our imperfect data many Fall River mill operatives have received wages too low to permit of family support by one wage-earner at " American " standards, but that their relative economic well-being has improved during the period of rising costs beginning in 1916. If wages were " insufficient " in 1919 and 1920 they were, of course, more insufficient in earlier years. When a family is larger than normal and when there are no additional bread-winners the situation is still worse. But when the family is not too large, and when women and children are supplementing the family income, a wage-earner's family in Fall River has had a choice between spending more now and saving for the future. Such is economic opportunity in Fall River cotton mills as judged

---

[1] Letter to the writer from Chas. E. Baldwin, Acting Commissioner of Labor Statistics, dated Aug. 18, 1922.

from data on economic opportunity in Massachusetts mills in general. It cannot be denied that there is opportunity outside the mills, but for the great mass of wage-earners in Fall River the cotton mill is the means of livelihood. A partial confirmation of this evidence of low earnings is seen in accounts of family expenditures in Fall River. It must be very carefully noted in this connection, however, that many families with low standards of living spend, even on low incomes, less than they earn. We shall find evidence of this among our Portuguese.

In the study of family budgets referred to above 158 Fall River families were included. 48 of those with incomes between $1200 and $1500 spent $624 annually for food, the largest sum for all the 91 localities listed in the study. For all families studied the average expenditure for food was $511 and the median $505. When only families of the same income ($1300)and of the same size are considered Fall River again stands first in the food expenditure of 43 communities. In expenditure for rent, on the other hand, Fall River stood 85th in the list of 91 localities.[1] This does not necessarily mean that wage-earners were not willing to spend more for rent. Says the Conference Board of Fall River tenements:

The ordinary tenement in Fall River contains from three to five rooms with toilet, and rents range from $1.25 to $4.00 per week. For the larger sum a bath would be included. There are very few heated apartment houses, and rents for these would be more than $20 a month. The majority of wage-earners probably pay between $1.75 and $3.00 per week and do not have a bath. The demand for the larger apartments with baths far exceeds the supply. Many families are forced

[1] Ogburn, "A Study of Rents in Various Cities," in the *Monthly Labor Review*, Sept., 1919, p. 10.

to live in inferior and crowded quarters at the present time [October, 1919], because no others are to be obtained.[1]

The above was written at the beginning of a period of rising rents in Fall River and corresponds with the writer's investigation except that rents had risen somewhat by 1920. In 1919, according to the study of the Bureau of Labor Statistics, the average rental paid by Fall River families was $2.56.[2] No exceptional overcrowding was shown, the families averaging 1.1 persons per room or about the same as for families in general.

The Bureau of Labor Statistics also rates thirty cities according to the amounts spent by families for the miscellaneous items in the budget. Here Fall River stands first in the list of expenditures for church, 18th for insurance, 23rd for amusements, 25th for uplift and education, 26th for street-car fares, 28th for charities, 29th for sickness and last for " patriotic purposes ".[3] Such ratings do not show, however, the reasons why little was spent for some of these items. The reason might conceivably be lack of need, lack of desire, necessity for spending more for other more pressing needs, or because the community furnished some of these things gratis. Perhaps Fall River families spend more for food because they are obliged to; but it is equally likely that they prefer eating well to living well.

Opportunity to Find a Desirable Home

Other opportunities and handicaps in Fall River are in part dependent on this fundamental economic situation which we have described and in part independent of it. Thus the opportunity to secure a sanitary and attractive

[1] *National Industrial Conference Board, op. cit.,* pp. 5-6.

[2] Ogburn, *op. cit.,* p. 10.

[3] *Monthly Labor Review,* vol. ix, Nov., 1919, p. 18.

home is in part limited by income and in part by the number of homes available at a reasonable rental. We have noted above the scarcity of desirable homes in 1919. As is well known this scarcity of the better sort of houses was at that period characteristic of most communities in the United States. On the other hand, as we have seen, rents are low in Fall River.

No one will deny that the sections of the city where most of the Portuguese live are unattractive. There is a dreary monotony of plain two and three story frame buildings with accommodations for from two to twelve families, sometimes fronting the street, and sometimes ugly alleys. In most yards the tramp of many feet has prevented the growth of grass although there are exceptions to this. Even where the interiors of the tenements are well-kept, hallways are apt to be defaced and uncleanly. What is everybody's business is no one's business.

Unfortunately, we have no reliable study of housing conditions in Fall River. Early in 1912 a supposedly scientific study of housing was indeed made by the Director of the Bureau of Social Research for New England. Unfortunately, an examination of the methods of this survey, at least in the parts of the city with which the present writer is acquainted, does not inspire confidence in the representative character of this study. Under the head of " Field of investigation " the author says:

The desire of the committee was to ascertain general conditions rather than startling abuses. It was therefore found advisable, in fairness to the city, not to pick individual houses but to take whole sections and record both sanitary and unsanitary conditions, normal and abnormal structures, and base conclusions upon an average.[1]

[1] Aronovici, *Housing Conditions in Fall River* (Fall River, undated, but study made in 1912), p. 2.

A map is then presented showing areas covered, and while a little thought would tell the reader that these areas must contain far more than the 279 buildings investigated, he is given the impression from the text that practically all houses in the areas indicated were studied. The present writer knows nothing of the representativeness of this study except as it refers to fifteen city blocks bounded by Broadway, Columbia, Hunter and Division Streets. Within that area he feels sure, however, that very far from all buildings were examined, and, what is much more important, that those examined were not a fair sample of the whole district. These fifteen city blocks contain to-day not far from 300 numbered dwellings. The writer examined the original schedules for the housing survey and found that, leaving William Street out of consideration,[1] a total of 29 dwellings had been investigated. But these 29 can hardly be considered representative. In general the living conditions in this district grow worse as one approaches the corner of Broadway and Columbia Streets and improve as one goes either south or east from that point. But an examination of the schedules shows that no less than seventeen of the twenty-nine houses investigated were located in the one block bounded by Broadway, Columbia, Eagle and Hope Streets—by far the worst block of the fifteen. Moreover, although the whole section is included in the shaded area on the map, as though all parts had been examined with equal care, no schedules were found for Division, Hunter or Grant Streets within the boundaries mentioned above. These streets are, according to the present writer's investigation, decidedly the best streets in the section. With great regret, therefore, we are obliged to forego the use of

---

[1] The present writer inadvertently omitted to include this street when examining the schedules.

this housing survey, in our attempt to appraise the opportunity which Fall River offers to its wage-earners to secure homes. Neither have we any study of our own to offer in its stead, except the information given below as to living conditions among about 100 Portuguese families in the Columbia Street district.

It is a matter of general knowledge, however, that housing conditions of mill workers in Fall River are not ideal. The general appearance of the houses is unattractive. The general absence of a bath has already been noted. In one of the worst types of dwellings the toilet is in a corner of the pantry with only a curtain separating it from the room. During the high rent period tenants complained of the difficulty in getting landlords to make repairs. If he were to consider the houses themselves alone, the writer would prefer life in the farm houses of Portsmouth without running water, to life in the mill houses of the city which he has seen;—at least he would prefer it if he could live there before the Portuguese had occupied them.

Thus one's estimate of the opportunity for normal home life in Fall River will depend upon one's idea of what constituted "normal" home life. The homes seem to be poor and unlovely, but not generally unsanitary. The proportion of the sexes is approximately equal with a slight excess of females. The low wages, no doubt, do tend to compel a postponement of marriage and to limit the possibility of occupying an "American" type of home. On the whole, the writer would consider the opportunity poor and such as to satisfy only a people accustomed to adverse living conditions.

Opportunity for normal home life in Portsmouth is perhaps better than in Fall River. The homes of the farming population there are of various types. It has seldom been necessary for newcomers to build new homes unless they have so desired, because the native population has moved out leaving ample accommodations. Many of the houses left are old and poorly equipped and most are, of course, lacking in modern conveniences, but these conditions are the typical rural situation. In place of more modern plumbing in Fall River, the inhabitant of Portsmouth has country air, ample space indoors and out, low rents, variety in type and location, and attractive rural surroundings. The condition of one's home in Portsmouth depends much more upon one's own ability to make something of it than does that of a Fall River tenement. A state investigation published in 1907 showed about two rooms per person in Portsmouth or about twice the space available in the city.[1] With the growth of large Portuguese families the ratio of people to rooms has possibly increased somewhat, but not greatly, for the population has declined in the last ten years.

Opportunity for Education

In educational opportunities offered there is naturally a considerable contrast between the two communities. In Portsmouth the schools are small, the distances in some cases considerable, and the school committee in charge apparently increasingly indifferent. The writer has been told that the committee takes the attitude that there is no use improving schools for the Portuguese to utilize. Without reflecting in the least upon the conscientious work of the teaching staff, the quality of instruction to be expected in Portsmouth may be judged from the fact that the highest salary paid to any teacher in 1920 was $695, as compared with $1500 paid to teachers in Fall River elementary schools after five years of service.[2] The town has seven

[1] R. I. Bureau of Industrial Statistics, *Annual Report for 1907*, Part I, Bulletin iii, p. 333.

[2] Portsmouth, R. I., *Report of Town Officers* (Newport, 1920), p. 14. Fall River, Mass., *Report of the Public Schools*, 1920 (Fall River, 1921), p. 69.

elementary schools for the first four grades, one of which also cares for all the fifth grade pupils. In addition there is one school for grades six to nine but no high school. Pupils wishing secondary education go either to Newport where they can get tuition free, or to Fall River where a fee of $125 a year is charged. The Superintendent of Schools is paid a salary of $300. Six of the school houses are old-fashioned one-room buildings. The more central school at Newtown is more modern and the Quaker Hill School near the Town Hall is, in physical appearance, a fairly up-to-date establishment with running water, flushed toilets and well-lighted rooms. Granting a fair amount of conscientious work on the part of teachers, Portsmouth can hardly be said to stimulate the love of education as well as might be wished.

In Fall River we find the relatively high-grade schools characteristic of Massachusetts cities. A special survey of Fall River Schools by an unusually competent committee, though never published, has enabled the writer to get a fair estimate of the quality of educational opportunity in Fall River, as late as 1917. This survey reports the Fall River tax rate for school purposes as next to the highest among cities of its size in the United States. The report criticized the distribution of the money obtained, however, on the ground that a disproportionate amount ($87.49 per student) was spent for secondary education, as compared with the sum ($34.91 per student) spent for elementary education.[1] Of 36 Massachusetts cities Fall River had the largest staff of high school teachers per unit of all but three. She also stood third from the last among these cities in the proportion of the population in the high schools (125 per ten thousand) being followed only by Chicopee and New

[1] Lincoln, *et al., Survey of the Schools of Fall River* (Report submitted May 25, 1917), ch. ii, p. 26.

Bedford. Of cities in the United States with a population of between 100,000 and 150,000 Fall River was fourth from the end in this respect being followed by Memphis, New Bedford and Bridgeport. The survey also lays special stress upon the great exodus of children from Fall River schools as soon as they reach the age of fourteen. " Probably three-fifths of the children of Fall River leave school as soon as they reach the age of 14." The committee found but 2125 children aged 14-18 in school out of a possible 10,000.[1] The following table showing the pupils enrolled in Fall River schools by grades indicates the great falling off in registration as soon as the sixth, seventh and eighth grades are reached. Commenting

TABLE 50

FALL RIVER, MASS., PUPILS IN PUBLIC SCHOOLS BY GRADES,
DECEMBER, 1916 [2]

Grades	Boys	Girls	Total
Kindergarten	196	202	398
Grade 1	1288	1179	2467
" 2	1068	1141	2209
" 3	974	989	1963
" 4	1076	1098	2174
" 5	1143	993	2136
" 6	685	757	1442
" 7	465	470	935
" 8	355	337	692
High 1	224	255	479
" 2	168	192	360
" 3	130	184	314
" 4	104	155	259
Post-graduate	6	16	22
Special	291	245	536
Sub-Freshmen	14	18	32
Totals	8187	8231	16418

[1] *Ibid.*, p. 121. If continuation schools are counted this number has presumably increased since 1917.

[2] Lincoln *et al., op. cit.*, ch. iv, p. 8.

upon this situation the Committee says: " It is believed by the survey committee that this [leaving school at the age of fourteen] is not due so much to financial necessity as to the fact that the education provided in grades seven and eight is not of a character suited to encourage pupils to continue this education." [1] Be that as it may, there is no question that children leave school to go to work as the following table makes evident.

Table 51 shows a very considerable exodus of children into industry in 1916. That this was not a year when an abnormally large number of children went to work is shown by the fact that the annual reports of the Public Schools for 1919 and 1920 show respectively 3174 and 2978 employment certificates issued to different children between the ages of 14 and 16. These numbers were exclusive of vacation employment certificates and home permits. The table also brings out the degree to which the cotton mill is the goal of such children, in that more than four-fifths of all children going to work entered the mills. The proportion of girls entering cotton mills was larger than that of boys.

So far as recent school reports show the educational policy of recent years, there seems to be a curious conflict between a desire to keep the children in school longer, and a fear lest what they learn shall make them dissatisfied with the life of a mill operative. This latter fear has led to a demand for increased emphasis upon practical and industrial courses. The following from the report of 1919 [2] is worth reproducing:

Manual training is vital to Fall River. No industrial com-

[1] *Ibid.,* ch. iv, p. 8.
[2] P. 15.

munity can lay the proper educational foundations for its youth without that training. Fully four-fifths of the wage-earners of the city are engaged in the manufacturing industries. An exclusively bookish education has created in the minds of many of them a radically wrong attitude towards life. It is undeniable that working at cotton manufacturing is looked upon as a necessary evil, as a last resort, as something to be given up if possible.

TABLE 51

FALL RIVER, MASS., OCCUPATIONS ENTERED BY CHILDREN LEAVING SCHOOL,[1] 1916

Cotton Industries	Boys	Girls	Totals
Weaving room	100	161	261
Doffing	53	179	232
Sweeper (spinning room)	176	7	183
Spinner	26	82	108
Spool attendant	1	98	99
Drop wiring (weave room)	54	4	58
Cleaner	32	16	48
Braider	9	34	43
Bobbin boy	19	2	21
Winder tender	10	12	22
Filling carriers	12	1	13
Trimmer	0	16	16
Work on rollers	11	1	12
Harness maker	3	12	15
Table boy	13	0	13
Hanking cord	10	0	10
Shuttle boy	10	0	10
Drawing-in tender	4	8	12
Cloth handler	11	2	13
Single-end piler	11	0	11
Heddle boy	4	6	10
Envelope filler	1	8	9
Yarn carrier	7	0	7
Back boy	7	0	7
Tuber	9	1	10
Finisher (shirt waists)	0	9	9
Bale sewer	5	0	5

[1] Lincoln, *et al.*, *op. cit.*, ch. iv, p. 12.

Waste boy	7	1	8
Cutter-off (cloth bags)	0	7	7
All others	59	28	87
Totals ("cotton")	664	695	1359

Non-cotton occupations	Boys	Girls	Totals
Clerk	45	4	49
Helper	24	2	26
Errand boy	21	0	21
Messenger (business)	10	0	10
" (telegraph)	16	0	16
Office boy	10	1	11
House work	0	16	16
Machine shop work	8	0	8
Home work (estimated)	0	50	50
Hat factory (mostly ironing machines) ...	15	4	19
Helper on wagon	5	0	5
Bobbin Co.	10	0	10
All others	47	22	69
Total ("non-cotton")	211	99	310
Grand totals	875	794	1669

The educational problem suggested by this quotation is too large for discussion in this study. Is the educational problem of Fall River to make "educated" people love to tend looms? Or is it to make them dissatisfied with the cotton mill, and if so who is to tend the looms? Or is it rather, as Arthur Pound would have us believe, to teach them how to use their leisure time profitably and intelligently? If cotton mill work is all which these people are capable of performing, it is surely no kindness to them to lead them to despise it. If, on the other hand, they can be fitted for more exacting work they should be given the opportunity. The writer makes no pretense of answering these questions. The above quotation is of interest to us as indicating that education in Fall River had seemed to lead to dissatisfaction with cotton mill work, and as showing a possible change in educational policy. Perhaps Fall

River needs different kinds of education adapted to the different mental capacities of different types of population. In addition to its regular day elementary and high schools, the public school system also affords special classes for subnormals in which 115 pupils were enrolled during the school year 1919-1920; an independent evening industrial school for women with an enrollment of 1075 and an average attendance of 663; one for men with an attendance of but 40; elementary evening schools with an enrollment of 1150 and an average attendance of about half that number; and classes in agriculture attracting 225. In addition a small day industrial school gives instruction to some 34 boys in interior decorating and cabinet making.

Fall River also has numerous parochial schools attended chiefly by French Canadians but not as a rule by Portuguese, although there is one such school especially for that nationality. The quality of the instruction in these schools need not be discussed here for they are merely an alternative to instruction in the public schools for those who wish a combination of religious and secular training and who can pay the fees asked. There are practically no other private schools in the city, and the children of the wealthier parents invariably attend the public schools.

Also located in Fall River is a state institution—the Bradford Durfee Textile School. This school has both day and evening classes. The entrance requirements for the day school are that the candidate must be at least 16 years of age and must either present a high school certificate or pass an examination in Arithmetic and English. Actually, most pupils have had at least two years of high school training. Four courses are offered: one in general cotton manufacturing requiring three years of attendance, and two-year courses in designing and weaving, the chemistry of dyeing and engineering. In the year ending Nov.

30, 1920, 97 students were enrolled, 57 of whom were residents of Fall River. The evening classes attract a larger number and very different type of students. Very many are mill operatives who wish to prepare themselves for some particular mill occupation. There are 13 or 26 week courses in one particular subject and most students take but one course. In 1921, 1292 students were enrolled in these classes nearly all of whom were residents of Fall River. The actual attendance, however, was but 755.

In accordance with a state law passed in 1918, continuation schools were established in Fall River in 1920 to provide schooling for minors between the ages of 14 and 16 who are employed not less than six hours per day, or who remain at home under special home permits.[1] Boys may go to either of two schools—one where carding, spinning and weaving are taught, and one where automobile repairing, electrical work, woodwork, mechanical drawing, and commercial branches are the subjects. The girls in the same group receive instruction in home nursing, care of infants and home management, and the regular academic subjects which are required; and in cooking, sewing, millinery and commercial subjects which are electives. " The entire school in its three divisions has had over 2500 pupils per week, making it by a considerable margin the largest school of its kind in the state, exception being made of the Boston school which has about twice its membership." [2]

Special educational work for immigrants is also carried on in the Fall River evening schools and by the Fall River Immigrant Committee. The latter organization was until recently financed by some of the cotton mills but is now

[1] *54th Annual Report of Public Schools of Fall River* (Fall River, 1920), p. 27.

[2] *55th Annual Report of the Public Schools of Fall River* (Fall River, 1921), p. 17.

(1922) on an independent basis. According to its annual report for 1920, 350 aliens had been in attendance in its English classes and 288 in advanced or citizenship classes. This organization seems to have been able to get the interest of the different nationalities to some degree by establishing classes in clubs or in shops. Their attendance records are more satisfactory than those of the classes in the public schools where the work has been handicapped by the lack of a full-time director of Americanization work. The Immigrant Commission is useful to immigrants in many other ways besides this, such as aiding in the transmission of money home, assisting candidates for citizenship in the courts, conducting public receptions for new citizens, handling foreign letters and cables, issuing affidavits, co-operating with other social agencies, delivering formal and informal lectures on various subjects, et cetera. All these aids are lacking in the rural community of Portsmouth, except as the people go to Fall River or elsewhere for them.

Thus, as would be expected, Fall River offers much more in the way of educational advantages to the newcomer, than does Portsmouth. Whether the new emphasis upon practical education is desirable, whether too great stress is given to high school education or not, it cannot be denied that there is much more educational opportunity in Fall River than the population takes advantage of.

Opportunity to Keep in Good Health

We may get a rough idea of the health opportunity in our two communities by noting natural and sanitary conditions, by referring to such vital statistics as are available, and by examining the organized efforts to promote health in each community. We shall do this very briefly.

Portsmouth impresses one as a healthful community. Except at one marshy spot the island is high and dry and the hills and part of the shore line are a summer resort for the well-to-do, including a few of great wealth. The winter's cold is no doubt trying for those who have seldom known frost at home. As in most rural communities sanitary conveniences are within the reach of only a few; and whether the lack of them will be a menace to health will depend upon the intelligence with which people live, and the enforcement of health regulations by the community. This enforcement is probably less strict and less necessary than in the city.

Death rates for a single year would be without significance for Portsmouth because of the small population.

Table 52 shows a total of 1315 deaths in Portsmouth in 36 years. By dividing the last thirty years into three periods of ten years each we find an average of 27.1 deaths per year during the first decade, 41.5 during the second and 48.2 during the third. If we should assume the absolute growth of population to have been constant between the Census years of 1890, 1900, 1910 and 1920 and should use the estimated population for about the middle of our decades (1896, 1906 and 1916 respectively) as a base, we should get very roughly the following average death rates for each of the three decades: 13.3, 16.9, and 18.4, respectively. A moment's thought, however, will show that we cannot consider these rising rates as indices of an increasing menace to health in the community, but as indications of a great change going on in the characteristics of the population of the town. A glance at tables 41 and 42 [1] shows the marked difference to-day between the age distribution of the Portuguese and that of the non-Portuguese. Reference to our chapter on infant mortality [2] will also show the marked difference in the number of infant deaths

[1] Page 155.

[2] *Cf.* especially pp. 197-8.

TABLE 52

PORTSMOUTH, R. I., DEATHS BY NATIVITY, 1885–1920 [1]

Year	Native Non-Portuguese	Portuguese Descent	Other Foreign	Negro	Unknown	Totals
1885	28	1	2	0	2	33
1886	23	1	1	0	0	25
1887	15	2	0	0	1	18
1888	20	1	0	0	3	24
1889	19	1	1	0	0	21
1890	23	1	2	0	0	26
1891	20	1	2	0	1	24
1892	29	1	1	0	0	31
1893	18	1	0	0	1	20
1894	17	1	2	0	0	20
1895	17	3	1	0	0	21
1896	24	6	1	0	0	31
1897	15	5	0	0	0	20
1898	22	5	1	0	0	28
1899	26	9	4	0	0	39
1900	26	8	2	0	1	37
1901	24	7	2	0	1	34
1902	21	16	1	0	0	38
1903	26	11	2	1	2	42
1904	29	4	5	0	0	38
1905	17	24	2	1	0	44
1906	31	12	1	0	1	44
1907	20	9	1	1	0	31
1908	20	10	4	0	0	34
1909	35	15	4	0	2	56
1910	30	20	4	0	0	54
1911	33	13	13	0	2	61
1912	18	16	4	0	0	38
1913	31	13	5	0	0	50
1914	21	23	5	0	2	51
1915	20	24	5	0	1	50
1916	20	16	2	0	0	38
1917	28	26	4	0	0	58
1918	19	24	3	0	1	47
1919	28	14	3	1	1	47
1920	24	16	2	0	0	42
Totals	837	360	92	4	22	1315

[1] From Register of Deaths for Portsmouth, R. I., 1885-1920.

among Portuguese and non-Portuguese. The marked rise in the death rate for Portsmouth can probably be explained, therefore, as a result of (1) the exodus of the younger native stock leaving an abnormal proportion of aged among natives; (2) the coming of a people with a high birth rate and hence the opportunity for many infant deaths; and (3) the coming of a people with an abnormally high infant death rate. These forces have apparently more than offset the fact that the Portuguese bring few aged with them. If we may assume that in the first of our three decades Portsmouth had a normal population, we may say that a death rate of 13.3 was low at that time, and that, so measured, the community may be rated as healthful.

As for organized public health work in Portsmouth it is almost nil. Reasonably competent physicians are on call, children in the schools are given simple eye and ear tests; and an experiment was once tried with a Red Cross nurse from Newport to visit families and examine children in the schools. This experiment proved a failure, however, because of lack of interest on the part of the community. In 1920 the Child Welfare Bureau of the State of Rhode Island began sending a nurse to look up new-born infants and to advise mothers as to their care. Her visits are but once a year, however, and while the work is greatly needed such a nurse can not have the influence of a resident district nurse. Beyond this and individual efforts of teachers and other residents little has been done to promote health in Portsmouth.

Turning to Fall River we find a city unattractive but not noticeably unsanitary. Its degree of healthfulness may be judged from the following table showing the city's death-rates for successive years from 1911 to 1919 inclusive and for the period 1906 to 1910, compared with corresponding rates for other cities of Massachusetts.

TABLE 53

DEATH RATES OF FIVE MASSACHUSETTS CITIES [1]

Cities	Average 1906-10	1911	1912	1913	1914	1915	1916	1917	1918	1919	1
Boston	17.9	17.3	16.6	16.8	16.6	16.7	17.6	17.4	23.6	15.7	
Cambridge ..	15.1	15.3	13.3	13.8	13.6	13.6	14.2	14.8	21.1	13.4	
Fall River ...	19.7	17.9	16.6	17.8	18.1	16.8	18.1	17.6	23.8	14.4	
Lowell	19.4	18.0	17.6	16.2	16.2	16.6	17.7	17.5	22.2	15.2	
Worcester ...	17.1	15.7	16.1	16.1	15.5	15.0	17.3	16.3	21.6	14.8	

This table shows Cambridge to have had the lowest death rate of these five cities, Worcester next with Boston, Lowell and Fall River running close together but with Fall River showing slightly the highest rate for the early five year period and for six of the ten more recent years. Fall River has, however, improved her relative standing in the state during the years 1919 and 1920. These five cities are the only ones in Massachusetts for which the Census Bureau computed rates. For the year 1920 the writer has computed rates for the other two cities in the state having over 100,000 population and finds a rate for Springfield of 13.2 and for New Bedford of 14.4. In using these rates we are in danger of assuming that we are measuring only the healthfulness of the community when we may as well be measuring the health habits of its inhabitants. We may also be seeing the result of peculiar age and sex distributions of the population. Fall River may conceivably have had a slightly higher death-rate in many years for any of the following causes or for a combination of them: because she is naturally slightly less healthful; because less efficient efforts have been made to promote public health there; because the Portuguese (or other types) live there

[1] Rates for all years except 1920 are from Bureau of the Census, *Mortality Statistics 1919* (Washington, 1921), p. 12. For the year 1920 the writer computed the rates from an advance report on deaths for 1920 published by the Bureau using the figures for population given in vol. i, of the *Census of Population for 1920*.

in large numbers; or because the total population is at those age periods when the death-rate is normally higher. In order to enable us to judge whether age and sex have been factors in the difference between Fall River's death-rates and those of other cities, the writer has computed the following table of corrected death-rates.

TABLE 54

CORRECTED DEATH-RATES FOR FIVE MASSACHUSETTS CITIES [1]

ies	Average 1906-10	1911	1912	1913	1914	1915	1916	1917	1918	1919	1920
ston	19.8	19.2	18.4	18.6	18.4	18.5	19.5	19.3	26.1	17.4	17.2
mbridge ..	16.2	16.4	14.3	14.8	14.6	14.6	15.2	15.9	22.6	14.4	16.0
ll River ...	22.1	20.1	18.7	20.0	20.3	18.9	20.0	19.8	26.8	16.2	16.5
well	21.4	19.9	19.4	17.9	17.9	18.3	19.5	19.3	24.4	16.7	17.4
orcester ...	18.6	17.1	17.5	17.5	16.9	16.3	18.8	17.7	23.5	16.1	16.1

[1] The crude death-rates presented in Table 53 were corrected for age and sex as follows: The distribution by age and sex of the total population of New England for 1910 was assumed to be a standard age and sex distribution, and the deaths per 1000 male and female in each age group were assumed to be standard mortality rates. The age and sex distribution of the population of each of the five cities in 1910 was assumed to be representative of the age and sex distributions of these cities' populations for the period 1906-10, and for each of the years 1911 to 1920 inclusive. This latter assumption probably involves a small error, since the age and sex distributions of the populations of the five cities doubtless varied slightly from year to year. However, it was felt that the 1910 distributions were sufficiently representative as bases for calculating death-rates, and since the actual distributions for the other years would necessarily have been based upon population estimates, the 1910 figures have been used. It should be added that the 1920 Census volumes on population now available do not classify populations by the age groups 15-24, 25-44 or 45-64. Since these age groups are significant in refining mortality rates, the 1920 figures were not used. A "factor of correction" was computed for each of the five cities by dividing the death-rate of the standard population by the calculated standard death-rate of each city. The "corrected" death-rates in Table 54 are the products of the crude rates (Table 53) by these "factors of correction." The "corrected" rates, therefore, show variations due to other factors than age and sex.

A more detailed description of this method of correcting crude death-rates will be found in Newsholme, *Vital Statistics*, Chapter XII, page 109 *et passim*.

This table shows the same relative standing of the death-rates of the five cities, even when allowance has been made for the influence of age and sex upon mortality. If Fall River's death-rate has been higher than that of some other communities, it has not been due to an abnormal distribution by sex or to an abnormally large proportion of people at those age periods when death-rates are high. As compared with the other five cities, the refined death-rate for Fall River is relatively higher than the crude death-rate. The difference is not, however, great. To the writer it seems that the somewhat higher death-rate in the earlier years in Fall River may be largely explained as due to excessive infant mortality which we have discussed elsewhere. The decline in general death-rate of recent years has been paralleled by a decline in infant mortality.

As Fall River is a textile manufacturing city an especial interest attaches to the data on tuberculosis risk. The Federal Study of Women and Child Wage-earners made about 1906 concludes that work in the cotton mills is injurious to women and that the risk from tuberculosis is especially high.[1] To obtain an estimate of the tuberculosis rate for the city of Fall River we have taken the five-year period 1915-1919 inclusive. During the decade 1910-1920 the population of Fall River increased only by 1190. There can, therefore, be no great error involved if we assume that the population increase was evenly distributed during this period and that the population increased by 119 annually. During these five years there were in Fall River 907 deaths from tuberculosis.[2] This gives us an average tuberculosis rate for the period of 140 per 100,000 popula-

---

[1] Senate Document No. 645, in *Senate Documents*, vol. xcix. *Women and Child Wage Earners in the United States*, vol. xiv, pp. 31-3.

[2] From the annual reports on Mortality Statistics of the United States, 1915-1919.

tion. For the same period the rate for the registration area of the United States was 124. To the extent that this difference is due to external conditions of life in Fall River, we may say that there is a somewhat abnormally great tuberculosis risk in this cotton mill city. It is obvious, however, that there are other possible explanations of this somewhat higher rate, such as that of a peculiar susceptibility to this disease on the part of the inhabitants of the city.

Fall River is fortunate in having organized public health work on a considerable scale. The chief organizations doing this work are a reasonably efficient Board of Health and medical and hospital service, and a remarkably well-organized District Nursing Association supported partly by private philanthropy and partly from the fees of patients who can afford to pay. In 1920 the Board of Health reported besides its agent, an inspector of plumbing, two sanitary inspectors, one inspector of slaughtering, one bacteriologist, two milk inspectors, one market inspector, three consulting specialists, one tuberculosis nurse, two infant welfare nurses and a medical inspector of schools for each of the eight districts.[1] The writer has made no special study of the work of these officials but those interested consider it reasonably efficient.

The District Nursing Association reported in March 1921 : " Beside the nine nurses working in the factories, which are fully paid for [by the corporations], there are thirteen nurses doing general work and three doing child welfare work only, and a superintendent and supervisor ". These nurses ministering both to the very poor and to those able to pay part or all of the sixty-five cents average

[1] *Annual Report of the Board of Health for the Year Ending Dec. 31, 1920.*

cost of a visit, attended to the needs of prenatal cases, the mother and new-born child, the pre-school and school child, the youth, the middle-aged and elderly people. In the year ending March 1921, " 39,998 visits were made to the homes of 5,701 individuals, not counting the 15,338 visits made by the child welfare nurses." In addition to this regular nursing service this organization supervises the work of a tuberculosis nurse partially maintained by the Anti-tuberculosis Society, employs a visiting housekeeper, a domestic science worker and a summer director of boys' work. It also conducts six infant welfare stations besides its own headquarters, and a social settlement.[1]

A newcomer to Fall River, then, even though himself somewhat ignorant of health problems in an industrial city, finds not a few whose duty it is to safeguard his health, and many others on whom he may call for assistance in time of need. Such help must be listed among the assets of life in Fall River.

Opportunity for Recreation

Life is not complete without the opportunity for a normal amount of recreation. In Portsmouth there is no public provision for recreation of any kind, nor is there commercialized recreation except for a summer resort at the extreme northern end of the island. But as in most rural communities nature affords ample space for self-directed play and in Portsmouth the ocean adds its special attractions. Recreation, therefore, is just what the inhabitants make it. " Foreigners " are not welcome at one or two points where natives or summer residents have monopolized choice bathing places, but there is ample space for them elsewhere, though at less attractive spots.

[1] *Annual Report of the District Nursing Association of Fall River*, 1920-21, *passim*.

In Fall River recreation is both public, private and commercialized. The city possesses three parks and some smaller greens and playgrounds comprising some 100 acres of land. There is a special playground director with headquarters at the Boys' Club. Five years ago there was some complaint that the playgrounds were not easily accessible for all the children, a defect which was partially remedied at that time.[1] When the writer asked representative social workers of the city what sort of social survey would most aid their work, they were unanimous that a study of recreational facilities was most needed. They emphasized the necessity of protecting the water supply from pollution, the danger to bathers from sewage deposited in the bay and the restricted bathing area which is therefore beyond walking distance for large numbers of people.

The chief form of commercialized amusement in Fall River is moving pictures.

There are a dozen houses in the city to which admission is usually fifteen cents with the war tax. Children are admitted to the smaller houses on Saturday afternoons for six cents. . . . One or two of the theatres frequently offer vaudeville shows and plays for which prices of admission range as high as $2. There are also a number of public dance halls to which admission is twenty-five cents.[2]

The opportunities to hear concerts at reasonable prices are numerous and such concerts are well attended, while during the summer months band concerts in the public parks are provided by charitable citizens.

In addition to these public and commercialized amusements the very size of the community makes possible a

[1] *Cf.* Dwight, "First Aid to 30,000 Children," in the *Child Labor Bulletin*, vol. v, p. 214.

National Industrial Conference Board, op. cit., p. 9.

greater number and variety of social organizations for recreational purposes. Aside from those organized by the churches or by the wage-earners themselves several others are worth noting. The Boy Scouts who are 600 strong in Fall River, have but few Portuguese members. The leaders of this organization say that this is not because the Portuguese are not wanted, but because they do not know of the opportunity. The fact that many of the troops have their headquarters in Protestant churches and that the leadership is Protestant for the most part, no doubt discourages the Portuguese from taking advantage of membership in this organization, although it is avowedly non-sectarian. But the most important recreational organization organized for rather than by the mill population is undoubtedly the Boys' Club. Here the Portuguese and other foreign nationalities are welcome and feel at home. The Club has a total membership of some 2800 of whom 1500 are boys under 14 years of age. A reasonably well-equipped and much-used building is provided with a small library, baths, swimming pool, gymnasia, pool and billiard tables, bowling alley, and facilities for playing many other games. No similar club exists for girls or women of this class, although they have the use of the baths at the Boy's Club at certain times.

Recently it has been complained that there is a tendency towards professionalism in recreational activities, the people seeming to prefer watching sports to actively participating in them. But this tendency is of their own choosing and is regretted by recreational leaders in the community. All in all, Fall River offers considerable opportunity for recreation. Playgrounds should be better located perhaps, bathing facilities might well be provided nearer to the center of the city, a girls' club corresponding to the Boy's Club is needed, and possibly the right leadership might educate people to demand more elevating forms of amusement than some of those which are now patronized. We shall refer briefly later to recreation as provided by the Portuguese themselves or by them as they are organized into churches.

Summarizing this imperfect picture of opportunity in our two communities we may say:

1. In Portsmouth the Portuguese come to a rural community with few contacts but with some opportunity to learn from the American farmers. Contacts are most numerous for children and for men, and least frequent for the women. In Fall River they find a more complex environment with few contacts with native-born but with many contacts with other foreign groups, and with more effort than in Portsmouth, at least, to assist them in solving their real problems.

2. In both communities they find a somewhat unaccustomed and trying climate to which it is not easy to adapt themselves.

3. Economic opportunity in both communities is somewhat narrow, but is of a sort to which they are either accustomed or can easily be adapted. Chance for economic success in Portsmouth depends upon hard work and upon a willingness to live at a low standard of living. Success comparable with that which they see among native farmers is not beyond the range of possibility, however. In Fall River they can expect but low real wages, albeit higher than those to which they have been accustomed. If they marry they must either live on a very low plane or expect their wives and children to continue to work outside the home as they have been accustomed to do in the Islands. Their chance for much advancement in the mills is not great, but after several members of the family have been working some time they may hope to accumulate savings by dint of economy.

4. The housing problem is not apparently acute in either

community.   The city affords more conveniences but dwellings are more attractively located in the rural community. Approximate equality in the numbers of the sexes favors normal family life, but low income may be expected to delay marriage.

5. In each community the numbers of their own people are sufficient to insure religious and social leadership by leaders of their own nationality, so far as the right sort of men are available.

6. The educational opportunity in either community is far superior to what the Portuguese have known in the Azores.   Judged by modern standards that offered in Portsmouth leaves much to be desired, however.   In Fall River reasonably efficient elementary schools are found.   A recent change in educational policy seems to stress practical education and some small effort is made to meet the special needs of immigrants.   For those who go on to advanced work, secondary and some specialized education is open, but only a small proportion of wage-earners are able or wish to take advantage of the opportunity.   The mores of wage-earners in Fall River are strongly set against higher education.

7. The health risk in Portsmouth does not seem to be great but the rapidly changing composition of the population makes death rates but poor indices of health conditions. There is practically no organized public health work there. In Fall River there is a possible tuberculosis risk to consider, but the city has had a death rate only slightly higher than other cities of its size in the state of Massachusetts. Such difference as there is is not due to an unfavorable age distribution of the population.   While there are other possible causes it would seem that the excessive infant mortality discussed in another chapter might account for a higher death rate in Fall River than in the other cities.

Moreover, the Fall River death rate has decreased considerably very recently.

8. Recreational opportunity in Portsmouth is that of a typical rural community by the seashore. In Fall River there are some handicaps in this respect, although the city is not without efforts to give immigrant children and adults a normal opportunity to play.

It is difficult to say whether total opportunity is greater in Portsmouth or in Fall River. Opportunity cannot be evaluated except in relation to the type of people who are to use it. It behooves us, therefore, to consider characteristics of the Portuguese and their achievement in the two communities.

Portuguese Achievement

As noted in another place, our information as to Portuguese achievement is derived partly from an analysis of statistics for Fall River and Portsmouth as wholes and partly from a survey of selected Portuguese families in Fall River, and of all Portuguese families in Portsmouth. It is necessary at this point to justify the choice of the 102 families studied in Fall River. These families all lived within fifteen city blocks bounded by Broadway, Hunter, Columbia and Division streets. This district was chosen on the advice of the District Nursing Association and the Association for Community Welfare [1] of Fall River as one which would be representative of the home life of typical Portuguese mill hands. Both organizations agreed that it would not illustrate either the worst or the best Portuguese homes though it would include a wide

---

[1] While the writer must acknowledge much friendly assistance on the part of these and other organizations, it must be understood that they are in no way responsible for the present study. Indeed, the writer knows of some statements with which some of them are not in sympathy.

range of living conditions. A little more than half the families were visited in company with a nurse and the balance with a kindergartener. The former were a selected group in so far as families reached by public health nurses are a selected group. Families which had had neither births nor illness in recent years were less likely to be on the Association's list, but such are comparatively few in this community. As the nurses visit poor and well-to-do alike in this section there was little if any selection of economic class. The highest grade houses were perhaps a bit less likely to be visited but these proved also least likely to house Portuguese.

Such selection as was involved in the co-operation of the nurses was largely overcome by the visits with the kindergartener. These were made later than most of the visits with the nurses and a deliberate attempt was made to include streets and houses which had been neglected previously. Nevertheless, the number of families visited in a block was roughly related to the number of Portuguese living in that block. Except for the fact that families and not single men or women were visited, and the likelihood that the interest of the nurses in young children and mothers may have selected families of the younger generation, the writer believes that a representative group of Fall River Portuguese has been studied. The age selection involved may be judged by comparing the age distribution of Portuguese given in table 43 [1] with the following for the members of the 102 families we have visited. We see from this comparison that the group we have studied contains an abnormally large number of children under ten years of age, a small proportion of young people 15-19, an abnormally small proportion of men and women over 45 and a normal

---

[1] Page 199.

TABLE 55

FALL RIVER, MASS., AGE DISTRIBUTION OF MEMBERS OF THE
102 FAMILIES STUDIED

Age	Number	Per cent
Under 1	33	6.9%
Under 5	131	27.3
5–9	77	16.0
10–14	48	10.0
15–19	25	5.2
20–44	181	37.7
45 and over	18	3.8
Total	513	100.0%

percent in the other age groups including the important one of those aged 20-44.

In addition to this evident selection of the younger age groups, there is a possible selection of the St. Michael type of Portuguese. All information which the writer has gathered indicates that this type predominates in the whole city, but if there are colonies of Portuguese from the other islands elsewhere our study of these families is not representative of them. On the whole, it will be wisest to distinguish our study of families from our data for the whole city by calling the former a study of families of the younger generation of Portuguese who have, for the most part, emigrated from the island of St. Michael's. 80 out of 88 fathers whose birthplace was noted had been born in St. Michael's.

Occupations

We have already described in Chapter 4 the occupations in their homeland of Portuguese immigrants to the United States,[1] and those of Massachusetts Portuguese after they

[1] Pages 106-8.

have settled here.[1] The 193 heads of families studied in Portsmouth comprised: 2 proprietors (not farmers); 14 skilled laborers, including 9 on farms and 5 mechanics or carpenters; 92 farmers, 38 of whom owned their land, 47 of whom rented it, and 7 whose status was unknown; 78 unskilled laborers, including 27 farm laborers, 16 laborers at the coaling station, 8 railroad laborers, 4 working in a shipyard, 3 truckmen, 19 unclassified laborers, and one woman doing home sewing. We find, therefore, that the Portuguese of Portsmouth are engaged in similar occupations to those they left in the Azores, but that the proportion of those in independent farming has greatly increased if we may trust our data on occupations abroad.[2] It is, of course, possible that a larger proportion of those owning or renting land in the islands took up farming in this country, than of those who had been laborers at home.

Information as to the occupation of fathers in Fall River was nearly always obtained from the wife and her knowledge of or ability to describe the exact occupation was often unsatisfactory. The following table, which gives these occupations exactly as the women gave them, undoubtedly contains some duplications of occupational groups especially where the room or mill in which the husband worked is the only basis for classification.

While some of these classifications are unsatisfactory it is evident that about three-quarters of these men were employed in the cotton mills or the print works. Whether this occupational distribution indicates a rise in occupational status over that in the islands depends chiefly upon whether one rates the typical mill work performed by these Portuguese as more or less skilled than that of unskilled laborers in the Azores.

[1] Pages 126-136.
[2] Cf. tables 16 and 17, pp. 106-7.

TABLE 56

FALL RIVER, MASS., OCCUPATIONS OF FATHERS

Laborers	16
Doffers	11
Weavers	6
Print Works	6
Firemen	5
Bleach room	5
Clerks	4
Unknown	4
Dyers	3
Spinners	2
Second hands	2
Insurance agents	2
Barbers	2
Folders	2

Piler, third hand, stone mason, cobbler, card room, foundry, boxer, starcher, grocer, cloth room, real estate, garage, packing room, dental laboratory, sampler, cotton sheds, rag factory, shaft cleaner, sexton, hotel worker, N. Y. boat, baker, inspector, conductor, paint room, truckman, yard hand, lunch room proprietor, and dead, one each. One man was also at home unoccupied.

Economic Achievement

Wage data are always difficult to obtain through family interviews. No attempt was made to do so in Portsmouth, partly because so large a proportion of the men were independent farmers, and partly because the conditions under which the families were visited gave no excuse to question the wage-earners about their income. We shall give below estimates of economic achievement in Portsmouth as measured by living conditions and ownership of property.

In Fall River an attempt was made to secure data as to income directly from the women interviewed wherever possible. Wage information was thus obtained for 53 out of 101 fathers. The ignorance of some of the mothers, the importance of some of the cases where the information was not obtained, and especially the fact that the interviews covered three summers during a period when wages were changing rapidly make the results of little value except for very rough calculations. Four men only were reported as receiving $30 a week or over, 33 between $20 and $29, and the balance under $20. Most of the latter were probably recorded before the rise in wages of 1920. Doffers, weavers and spinners are the only groups for which we have presented wage statistics earlier in this chapter. Reference to table 47 [1] will show that men in these three occupations were paid between $20 and $30 in 1920, in Massachusetts mills. In our chapter on infant mortality we have presented some evidence that the Portuguese are the lowest-paid nationality in Fall River with the exception of the Poles.[2] We find an individual instance, however, among our 101 men of a wage of $55 a week paid a mason.

[1] Page 214.

[2] *Cf. supra*, p. 168.

The Immigration Commission studying 3,125 male Portuguese employees in mining and manufacturing found average weekly earnings of $8.10 which was the lowest figure among 61 nationalities except that for the Albanians ($8.07) and for the Turks ($7.65). The average for all foreign-born was $11.92.

The Portuguese family income, however, was relatively high, averaging $790. Twenty-one out of 34 nationalities showed a lower average, and that for the foreign-born as a whole ($704) was lower than that for the Portuguese.

This contrast between individual wages and family incomes is apparently accounted for in part by the fact that except for the Syrians and French, the Portuguese had the largest proportion of families (27.9%) with income from wives. Twelve other nationalities had a larger proportion of families receiving income from children, but the Portuguese had the largest proportion, except the Syrians, of children aged 6-16 at work. Thus the youth of the children rather than any disinclination, or lack of need to send them to work, seems to account for the somewhat better standing of the Portuguese with respect to child labor. Only 120 Portuguese families were included in this last study, so that one must use the data with caution. *United States Immigration Commission Report*, 61st Cong., 3rd Sess., Washington, 1911, vol. i, pp. 367, 412, 414 and 472.

It must be confessed that these data on wages are far from satisfactory. It is all the more important, therefore, that we use other means to measure economic success or failure. We may first inquire as to the reputation of the Portuguese as workmen.

Everyone agrees that the Portuguese are capable farmers and good farm laborers. Testimony to this effect comes not only from the inhabitants of Portsmouth, but from those who have observed them on the farms of Cape Cod and elsewhere. They are in the fields as long as it is light and employ the labor of every member of their families old enough to wield a hoe. Being in addition exceedingly frugal and understanding intensive farming they are successful on New England farms where the native farmer has either failed or found more lucrative employment in the city. Their economic success is often, however, at the expense of the health and happiness of wives and children, and it spells hard work with little recreation for the whole family.

When the Portuguese first came to the cotton mills of Fall River their labor was much prized. Some employers complain to-day that they lose their energy and docility when they become half-Americanized and that the second generation are a " bad lot " in the mills. At the time of our study the Portuguese had been especially active in the doffers' strike in 1919, and that fact may possibly account in part for the relatively low esteem in which they were held by some employers at that time. It is also complained in some quarters that the Portuguese are frequently guilty of the larceny of cloth from the mills. Our evidence for arrests given below [1] does not bear out this alleged criminality, but it is argued that arrests are only made occasionally,

---

[1] *Cf. infra*, p. 327 ff.

for such offenses as these have come to be incidents to be expected where the Portuguese are employed. Even these critics admit, however, that the Portuguese are a frugal folk who are making good industrially. The frugality and economic success of the Portuguese of Portsmouth is attested not only by general observation, but by their rapidly increasing purchases of land. The writer examined the original census schedules showing the ownership of homes in Portsmouth and found 171 homes recorded which he classified as occupied by families of Portuguese descent. Of these 118 were rented homes, 26 were owned but mortgaged, 24 were owned without encumbrance, and in three cases the nature of the tenure was unknown. Considering the short length of time that these people have been in Portsmouth [1] and the small capital with which most of them start this would appear to be a remarkably good showing. Table 57 taken from the Portsmouth Tax Book shows the assessed valuation of property of Portuguese

TABLE 57

ASSESSED VALUE OF PROPERTY, 1920, PORTSMOUTH, R. I.

Owner	Land Value	Buildings and Improvements	Tangible Personal	Intangible Personal	Tota
Corporation	$183,275.	$266,775.	$16,000.	none	$466,
Portuguese	132,850.	65,550.	36,850.	2,500.	237,
Non-Portuguese .	1,345,315.	1,158,300.	192,450.	736,100.	3,432,
Totals	$1,661,440.	$1,490,625.	$245,300.	$738,600.	$4,135,
Portuguese Paying	84	74	49	4	
Portuguese Av. Value	$1582.	$886.	$752.	$625.	$2,
Portuguese % Total value (Omitting corporations) ..	9.0%	5.4%	16.1%	.3%	6.

[1] *Cf. infra*, pp. 275-6.

and non-Portuguese for the year 1920. In that year there was a total of 1194 different individual taxpayers exclusive of business concerns and corporations. Of these 1194, however, no less than 488 were non-residents and were chiefly owners or renters of small shore lots which they occupy during the summer months. Of resident tax-payers 601 were of non-Portuguese descent and 100 of Portuguese descent and there was also a single non-resident Portuguese taxpayer. The Portuguese thus make up about a seventh of the total resident tax-payers. They own about a sixteenth of the total assessed value of the property of individuals and something over one-fourteenth of that of resident individuals. If we were to deduct the value of the property of the two Vanderbilt families, then the Portuguese would be seen to own nearly an eleventh (in value) of the remaining property of residents. The Portuguese of Portsmouth, as we have seen, make up about a third (32.5 per cent) of the total male population fifteen years of age and over.

Starting with these facts we may make several comparisons. In the first place, we note that over half of the Portuguese families of Portsmouth (100 out of 194) own property through the person of one of their members. 84 are taxed for land, 74 for buildings and improvements, 49 for tangible personal property and only 4 for intangible personal property. They thus own about one-seventh of their normal proportion of land according to value; about one-sixth of their proportion of buildings and improvements; almost exactly a half of their proportion of tangible personal property; but only one one hundred and eighth of their proportion of intangible personal property. More significant, perhaps, is the fact that the value of their total assessed property is just one-fifth of its normal value. That is to say, the Portuguese who make up 32.5 per cent of the total male population fifteen years of age and over, are assessed for 16.2 per cent of the total assessed value of property. This figure becomes two-ninths if we consider only resident tax-payers; and three-elevenths if we leave out of consideration the two Vanderbilt properties. In all probability there are other large estates which should be disregarded on the ground that they are really summer residences only. So that it probably somewhat understates the case for the Portuguese if we say that they should have something less than four times their present property holdings to make as good a showing as do the typical non-Portuguese residents. All, of course, both Portuguese and non-Portuguese, who have insufficient property to be taxed are omitted from this calculation.

We must guard against too dogmatic conclusions from these data. There is no doubt that the Portuguese are still far below the natives in respect to property ownership. There is little doubt, also, that some of the most able natives have left the township. Nevertheless, when we consider the recent immigration, illiteracy, low standard of living, and other handicaps of the Portuguese, their degree of success in accumulating property seems remarkable. We know that much of the land, both Portuguese and native, is mortgaged; but we do not know which is the more heavily mortgaged. We do know that the Portuguese holdings are rapidly increasing and that the normal progression among these people is from the status of farm laborer, to that of tenant, to that of owner with mortgage encumbrance, and often to that of owner without encumbrance. A change from the situation in 1885 where there was but one Portuguese landowner, to that of 1920 with 84 is startling. If this tendency continues Portsmouth will soon not only be a community of Portuguese people but will be Portuguese-owned.

Ownership of landed property is a better index of economic progress in a rural community than in the city where many families occupy a single tenement block, and where savings are put into other forms of investment than land. No study of the tax books of Fall River has been made, but we have examined the property plot books for the fifteen city blocks where our 102 families live. It is a cause for some surprise that more than half of this land is found to be owned to-day by Portuguese. We do not know how many of these landowners accumulated their capital out of savings from mill wages. Possibly none at all. But such a showing indicates that some Portuguese, at least, "are making good " in this respect. The records also show that the transfers of land in this district from non-Portuguese to Portuguese ownership have increased rapidly during and since the recent period of relative prosperity among Fall River mill hands. A prominent Portuguese citizen of Fall River informed the writer that 80 per cent of the purchases of land in Fall River during the five-year period (1917-1921) had been made by Portuguese, and that the Portuguese are proprietors of 128 business establishments in the city. He also stated that 60 per cent of the deposits in savings banks had been made by them. An attempt was made to check up this last statement by reference to bank treasurers. Unfortunately the bank in which the Portuguese have the largest amounts deposited declined even to estimate the proportion of their deposits made by these people. The estimates of the other banks fell far below the figure given above but were based upon total deposits and not upon money deposited in recent years. All agreed also that the Portuguese have increased their savings greatly since the war.

Another method of estimating the economic success of the Portuguese is to examine the lists of business and professional men given in a city directory. For this admittedly crude test data from New Bedford [1] was used instead of

---

[1] It must be admitted that this procedure is open to the serious objection

from Fall River, partly because the information was more readily obtained from the former source and partly because the Portuguese have had more time in which to attain such success in New Bedford. As we were compelled to use the directory of 1918 our data does not reflect the effects of the period of post-war-time prosperity. Table 58 shows the results of this effort. This table probably somewhat understates the proportion of Portuguese in these professions and businesses, and for two reasons. In the first place, in the case of partnerships and corporations as well as of concerns where the owner's name does not appear it is impossible to tell when there are Portuguese associated in the business. Such firms appear in the totals and so the proportion of Portuguese names is understated. The number of such cases is not so great, however, as seriously to affect the general impression given by the table though it may be of some importance in connection with a few particular occupations. Secondly, some Portuguese may have anglicized their names, and while we have seen that this process usually does not affect the first name, it is perhaps slightly more liable to do so in the case of business men than among the general population.

TABLE 58

PORTUGUESE IN BUSINESS AND PROFESSIONS, 1918,
NEW BEDFORD, MASS.

Occupations	Portuguese Names	Total Names
Architects	0	11
Artists	0	5
Accountants	0	6

that we do not know whether the proportion of St. Michael Portuguese is as great in New Bedford, as in Fall River. It probably is not. But as all our data tend to show that the St. Michael Portuguese are among the least advanced type, and as the New Bedford data show but a mediocre achievement, the table possesses some value despite this weakness.

Auto accessions	1	9
Auto repairs	2	37
Auto stations	1	10
Autos	1	15
Bakers	17	62
Bicycles and repairs	3	15
Billiards and pool	5	20
Blacksmiths	2	30
Boatbuilders	1	4
Carpenters and builders	3	48
Clergymen	3	62
Clothing	1	47
Comber supplies	1	3
Constables	1	3
Contractors and builders	4	33
Coopers	1	1
Cream	1	2
Dairy	1	2
Dentists	3	57
Dressmakers	5	122
Druggists	6	82
Dry goods	1	64
Electricians, etc.	1	16
Engraving	1	2
Expresses	1	11
Fish and oysters	26	41
Florists	1	21
Fruit	1	52
Furniture	3	52
Garages	3	43
Gas-fitters	1	3
Retail grocers	98	366
Hairdressers	54	183
Hardware	2	28
Justices of peace	1	28
Lawyers	6	72
Machinists	1	12
Manufacturing companies	1	47
Market gardeners	1	2
Masons	1	13
Men's furnishings	1	17
Milk	2	18
Millinery	2	45
Musical instrument makers	1	1

Notaries public	1	22
Nurses	3	96
Painters	3	54
Phonographs	1	7
Photographers	3	21
Physicians	6	128
Pictures and frames	1	11
Printers	2	21
Publishers	1	5
Real estate agents	7	59
Restaurants	8	75
Sausage manufacturers	3	6
Second-hand goods	1	8
Shoe dealers	3	40
Shoemakers and repairs	17	94
Stables	2	15
Steamship agents	3	6
Tailors	2	65
Teachers	0	?
Teamsters	1	20
Undertakers	2	20
Variety stores	17	203
Wines and liquors	10	110
Wood and coal	3	26

When all allowances are made, however, the table seems to show that the Portuguese have by no means entered the business or professional world in a ratio proportionate to their share in the total population. The Portuguese make up not far from a quarter of the total population of New Bedford. In only fifteen of the seventy-one categories of the table have they this or a larger proportion of names. With the exception of hairdressers and retail grocers these fifteen do not include the numerically important occupations, nor do they as a rule include those occupations requiring most training. Among the professions we note that there are but three Portuguese dentists out of fifty-seven; but six lawyers out of seventy-two; but three nurses out of ninety-six; and but six physicians out of one hundred twenty-eight. Similar differences are found for most of the skilled trades.

It seems remarkable that not a single Portuguese name is distinguishable among those of teachers in New Bedford. In partial explanation of this poor showing we may note that while it is true that a number of Portuguese have lived in New Bedford for many years, and not a few have been born and reared there; nevertheless the great bulk of them are comparatively recent immigrants who could hardly be expected to have acquired the capital for business nor the education for the professions. Moreover, all the handicaps discussed elsewhere are stumbling blocks along the path from the laborer's or peasant's hut where no one reads or writes, to the status of a learned profession, skilled trade or business.

The Standard of Living of the Portuguese

An investigation of living conditions is still another method of estimating the economic achievement of a people.

In order to study living conditions among the Portuguese a house-to-house visitation was made of practically every Portuguese family in Portsmouth and of the 102 families in Fall River the selection of which has already been described. Necessarily the women were more often interviewed than the men, because the men were usually at work in the fields or in the mill.

The writer was fortunate in securing as interpreter a woman of Portuguese descent with the training of a district nurse. She had had practice in taking family histories and readily adapted herself to the purposes of the investigation. Much credit is due her for her untiring energy and for her intelligent interest which did much to make possible such success as was obtained.

The entire township of Portsmouth was covered once in the summer of 1919. Experience showed, however, the desirability of adding one or two questions to our schedules, and a second visitation was made to all but one small section of the township the following summer. In this way an almost complete census of the Portuguese in the community was secured. Indeed, the total population of Portuguese descent which we enumerated was 1171 including 41 boarders, or 94 more than the Federal Census records. The date of enumeration was not exactly the same, however.

The following information was obtained on our schedules wherever possible although it was not all used in the tabulation: names, ages, occupations and dates of immigration of all members of the family; the number of persons in the household with boarders distinguished; the number of rooms; how long the father and mother had been married; whether the home or farm was owned or rented; and a rating of the standard of living as explained below. On the second visitation the birth place was determined more definitely so as to give the name of the island in the Azores or elsewhere from which the father or mother came.

In probably 95 per cent of the cases the writer personally entered the home and when he did he always personally made the rating for standard of living. The few cases where the nurse went alone were mostly houses where the writer was personally acquainted with the occupants and already knew the conditions.

Where the Portuguese seemed sufficiently intelligent and spoke English, the purpose of the investigation was explained to them. This was impossible in very many cases, however, as it would have been impossible to make the real meaning of the study intelligible to the people. In such cases one of two methods were adopted: either the nurse entered the home as a friendly visiting nurse and took the family record in the course of her " official " duties; or else the family were informed that " a census " was being taken.

The method of rating the standard of living of these

people was admittedly imperfect, though possibly the best which could have been employed under the conditions of the investigation. The writer had visited a number of Portuguese homes before this actual study was begun. He had thus a general notion of living conditions among them. These had included a few of the best and a few of the worst types of homes which were found. Taking the best home as an upper standard and the worst as a lower, nine classes were distinguished beginning with class " a " as the best and ending with class " a minus 8 " as the worst.

The judgments which were made were based upon at least three different elements: neatness; quality and variety of furniture and other household equipment; and evidence of artistic or intellectual taste such as pianos, books et cetera. The appearance of the exterior of the house was also considered but probably more weight was given to interior than to exterior conditions. So far as exteriors entered into the rating the appearance of the house rather than that of the barns or outhouses was considered. This was for two reasons. In the first place our ostensible errand was often to see the baby, and this errand did not make a request to see the barns natural. Secondly, since the interview was usually with the mother it seemed advisable to confine the judgment somewhat to those parts of the household over which she had more immediate oversight. It is admitted, however, that a well-mowed lawn—a rare occurrence—and a flower garden weighed somewhat in the higher ratings. Also it is difficult to prevent the presence of such obstacles as garbage and tin cans in the yard from influencing one's impression, even though the wife may not have been responsible for them.

The following hypothetical pictures of five of the classes of homes may give some idea of the standards used:

Grade " a ".   House may be small or large but usually recently painted; lawn mowed as a rule; porches and entrance
free from litter; kitchen or living room furnished with modern
conveniences such as would be available in the country; alu-
minum tea-kettle or other shining kitchen ware, a stove well-
polished; cans of preserves; floors spotless or nearly so; neat
wall paper; books and reasonably artistic pictures; musical
instruments visible if parlor is seen; perhaps a camera on the
table and good family photographs; occupants neatly dressed,
the mother perhaps apologizing for being caught in a somewhat soiled apron; children under control and attractively
dressed; interest in the study which was being made; not necessarily evidences of wealth but of reasonable comfort.   In
brief the writer's idea of the standard of living of a reasonably well-to-do, intelligent American farmer's home with a
neat woman presiding over it but without frills.

Grade " a minus 2 ".   Either a home with grade " a " standards of neatness and intellectual interest, but with considerably lower degree of variety and quality of equipment and
with evidences of low income; or a home with evidence of
considerable spending but with some slovenliness such as
children's underclothing lying on a chair, crumbs not swept
up or soiled upholstering on furniture.   The walls, however,
will be papered or else painted and scrupulously neat.   The
lawn may or may not be mowed—more often not.   The house
perhaps in need of paint but nowhere falling to pieces.   The
atmosphere perhaps comparable to that of a third-class hotel
with which one puts up but which one cannot be said to enjoy.

Grade " a minus 4 ".   This grade is the modal grade.   It
therefore is the one of which the writer thinks most frequently as the home of the typical Portuguese farmer and his
numerous family.   It is usually the former residence of some
Anglo-Saxon who has died or given up the struggle with the
soil.   The house is not the better for its new owners.   The
yard is somewhat littered and full of hens and ducks.   The
paint is wearing off the exterior of the house and one of the
front blinds is broken.   The walls inside are painted dark blue

or green, but have a number of rather cheap pictures upon them in somewhat gaudy frames. The pictures represent religious subjects. The rooms are furnished reasonably well, but everything is dingy and in poor taste. One suspects that the corners of the room and especially a crack or two in the plaster may house creeping things. Large tubs stand in the yard with a rather corpulent woman bending over one of them. Her children are numerous and barefooted. She, however, has both shoes and stockings on, is genial and well-mannered. In the kitchen, conveniences are few and the mother wipes crumbs off a wooden chair for her guests to sit upon. Everything has the appearance of being made for use and of being everlastingly used. If one gets a peep into a bedroom or livingroom, however, there is some attempt at decoration, albeit cheap and gaudy. The beds are often tumbled and do not look inviting to the scrupulous. No books are seen. There are lace curtains at the windows though sometimes they are a bit soiled. The walls are fairly sound and some of the rooms are papered, but the paper has several tears in it.

Grade " a minus 6 ". This grade may best be described as intermediate between grade " a minus 4 " and " a minus 8 ". Either no papered walls are seen or the paper is very much torn and soiled. The plastering is broken in a number of places, and you are very certain that the bugs are playing there. Furniture is of the simplest, but there is always a sewing machine. There is an unpleasant odor quite evident, of which you had a slight suspicion in some of the grade " a minus 4 " houses—an odor of Portuguese soup and people and probably other things. What a wreck they have made of the house—but then they do work everlastingly hard—and what a swarm of children the mother does not care for. Some garbage has been left where it fell on the kitchen floor, and garments lie about in disorderly heaps. The older of the two women is without shoes or stockings and her hair is unkempt. You do not stay long after the statistics are taken, and brush past the chickens which are roosting on the doorstep.

Grade " a minus 8 ". A once respectable house has been

ruined by the occupancy of more people that it was intended to hold; or a larger building appears scarcely less disreputable although many rooms are unoccupied. The house is almost literally without furniture except one or two chairs and a littered sewing machine. The plaster has not even been painted for years. One room has a few shreds of its former paper hanging in tatters on its walls. The floor is covered with garbage and old clothes, and the former has attracted the chickens indoors. The odor is almost unbearable. Occupants are dirty and half-clad, and give every evidence of ignorance. Women are bare-footed, but they will try to hide their feet behind the table as they talk to you.

Classes intermediate between the above five were sometimes distinguished. The factors which determined the rating of particular homes varied greatly and independently of one another. For example, the house of the largest Portuguese tax-payer in the town was rated " a " because the evidence of means outweighed a certain degree of disorder in the kitchen, which, as it happened, was the only room seen in that home. Similarly one grade " a minus 4 " house might be neat but with unusually meager equipment, while another might be fairly well stocked with furniture et cetera, but unusually untidy.

The standards used are open to the objection that they are subjective—based upon the judgment of the visitor made during a rather brief interview. The writer believes, however, that they are more satisfactory than more objective measures alone would have been; for it is often little intangible differences or seemingly petty details which make up the real difference between a low and a high standard of living. At any rate, the nature of the inquiry precluded the use of the same objective measures of living conditions in all homes, for the occasion was often merely a friendly call which made it impossible to request permission to examine bedrooms or toilets or other possible criteria.

Undoubtedly, the greatest difficulty in this attempt to rate homes, however, was the fact that the homes were visited on different days and at different hours of the day. No woman's kitchen looks the same just after the soiled dinner dishes have been piled in it as it should look at four o'clock in the afternoon; and Monday is usually a less satisfactory day for a call than some other days in the week. Because of these difficulties injustice has no doubt been done in some of the ratings. We can only say that such injustices were inevitable and that they probably affected all grades of homes about equally. The fact that when a second visit was made to a large number of the homes in the following summer scarcely any occasion was found to change the first ratings seems to show that they were approximately correct. No assumption is made, however, that they represent more than approximate estimates of standards of living.

The same methods were used in the house to house study in Fall River as in Portsmouth. No grade of home in Fall River is, of course, exactly like the corresponding grade in Portsmouth because city tenements are not like rural farmhouses. Comparisons between the two are therefore less justified than comparisons between different classes in the same community.

The percentages of homes in each of the nine classes is shown in the following table:

	a	$a-1$	$a-2$	$a-3$	$a-4$	$a-5$	$a-6$	$a-7$	$a-8$	Total
Portsmouth	7.1%	7.1	16.5	15.9	22.0	15.4	11.0	1.6	3.3	99.9
Fall River	2.9	18.6	21.6	21.6	28.4	2.0	4.9	0.0	0.0	100.0

This table shows that while the average rating for Fall River homes was higher than that for Portsmouth, the proportion both of very good and very bad homes was greater in the rural community. As our rural study included all types of homes while our urban was somewhat selected as a community which would contain typical Portuguese mill hands, this is the result which would be expected. It is also probably true that the city would not permit many families to live in the filth in which our grade " a minus 8 " families in Portsmouth are found. The writer did visit one family in Bristol, Rhode Island, however, for whom he would have had to create an " a minus 9 " grade.

It is possible also to compare Portuguese homes in Portsmouth with those in Fall River with respect to the number of persons found in them per room. Unlike the above ratings, however, this comparison is influenced very much by the homes available—a factor largely out of the control of the Portuguese. In Portsmouth the average number of persons per room in 193 Portuguese homes was found to be 1.11 and the median 1.00. In Fall River the corresponding figures for 100 families are 1.42 and 1.40 respectively. This figure is very close to that found by the Immigration Commission (1.38). They also found a higher degree of overcrowding among 14 out of 39 nationalities investigated than they found among the Portuguese.[1] The following table shows the percentages of total Portuguese families in each community having given numbers of persons per room.

TABLE 59

PER CENT OF PORTUGUESE HOMES HAVING GIVEN NUMBER OF
PERSONS PER ROOM

	Number Families	Under 1	1–1.50	1.51–2.00	Over 2	Totals
	Number		Per cent			
Portsmouth	188	38.	47.	11.	5.	101.
Fall River	100	12.	53.	27.	8.	100.

While no shocking overcrowding was found in either community it is evident from the above table that more space was available in the rural community. This is just what would be expected.

[1] *United States Immigration Commission Report,* 61st Cong., 3rd Sess., Washington, 1911, vol. i, p. 431.

No data on rents were secured in Portsmouth because rent there would include the rent of the farm land. In Fall River 100 families were found to be paying an average of $3.22 per week rent and the median rental was $3.20. As about three-quarters of these data were secured in 1920 this situation reflects in part the effect of the rising rents in that year. Similar data for 1921 would, however, have probably shown somewhat higher rents.

We may now correlate standard of living as we have measured it, with other factors in the lives of the Portuguese. The correlation between occupation and standard of living for 172 families in Portsmouth is shown in the following table.

TABLE 60.

PORTSMOUTH, RHODE ISLAND, OCCUPATION AND HOME RATINGS OF PORTUGUESE FATHERS

	a	a-1	a-2	a-3	a-4	a-5	a-6	a-7	a-8	Totals
Proprietors	1	0	0	1	0	0	0	0	0	2
Skilled laborers	2	3	3	2	1	0	0	1	0	12
Gardeners, head farmers, dairymen	2	1	3	0	1	0	0	1	0	8
Mechanics, carpenters	0	2	0	2	0	0	0	0	0	4
Farmers	10	7	15	8	20	14	7	2	3	86
Renters	1	2	5	5	10	10	7	1	3	44
Owners	8	5	8	3	9	2	0	0	0	35
Status unknown	1	0	2	0	1	2	0	1	0	7
Unskilled laborers	0	2	9	12	16	13	10	0	3	65
Truckmen	0	0	0	2	0	0	0	0	0	2
Coaling station	0	1	2	2	4	3	1	0	0	13
Ship yard	0	0	0	0	1	3	0	0	0	4
Railroad	0	0	1	0	1	3	3	0	0	8
Farm laborers	0	0	1	4	5	2	4	0	3	19
Unclassified Miscellaneous	0	1	1	1	2	1	1	0	0	7
Totals	13	13	28	24	39	28	18	3	6	172[1]

In addition to these 172 fathers there were 22 families where the occupation of the fathers was not reported. These included 2 skilled laborers, 10 farmers and 10 unskilled laborers.

We find in this table that all proprietors, ten out of twelve skilled laborers, forty out of fifty-six farmers, three out of seven in miscellaneous occupations and twenty-three out of sixty-five unskilled laborers lived in homes of the four superior classes. They therefore rank in the order named. In the occupational subdivisions the contrast between owners and renters of farms is noticeable and as would be expected; twenty-four out of thirty-five owners living in homes of the four superior classes, as compared with only thirteen out of forty-four renters. Skilled laborers with ten out of twelve in the superior groups outrank even the owners of farms.

In our Fall River material the number of men in each occupational group was too few to warrant the construction of a table similar to the above. In Portsmouth it cannot be denied that there is a high degree of relationship between occupation and living conditions.

One of the most interesting questions, but one which our data will not permit us to answer satisfactorily, is the question of possible relationship between island of birth and economic achievement. In Fall River practically all of our Portuguese (80 out of 88 cases where the information was obtained) whose homes were studied were from St. Michael's, so that we cannot compare them with those from other islands. In Portsmouth no less than 110 out of 164 foreign-born Portuguese fathers, and 91 out of 102 foreign-born mothers whose exact home abroad was known were from St. Michael's. Tables 61 and 62 show for fathers and mothers respectively the relationship between home rating and source of immigration. The figures for many of the islands are too small to be of any significance. It is interesting to note, however, that 34 out of 110 or only 31 per cent of fathers from St. Michael's, as compared with 30 out of 59 or 51 per cent of fathers from other islands are found in the four superior types of homes. Similar figures for mothers computed from table 62 show 32 per cent of St. Michaelese mothers as against 51 per cent of mothers from the other islands in the better homes.

TABLE 61

BIRTHPLACE OF FATHERS AND HOME RATINGS, PORTSMOUTH, R. I.

Home Ratings	S.Mi.	S.Ma.	S.G.	F.	Ter.	P.	Gr.	Lis.	Mad.	Br.	Amer.	Un.	Totals.
....	4	2	3	1							1	2	13
-1	4		2	2						1	1	3	13
-2	11	1	3	3	3	1	1				2	5	30
-3	15		3	3					1		1	6	29
-4	22	1	6	1	1				1	1	1	6	40
-5	26		1									1	28
-6	14	1	2	1								2	20
-7	2		1										3
-8	3		1									2	6
Unknown	9		1									2	12
Totals	110	5	23	11	4	1	1	1	2	1	6	29	194

Key to Tables 61 and 62
S. Mi.—St. Michael's
S. Ma.—St. Mary's
S. G.—St. George
F. —Fayal
Ter.—Terceira
P.—Pico
Gr.—Graciosa
Lis.—Lisbon
Mad.—Madeira
Br.—Brazil
Amer.—America
Ire.—Ireland
Un.—Unknown

TABLE 62

BIRTHPLACE OF MOTHERS AND HOME RATINGS, PORTSMOUTH, R. I.

Home Ratings	S.Mi.	S.Ma.	S.G.	F.	Ter.	P.	Gr.	Lis.	Mad.	Br.	Ire.	Amer.	Un.	Tot.
a	3		5	1								2	2	13
a-1	4		3	2								1	3	13
a-2	11	1	1	4	3						1	6	3	30
a-3	13		3	3			1		1			2	6	29
a-4	21	1	4	6	2								6	40
a-5	22		3						1			1	1	28
a-6	12	1	2	1	2								2	20
a-7	2		1											3
a-8	3		1										2	6
Unknown	7		1	1	1							1	1	12
Totals	98	3	24	18	8		1		2		1	13	26	194

In view of the contrasts between the islanders which we have discovered in other chapters, this difference is of considerable interest. Its importance is somewhat brought into question, however, by the fact that while the St. Michael's Portuguese fathers had averaged to be in this country 15.9 years, those from other sources had averaged 23.2 years. Perhaps the difference in living conditions between these groups is accounted for by the shorter residence in this country of those from St. Michael's. Nevertheless, it would be very interesting if we could compare the ratings of Fayalese with their brothers from St. Michael's. We had in Portsmouth but 11 fathers and 18 mothers from Fayal. Only one of these fathers had a home rated below " a minus 4 " while no less than 45 of the 110 from St. Michael's were so rated. Similarly only one of the 18 Fayalese mothers had homes of the lower ratings while 39 mothers out of 98 from St. Michael's did. We have information as to both the length of residence and island home of 9 of our 11 Fayalese fathers and find that they have averaged to be here 18.4 years against 15.9 for the St. Michaelese. This difference of but 2½ years is not very great and leaves one with just a suspicion that the difference in the ratings of families from these two islands may be due to a difference in type as well as to this slight difference in length of residence. We must admit that this evidence is but slender. It acquires weight, if at all, only when considered in connection with our other evidence of contrast in type between the different islands. Tables 63, 64, 65 and 66 show the relationship between the length of residence in the United States and the home rating of families in Portsmouth and Fall River. Table 63 shows that only 7 fathers and 11 mothers of Portuguese

TABLE 63

IMMIGRATION OF FATHERS AND HOME RATINGS, PORTSMOUTH, R. I.

Ratings	a	a-1	a-2	a-3	a-4	a-5	a-6	a-7	a-8	Totals	Unknown
Born in U.S.	1	1	2	2	1					7	
50-55 years	1									1	
45-50 "		1								1	
40-45 "		1	1							2	
35-40 "		3	2	1		1				7	
30-35 "		1		1	3					5	
25-30 "		4		5	2	2	4			17	
20-25 "		1		1	2	2	2		1	9	
15-20 "	1	3	7	9	15	6	13	1	4	59	3
10-15 "	1	2	3	6	8	4	2	1	1	28	5
5-10 "			4	5	7	4	1			21	2
1-5 [1] "		1		1	1	2				5	
Father dead		3	2	2	2		1			10	
Unknown			3	2	2	3				10 [2]	1
Totals	13	13	30	29	40	28	20	3	6	182	11
Average Years in U. S.	29.5	27.4	20.6	15.0	17.4	15.2	15.4	13.0	18.0	18.8	

[1] A single father who has been in this country somewhat less than a single year is included in this group.

[2] One woman with illegitimate son omitted.

TABLE 64
IMMIGRATION OF MOTHERS AND HOME RATINGS, PORTSMOUTH, R. I.

Ratings	a	a-1	a-2	a-3	a-4	a-5	a-6	a-7	a-8	Totals	Unkn
Born in U.S. .	2	1	5	2		1				11	1
46–50 years ..		1								1	
41–45 " ..			1							1	
36–40 " ..		1								1	
31–35 " ..	2									2	
26–30 " ..	2	1	2			2				7	
21–25 " ..	1		2	3	5					11	
16–20 " ..	3	7	5	6	15	5	8		3	52	5
11–15 " ..			2	5	5	5	2	1	2	22	6
6–10 " ..			6	2	9	7	4	1	1	30	5
1–5 [1] " ..	1			1	1	5	2			10	1
Mother dead ..		1		2				1		4	
Unknown	2	1	5	3	4	3	2			20	3
Totals	13	13	28	24	39	28	18	3	6	172 [2]	21
Average Years in U. S.	22.4	22.5	17.0	15.8	14.2	11.6	13.5	13.0	14.7	15.5	

TABLE 65
IMMIGRATION OF FATHERS AND HOME RATINGS, FALL RIVER, MASS.

Ratings	a	a-1	a-2	a-3	a-4	a-5	a-6	a-7	a-8	Totals	Unkno
Born in U.S. .		1								1	
31–36 years ..		1								1	
26–30 " ..	2			1	2					5	
21–25 " ..	1		5	1	2	2	1			12	
16–20 " ..			9	8	6	7	1	2		33	
11–15 " ..			2	4	8	7				21	
6–10 " ..			1	8	5	4		2		20	
1–5 " ..			1		2		1			4	
Father dead ..					2					2	
Unknown					3					3	
Totals	3	19	22	22	29	2	5			102	
Average Years in U. S.	26.3	19.1	13.0	14.8	14.9	14.6	11.0			15.5	

[1] A single mother who has been in this country somewhat less than a year is included in this group.

[2] One woman with illegitimate son omitted.

TABLE 66

IMMIGRATION OF MOTHERS AND HOME RATINGS, FALL RIVER, MASS.

Ratings	a	a-1	a-2	a-3	a-4	a-5	a-6	a-7	a-8	Totals	Unknown
Born in U.S. .		4[1]		3	2[1]	1[2]				10	
-30 years ..	2	1		1						4	
-25 " ..	1	3	4	2	3					13	
-20 " ..		5	6	1	6	1	2			21	
-25 " ..		2	3	12	9		1			27	
-10 " ..		4	6	3	3		2			18	
-5 " ..			3		3					6	
Unknown					3					3	
Totals	3	19	22	22	29	2	5			102	

descent in Portsmouth were born in America. For 155 foreign-born fathers whose length of residence in the United States is known the average period of residence was 18.8 years; while for 137 foreign-born mothers the corresponding period was 13.6 years. In Fall River the fathers had been here 15.5 years on the average and the mothers 14.6 years; while one father and ten mothers were born in America. On the whole these periods do not seem any too long for a people two-thirds illiterate to demonstrate their capacity for adaptation to a changed physical and social environment.

All four of these tables show some degree of relationship between home conditions and length of residence. Dividing our tables at the line between the " a minus 3 " and " a minus 4 " groups, we find that in Fall River 59 foreign-born mothers who lived in the better homes had been in this country 15.1 years on the average, while 30 whose home ratings were lower had been here 13.7 years. For fathers the corresponding figures are 15.9 and 14.6. In Portsmouth

[1] One of French Canadian parentage.
[2] Italian parentage.

the mothers in the higher grade homes had been here on the average 5.1 years longer than other mothers; while fathers in the better homes had been here 4.1 years longer. The correlation, measured in this way, is seen to be greater in the rural community than in Fall River, and greater for men than for women.

We have also figured the coefficients of mean square contingency [1] for each of these four tables.

---

[1] The coefficient of mean square contingency used in this study is a method devised by Karl Pearson for measuring the relationship between series of attributes. It is based upon assumptions and mathematical processes that make unity an expression of the utmost deviation from a pure chance relationship, where the number of attribute classes is infinitely great. For any finite number of classes the maximum value of the coefficient is less than unity but approaches unity as the number of classes is increased. Thus if "home conditions" were classified in only two grades and "length of residence" in only two classes, the highest possible value of the coefficient would be 707. If we should increase the number of classes for each attribute to 4, the maximum value of the coefficient would be .866, and so on with a greater and greater number of classes. On the other hand, if the numbers of cases found in all the classes, regardless of the number of classes into which the two attributes are divided, were exactly the numbers that could be expected there by pure chance, the value of the coefficient would be zero.

The dependence of the maximum value of the coefficient upon the number of attribute classes in the contingency tables necessitates the greatest caution in comparing coefficients derived from tables which have not the same number of classes. Thus, if the coefficient of mean square contingency derived from a table of four classes for each attribute were found to be .866 and the coefficient derived from a table of 8 classes for each attribute were also found to be .866, we should not be justified in saying that the degree of relationship was the same. In the former case the relationship would be perfect (the maximum value of the coefficient for four attribute classes being .866), while in the latter case the maximum value of the coefficient is .935.

Moreover, it should be noted that an insufficient number of cases brought under observation might cause deviations from the pure chance distribution by classes that would not in any sense indicate

Table 63 shows the relationship between the home ratings of families in Portsmouth and the length of residence in the United States of the fathers of these families. The coefficient of mean square contingency for this table is .55. The highest possible value of the coefficient for a table composed of this number of attribute classes is .949. The coefficient therefore shows a fairly high degree of relationship between the attributes, and indicates that, if other things are equal, the longer the time the Portsmouth fathers have been in the United States the higher, by the definition used in this study, will be the standards of living of their families.

The same reasoning and interpretation is applicable to Table 64 which shows the relationship between the home ratings of families in Portsmouth and the length of residence in the United States of the mothers of these families. Here the coefficient of mean square contingency is .461 and, with the same qualifications made for the coefficient described above, we may say that the longer the time the Portsmouth mothers have been in the United States the higher will be the standards of living of their families. It will be noted however that the degree of relationship between the attributes is slightly less for the mothers than for the fathers.

relationship, but merely the fact that the samples classified were not representative.

The coefficient of mean square contingency resembles the Pearsonian coefficient of correlation, but differs from it in that the contingency coefficient cannot be expressed with the algebraic plus or minus signs.

For the mathematical derivation of the coefficient of mean square contingency and a more detailed discussion of its significance and limitations, see Rugg, *Statistical Methods Applied to Education* (Boston, New York, Chicago, 1917), pp. 299-307; and Yule, *An Introduction to the Theory of Statistics* (6th Edition, London, 1922), pp. 63-72, and pp. 375-377.

Tables 65 and 66 show identical relationships for the Portuguese mothers and fathers of Fall River. The coefficient of mean square contingency for Table 65 is .405. The coefficient of mean square contingency for Table 66 is .421. In order to make clearer to the general reader the relationship shown in Tables 63, 64, 65 and 66, the attribute " home rating " or " standard of living " is divided into the three categories " good ", " fair " and " poor ", and the attribute, " length of residence ", into three categories, " 21 years and over ", " 11 years to 20 years ", and " less than 11 years ", in the supplementary Tables 63 A, 64 A, 65 A and 66 A. In these supplementary tables the absolute numbers are reduced to percentages. Comparison of the percentage columns of the tables shows that for Providence, Rhode Island, and for Fall River the longer the fathers and mothers have been in the United States, the higher the standard of living ratings of their families. Great caution must be exercised, however, in drawing conclusions from tables in which the percentages are based upon such small totals.

TABLE 63A

RELATION OF STANDARD OF LIVING (HOME RATING) TO LENGTH OF TIME
IN UNITED STATES OF FATHERS, PORTSMOUTH, R. I.

(FIGURES TAKEN FROM TABLE 63)

Length of Time Fathers Have Been in United States	Standard of Living									
	Good		Fair		Poor		Totals		Unknown	
	a a-1 a-2		a-3 a-4 a-5		a-6 a-7 a-8					
	No.	%	No.	%	No.	%	No.	%	No.	%
21 years and over	26	46.4	22	22.6	1	3.4	49	26.9	0	0.0
11 years to 20 years	17	30.4	48	49.4	22	75.9	87	47.9	8	72.7
Less than 11 years	5	8.9	16	16.4	5	17.3	26	14.3	2	18.2
Unclassifiable	8	14.3	11	11.2	1	3.4	20	10.9	1	9.1
Totals	56	100.0	97	100.0	29	100.0	182	100.0	11	100.0

TABLE 64A

RELATION OF STANDARD OF LIVING (HOME RATING) TO LENGTH OF TIME
IN UNITED STATES OF MOTHERS, PORTSMOUTH, R. I.

(FIGURES TAKEN FROM TABLE 64)

Length of Time Mothers Have Been in United States	Standard of Living									
	Good		Fair		Poor		Totals		Unknown	
	a a-1 a-2		a-3 a-4 a-5		a-6 a-7 a-8					
	No.	%	No.	%	No.	%	No.	%	No.	%
21 years and over	21	38.9	13	14.2	0	0.0	34	19.7	1	4.7
11 years to 20 years	17	31.5	41	45.1	16	59.2	74	43.1	11	52.4
Less than 11 years	7	12.9	25	27.5	8	29.6	40	23.3	6	28.6
Unclassifiable	9	16.7	12	13.2	3	11.2	24	13.9	3	14.3
Totals	54	100.0	91	100.0	27	100.0	172	100.0	21	100.0

TABLE 65A

RELATION OF STANDARD OF LIVING (HOME RATING) TO LENGTH OF TIME
IN UNITED STATES OF FATHERS, FALL RIVER, MASS.

(FIGURES TAKEN FROM TABLE 65)

Length of Time Fathers Have Been in United States	Standard of Living							
	Good		Fair		Poor		Totals	
	a a-1 a-2		a-3 a-4 a-5		a-6 a-7 a-8			
	No.	%	No.	%	No.	%	No.	%
21 years and over	11	25.0	8	15.0	0	0.0	19	18.7
11 years to 20 years	23	52.3	29	54.7	2	40.0	54	52.9
Less than 11 years	10	22.7	11	20.8	3	60.0	24	23.5
Unclassifiable	0	0.0	5	9.4	0	0.0	5	4.9
Totals	44	100.0	53	100.0	5	100.0	102	100.0

TABLE 66A

RELATION OF STANDARD OF LIVING (HOME RATING) TO LENGTH OF TIME
IN UNITED STATES OF MOTHERS, FALL RIVER, MASS.

(FIGURES TAKEN FROM TABLE 66)

Length of Time Mothers Have Been in United States	*Standard of Living*								
	Good		*Fair*			*Poor*			*Total*
	a	a-1	a-2	a-3	a-4	a-5	a-6	a-7	a-8
	No.	%	No.	%.	No.	%	No.		
21 years and over	15	34.1	12	22.6	0	0.0	27	2	
11 years to 20 years	16	36.4	29	54.8	3	60.0	48	4	
Less than 11 years	13	29.5	9	16.9	2	40.0	24	2	
Unclassifiable	0	0.0	3	5.7	0	0.0	3		
Totals	44	100.0	53	100.0	5	100.0	102	10	

It is encouraging to find this degree of progress made by these people in this country, for it leads us to hope that a longer residence may see their standards of living rising as those of other immigrant groups have risen. One who views the worst or even the typical Portuguese immigrant home in the country, may well fear for some of the standards of life which seem so essential to middle or upper class Americans. The pessimist sees only the onrush of a horde of low-standard peoples. The optimist may take heart, perhaps, when he finds that ten or twenty years on a Rhode Island farm or in a cotton-mill tenement may raise that low standard, not indeed to that which our idealism demands, but to something a little more respectable. A more rapid advance can hardly be expected until illiteracy and ignorance have been banished from among these immigrant populations.

The optimist may take heart also, if he confines his visits to a score or so Portuguese homes in Portsmouth where real advance, and even the beginnings of real cultural development may be seen. There are Portuguese homes with

smooth-mowed lawns, with a love of beauty, with aversion
to dirt, with pianos, and cameras and automobiles, and even
with small family libraries within the bounds of the little
town of Portsmouth. They and their examples are the
hope for the future.

Finally, we have data on the correlation between the size
of the family and the home rating. In the chapter on infant mortality and further on in this chapter we note that

TABLE 67

CHILDREN LIVING AT HOME AND HOME RATING, PORTSMOUTH, R. I.

Ratings Children	a	a-1	a-2	a-3	a-4	a-5	a-6	a-7	a-8	Totals	Unknown
None	2	3	3	2	2	3				15	2
One	1	1	4	2	4	1				13	1
Two	2	5	7	4	3	3	2			26	2
Three	1		6	8	2	6	3		1	27	3
Four	1	3	2	3	11	6	2			28	0
Five	3	1	3	3	5	3	6	1	1	26	1
Six	1			4	2	3	1		2	13	2
Seven	1		1	1	2	2	2	1	1	11	
Eight	1		3	1	6	1	2			14	
Nine				1	2		1			4	
Ten								1	1	2	
Eleven					1		1			2	
Unknown			1							1	
Totals	13	13	30	29	40	28	20	3	6	182	11
Average per Family	3.7	2.2	3.1	3.2	4.7	3.7	5.3	7.3	6.2	4.0	

3.3   4.7   4.7

The coefficient of mean square contingency for this table is .52.

the Portuguese are characterized by a remarkably high birth
rate, but that because of their high child death rate and of
the fact that many of the parents have been married but a
few years, the average size of the Portuguese family is
not as great as would be expected. Table 67 compares for
Portsmouth the number of children in the family with the
rating. The very large family is seen to be the exception
among those with the highest ratings, and the very small
family is unusual among those with the lowest ratings. A

wide distribution is found among the intermediate groups. The average number of children per family is seen to be 4.0, and the families with ratings ranging from "a" to "a minus 3" have but 3.3 children per family; while those with the rating of "a minus 4" as well as those with ratings higher than that have an average of 4.7 children per family.

TABLE 68

CHILDREN UNDER 10 LIVING AT HOME AND HOME RATING, PORTSMOUTH, R. I.

Ratings Children	a	a-1	a-2	a-3	a-4	a-5	a-6	a-7	a-8	Totals	Unknown
None	7	8	6	4	5	5	1	1		37	
One	2		7	8	7	3	2			29	
Two	2	5	8	6	5	6	2		1	35	
Three			4	5	8	6	7		2	32	
Four	1			4	8	6	6	2		27	
Five	1		1		6	1	1			10	
Six						1			2	3	
Seven							1			1	
Totals	13	13	26	27	39	28	20	3	5	174	
Unknown			2	1						3	16
Average per Family		1.5			2.8			2.2			

The coefficient of mean square contingency for this table is .598.

Table 68 was constructed in order to eliminate the influence of children in the family who were old enough to be useful on the farm. We find here that families with ratings of "a" to "a minus 3" average to have 1.5 children; while families with the lower grade of homes average to have 2.8 children. Similarly the coefficient of mean square contingency is a little higher (.60) for this table than for the other. It is thus the young children whose presence is associated with bad living conditions.

Interpreting the coefficient from each of these tables in the light of the explanation given above, we may say that there is a fairly high degree of relationship between home rating and the number of children in the family. In other words, the coefficients indicate that, if other things are equal,

TABLE 69

CHILDREN LIVING AT HOME AND HOME RATING, FALL 'RIVER, MASS.

Ratings Children	a	a-1	a-2	a-3	a-4	a-5	a-6	a-7	a-8	Totals	Unknown
None		1	2		1					4	
One		6	11	4	4	1	2			28	
Two	1	2	5	3	4					15	
Three		4	1	7	7		1			20	
Four	2	3	3	6	5	1				20	
Five		1		1	2		1			5	
Six		2		1	3					6	
Seven					3					3	
Eight							1			1	
Totals..........	3	19	22	22	29	2	5			102	
Average per Family	3.3	2.8	1.6	2.3	3.5	2.5	3.6			2.8	
			2.5				3.5				

The coefficient of mean square contingency for this table is .513.

the fewer the number of children in the home, the higher, by the definition used in this study, will be the standard of living of the family.

Tables 67, 68 and 69 have been converted, for the benefit of the general reader, into simple tables by combining the original classes of the two attributes into larger categories and reducing the absolute numbers to percentages. The results are given in the supplementary tables 67 A, 68 A, and 69 A, and show the same general relationship between

TABLE 67A

RELATION OF STANDARD OF LIVING TO NUMBER OF CHILDREN LIVING AT HOME, PORTSMOUTH, R. I.

(FIGURES FROM TABLE 67)

Number of Children Living		Standard of Living							
	Good		Fair		Poor		Totals		Unknown
at Home	a a-1 a-2		a-3 a-4 a-5		a-6 a-7 a-8				
	No.	%	No.	%	No.	%	No.	%	No.	%
No Children ..	8	14.3	7	7.2	0.	0.0	15	8.2	2	18.1
One to Three..	27	48.3	33	34.0	6	20.6	66	36.3	6	54.6
Over Three...	20	35.7	57	58.8	23	79.4	100	54.9	3	27.3
Unclassifiable .	1	1.7	0	0.0	0	0.0	1	0.6	0	0.0
Totals	56	100.0	97	100.0	29	100.0	182	100.0	11	100.0

standard of living and number of children in the home as was indicated by the contingency coefficients. Here, again, great caution must be exercised in drawing conclusions from percentages based upon such small totals.

TABLE 68A

RELATION OF STANDARD OF LIVING TO NUMBER OF CHILDREN UNDER
10 LIVING AT HOME, PORTSMOUTH, R. I.

(FIGURES FROM TABLE 68)

Number of Children under 10 Living at Home	Good			Standard of Living Fair			Poor			Totals	
	a No.	a-1 %	a-2	a-3 No.	a-4 %	a-5	a-6 No.	a-7 %	a-8	No.	%
No Children ...	21	38.8		14	14.7		1	3.7		36	20.5
One to Three ..	28	51.9		54	56.8		14	51.8		96	54.5
Over Three....	3	5.6		26	27.4		12	44.5		41	23.3
Unclassifiable ..	2	3.7		1	1.1		0	0.0		3	1.7
Totals	54	100.0		95	100.0		27	100.0		176	100.0

TABLE 69A

RELATION OF STANDARD OF LIVING TO NUMBER OF CHILDREN
LIVING AT HOME, FALL RIVER, MASS.

(FIGURES FROM TABLE 69)

Number of Children Living at Home	Good			Standard of Living Fair			Poor			Totals	
	a No.	a-2 %	a-2	a-3 No.	a-4 %	a-5	a-6 No.	a-7 %	a-8	No.	%
No Children ...	3	6.8		1	1.9		0	0.0		4	3.9
One to Three ..	30	68.2		30	56.6		3	60.0		63	61.8
Over Three	11	25.0		22	41.5		2	40.0		35	34.3
Unclassifiable ..	0	0.0		0	0.0		0	0.0		0	0.0
Totals	44	100.0		53	100.0		5	100.0		102	100.0

Table 69 for Fall River is comparable with table 67 for Portsmouth. We are first struck by the comparatively small families of the city Portuguese, who average to have but 2.8 children per family, as against 4.0 for rural families. This may be due in part to the possible selective effect of our method of study which probably included an abnormal proportion of young mothers who had not borne many children. The infant death rate is somewhat larger for the city than for the rural community also. Here families with ratings of from " a " to " a minus 3 " had on the average 2.5 children per family and those with the higher ratings 3.5 or exactly one child per family more. The coefficient or mean square contingency here was .51. Here again there seems little doubt that the over-large family is closely associated with undesirable home conditions, but whether it is the economic effect of the large family or the ignorance so often correlated with an excessive birth rate it is more difficult to say. At any rate there can be little doubt that very many Portuguese families would be better off with somewhat smaller broods.

Summarizing what we have had to say about the economic achievement and standard of living of the Portuguese, we may say that they are a low income group, with the asset of thrifty habits which perhaps yield somewhat after an exposure to American industrial environment; that they are still a relatively small but rapidly increasing factor in property ownership, savings bank accounts and the tax lists; that they are on an extremely low plane [1] in many cases but that their status improves very considerably as time goes on; that there is a strong possibility that the standard of living varies among immigrants from the different islands, so that our conclusions had best be confined to the large group from St. Michael's; that home conditions are related to occupation of fathers about as one would expect;

[1] The writer is unable to agree with the conclusion of the Immigration Commission in its study of 20 Portuguese families in Portsmouth, that the Portuguese have on the whole as good surroundings as native farmers who rent or own small farms. The Commission, however, was apparently giving more weight than this study gives to the appearance of the land itself. The present writer would agree that the Portuguese are second to none in their ability to make the land produce. United States Immigration Commission Report. 61st Congress, 3rd Session. Washington 1911. Vol. XXII, p. 451.

that they are somewhat better where the mother remains at home than where she goes out to work; and that there is a fairly high correlation between the over-large family and low-grade homes especially where that family is below the age where they can be assets on the farm or in the mill.

Vital Statistics and Health

In our discussion of infant mortality we have already commented on the high birth-rate of the Portuguese as a possible cause of their high infant mortality. It is important therefore to consider the rate of natural growth of these people in our two communities.

TABLE 70[1]

NATIVE, PORTUGUESE[2] AND OTHER FOREIGN BIRTHS,[3] PORTSMOUTH, R. I., 1910-1920

| | Native[3] | | Portuguese[1] | | Other Foreign | | Unknown | | Total | |
	Live	Still	Live	Still	Live	Still	Live	Still	Live	S
1910	19		31		6			1	56	
1911	12		42	1	13				67	
1912	14		44		12	1			70	
1913	17		54	1	7				78	
1914	15	1	60	3	5				80	
1915	14		48	1	2				64	
1916	30	1	51	1	5		1		87	
1917	19		61	2	4	1			84	
1918	20		73		5				98	
1919	25		61	4	10				96	
1920	29		49	2	1	1			79	
Totals	214	2	574	15	70	3	1	1	859	

Table 70 shows births in Portsmouth, Rhode Island for the eleven-year period 1910-1920. The number of births in

[1] Computed from the Portsmouth Birth Register in the Town Clerk's office.

[2] That is of Portuguese descent, including births to parents who though born in the United States were themselves of Portuguese descent.

[3] Omitting births where either parent was of Portuguese descent.

Portsmouth in a single year are too few to enable us to figure a useable birth rate. We must therefore content ourselves with a rough estimate of the average rate for the eleven years. We have not attempted to use birth data earlier than 1910 because before that date no canvasser was employed in Portsmouth to find births which had not been reported by physicians. The writer believes that reports of births and deaths are reasonably accurate for these eleven years provided they are obtained from the town records rather than from the state reports. Serious errors occur in the state reports because the figures are sometimes sent to Providence before the late birth returns are in. Rhode Island was dropped from the registration area for several years, not [1] because of inaccuracies in returns but because they were late.

Our table shows 859 live births during the eleven-year period or an average of 78.1 per year. The population of Portsmouth declined between 1910 and 1920 from 2681 to 2590. This decline was due to the closing of the coal mines early in the decade. The assumption that the loss of 91 people was evenly distributed throughout the decade is probably incorrect but the error involved is unavoidable. This assumption gives us a population in 1915 (the middle point in our eleven-year period) of 2636. On that figure as a base we have figured a very rough estimated birth-rate for the entire period of 29.6.

It is equally difficult to estimate comparative birth-rates for the Portuguese and the native-born non-Portuguese for we have figures which classify the population by nationality only for 1920. It is practically certain that during our eleven-year period the native non-Portuguese population has remained nearly stationary though it may have declined a

---

[1] Letter from the Bureau of the Census to the writer.

little. The loss due to the closing of the coal mines, however, was a loss mostly of foreign-born non-Portuguese. On the other hand it is even more certain that the Portuguese population has increased during this period. If, therefore, we figure birth rates on the incorrect assumption that both these elements in the population were in all years the same as they were in 1920 we shall get results which will be incorrect, but which will give us too low a rate for the Portuguese and probably one which will be approximately correct for the native non-Portuguese. The latter would be, if anything, too high. Therefore this procedure will tend to underestimate the contrast between the Portuguese and non-Portuguese birth-rates. Using this method, we get a native non-Portuguese crude birth rate of 14.5 to compare with a Portuguese rate (including all of Portuguese descent) of 48.5. In other words the natural increase of the Portuguese would seem to be more than three times that of the native non-Portuguese.

The assumption that the number of women aged 15-44 remained constant throughout the 11-year period is, if anything, one which would be still more liable to give a refined birth rate too low for the Portuguese and too high for the native-born non-Portuguese. This assumption gives us a average refined birth rate (births per 1000 women 15-44) for the non-Portuguese native-born of 74.1, and for those of Portuguese descent of 270.4. So estimated, the Portuguese refined birth rate is 3.6 times that of the " old stock " —a contrast even greater than that between the crude rates. The relatively high Portuguese rate in Portsmouth, then, is not due to the presence of a larger proportion of women aged 15-44. An examination of the age distribution given in table 42 [1] shows, however, that the Portuguese do have a larger proportion of women in the early part of the child-bearing period.

[1] Page 198.

We have computed from the original birth returns in the office of the City Clerk of Fall River the number of births to women of Portuguese descent, and to those of other than Portuguese descent for the year 1920. We find 1062 Portuguese births and 2524 non-Portuguese, both being exclusive of stillbirths. In determining these figures we had three checks on nationality or descent—the recorded birthplace of parents, the names of parents and of children and in some cases the employment of a Portuguese midwife. No case was found, however, where a Portuguese midwife was employed and where the birth was not clearly either Portuguese or non-Portuguese by the other criteria.[1]

The total population of Fall River in 1920 was 120,485 which gives us a crude birth rate of 29.8, which curiously enough is within .2 of the estimated rate for Portsmouth. Referring to table 43[2] we find that the population of Portuguese descent in Fall River in 1920 numbered 22,431 giving a crude Portuguese birth rate of 47.3, 1.2 points lower than our estimated rate for Portsmouth. The non-Portuguese population numbered 98,027 giving a rate of 25.7. This

[1] Forty-two out of the 1062 births recorded as Portuguese in the table would not have been so recorded under the usual definition of that term, because neither of their parents was born in Portugal nor in any of her possessions. These included thirty cases where both parents were born in the United States. In one of these thirty cases both parents were born in Hawaii; in another one parent was born there; and in two others one parent only was recorded—probably cases of illegitimacy. In the other eleven cases one parent was born in the United States and the other in some foreign country other than Portugal. All but one of these eleven were evidently cases of mixed marriages. The one doubtful case was where one parent was born in Bermuda and was quite probably also of Portuguese descent. The countries included in the mixed marriages were Canada (four cases), Syria (two cases), and one case each from Ireland, Scotland, France, Bermuda and Italy. The remaining case was one where one parent was born in France and one in Mexico but of Portuguese descent.

[2] Page 199.

rate is not comparable with the rate for the native non-Portuguese in Portsmouth since the former includes non-Portuguese foreign-born. The contrast between the Portuguese and non-Portuguese rates in Fall River is all the more striking, however, for that reason. Table 43 also enables us to figure refined birth rates for the Portuguese and non-Portuguese. There were in 1920 24,490 non-Portuguese women aged 15-44 inclusive in Fall River. There were 2524 births to non-Portuguese women which gives a refined birth-rate of 103.1. Similarly we find a refined rate for Portuguese women of 199.3. When it is remembered that among the non-Portuguese with whom our Portuguese are compared are very large numbers of other foreign groups including some who like the French Canadians are noted for their high vitality, this last comparison becomes very striking.

It is interesting at this point to turn back to our vital statistics from Portugal and the Islands [1] to see whether Portuguese vitality is adversely affected by removal to this country. For the five-year period 1913-1917 the highest crude birth-rate for any district was 36.64 for Ponta Delgada—the district from which most of the Portuguese we are studying come. But this rate is more than ten points lower than our crude rate for the Portuguese of Fall River and still lower than our estimated rate for Portsmouth. Similarly the highest refined rate which we found for any district in any year was 158.97 for Ponta Delgada in 1915 which compares with our 199.3 for Portuguese of Fall River and with our estimate of 270.4 for those of Portsmouth. We are, it must be admitted, insufficiently informed as to the reliability and comparability of the data from these Portuguese districts, but the differences are sufficiently great to suggest that the Portuguese of our communities have a higher rate of natural increase than their brethren at home.

[1] *Cf.* tables 6 and 7, pp. 53 and 55.

At least two possible explanations might be offered for this situation. The class of people who emigrate from these Islands are presumably of a higher vitality class than are the general population. Also the improved economic status of the Portuguese in America may affect their birth rate favorably. It is true that the long-time effect of rising standards of living is usually a decline in the birth-rate, but the immediate effect is usually just the opposite. No doubt both of these factors help to account for the high vitality of Portuguese immigrants.

It is still more important to compare the vitality of foreign-born Portuguese women in Fall River, with that of native-born women of Portuguese descent. We have 982 births recorded for 1920 to foreign-born Portuguese mothers,[1] and 111 to native-born women of Portuguese descent.[2] Table 44 [3] shows that there were in 1920 4523 foreign-born Portuguese women aged 15-44 and 805 native-born of Portuguese of mixed descent. We have then a refined birth rate for the former of 217.1 and for the latter of 137.9.[4] This difference is considerable and seems to show that the Portuguese, in common with other nationalities, reduce their birth-rates in the second generation. Moreover, this contrast seems to be in spite of the fact that the native-born women of Portuguese descent include a much larger proportion of women in the more fertile younger age groups.

[1] We have included among the Portuguese foreign-born mothers 12 born either in Brazil or Bermuda who were evidently of Portuguese descent.

[2] Unlike our other figures for births these births both include still-births. It would have been better to have eliminated them but as the proportion of still-births among Portuguese births was almost exactly the same in 1920 as among non-Portuguese, the idea of relative fertility given by the figures is not materially altered.

[3] Page 200.

[4] These figures are not comparable with our other refined birth-rates because they include still-born. See note (1).

Thus percentage computations from table 44 show that 84 per cent of native-born Portuguese women aged 15-44 were between the ages of 15 and 24 as against 39 per cent of native-born women of Portuguese descent. Unfortunately we are unable to further refine our data by considering the relative numbers in each group who were married. We show below [1] that foreign-born Portuguese women marrying after coming to this country average to marry two years later than do the native-born of Portuguese descent. On the other hand the fact that the proportion of native-born aged 15-19 is considerably greater than that of the foreign-born leads one to suspect that a larger proportion of native-born of Portuguese descent aged 15-44 are single than of foreign-born Portuguese. On the whole, however, considering the net effects of these various factors—the much higher refined birth-rate of foreign born; earlier marriage of native-born, but larger proportion of very young among the native-born women of Portuguese descent—there seems little doubt that Portuguese women of the second generation are considerably less fertile than those who were born abroad. This is an important conclusion, for it correlates with the rising standard of living which we have shown [2] to be characteristic of the Portuguese who have lived here for a considerable period.

In order to estimate roughly the proportion of a Portuguese woman's time which is normally devoted to child-bearing a study was made of the intervals between births to Portuguese women bearing children in Portsmouth in the years 1919 and 1920. It was not feasible to consider a longer period because of the many duplications of names and of the frequent recording of the same parents under different names. It would have been still better to consider

[1] *Cf. infra*, p. 305.
[2] *Cf. supra*, p. 275 ff.

all Portuguese births for a single year in a large city; but unfortunately both the New England cities containing a considerable number of Portuguese (Fall River and New Bedford) are located in Massachusetts where the number of the birth is not recorded when the birth is registered.

We show below [1] that Portuguese women of Portsmouth average to marry at the age of 21. Our very rough estimate of the birth interval was therefore made by subtracting 21 from the mother's age at the time of her most recent birth, and dividing the remainder by the number of the birth. Thus Mary Pimental's tenth child was recorded and her age given as 40. 21 from 40 leaves 19 which divided by 10 gives an average interval between births for this mother of 1.9. Whether we are justified in using this procedure even for rough estimates depends upon the representativeness of our data as to the age at marriage, the accuracy of the figures for age of mothers and number of birth, and the correspondence between the age at marriage in Portsmouth and the age at which mothers married before their immigration, were married. While all three of these sources of error undoubtedy exist there is no apparent reason why the first two should be more liable to result in an understatement of the interval between births than the opposite. As for the last source of error we can only say that if Portuguese women marry younger in the Azores than in Portsmouth, then our estimates of intervals are by so much too small.

Keeping the above sources of error in mind we may report that our study showed an average interval for Portuguese mothers reporting births in 1919 of 2.01 years and for those reporting in 1920 of 1.56 years, or 1.77 for the two years taken together. When it is remembered that pregnancies not resulting in child-birth are not considered, and that marriages where more than one or two children could

[1] *Cf. infra,* p. 304.

not be born for physiological reasons are included, it is seen that the normal state of the married Portuguese woman who is in good health is, in the rural community of Portsmouth —well-nigh continuous pregnancy or child-bearing. This fact is the more notable when it is remembered that these women were at all ages within the child-bearing period, although naturally among the Portuguese, as among all peoples, the earlier years of maturity are the more fertile. The average age of the women considered was 30.5 years. The distribution of ages of mothers and the corresponding average intervals are shown in the following table.

TABLE 71

ESTIMATED INTERVALS BETWEEN BIRTHS FOR PORTUGUESE [1]
MOTHERS OF PORTSMOUTH, R. I.

(1919 AND 1920 COMBINED)

Mothers Ages	Number of Mothers	Average Interval
Under 20	7	.73 [2] years
20–24	17	.97 "
25–29	24	1.45 "
30–34	32	2.29 "
35–39	18	2.73 "
40–44	6	2.81 "
Under 45	104	1.77 years

[1] Computed from the Register of Births of Portsmouth, R. I.

[2] Three mothers had their first child before they were 21 years old. These were recorded as having had an interval of one year although they probably will have more children before reaching that age. On the other hand intervals as small as .25 and .33 were averaged in with the rest where, for example, four or three children had been born by the twenty-first birthday. This latter procedure though based upon intervals which are physiologically impossible, is statistically justified. This is because such cases are presumably offset by those of women marrying above the average age, for whom intervals have been reckoned greater than those actually occurring. For example a woman marrying at the age of 24 and registering her first child in that year would be reckoned as having had an interval of three years when actually she might thereafter bear a child a year.

According to this table it is not far from the truth to say that married Portuguese women under 30 years of age who bear any children have a child every year, and that those in the higher age groups have one every two to three years.

Turning to mortality data we find the Portuguese also with an abnormally high death-rate. We have already discussed infant mortality among these people in a separate chapter. Earlier in this chapter [1] we have given a table of deaths classified by descent for Portsmouth. We also surmised that the coming of the Portuguese had been a chief factor in the apparent rise of the death rate in the town during the last thirty-six years. Unfortunately the changes in the number and age distribution of the Portuguese have been so rapid that it is not feasible to even estimate Portuguese death rates for ten-year periods, as we have done for the general population. Neither are the deaths in 1920 sufficiently numerous to enable us to figure a Portuguese rate for that year. All that we can say is that the range in number of deaths per year has recently been from 13 to 26 and that the Portuguese population has recently been in the neighborhood of a thousand. One gets the general impression that if the high infant mortality of the Portuguese could be eliminated, the death rate for higher age periods would not be very excessive; but whether the absence of aged people will account for this situation is not proven.

We can get some notion of the health of school children in Portsmouth from 232 school health cards filled out by a Red Cross nurse, following examinations of that number of children made in 1919. Of these 232 cards 145 were for Portuguese children and 83 for non-Portuguese mostly of the " old stock ". Four were for half-Portuguese children. 78 per cent of the non-Portuguese children were classed as having some physical defect, and 96 per cent of the Portu-

[1] *Cf. supra*, p. 238.

guese children. 81 per cent of Portuguese children and 54 per cent of non-Portuguese were reported as having one or more of the following defects—diseased tonsils, nasal obstructions or adenoids. Considering that about ⅗ of the children were Portuguese, we note that there was no striking difference between the Portuguese, and non-Portuguese in the prevalence of such troubles as eye defects, or defective hearing and discharge from the nose. But the Portuguese children showed more than their proportion with marked mental deficiency (5 out of 7); bad posture (18 out of 24); curvature of the spine (all of the six); malnutrition (20 out of 26); rickets (all of the three); suspected tuberculosis (4 out of 5); enlarged glands (all of the 3); pediculosis (all of the 9); ring worm (all of the 3); and cardioadenitis (24 out of 35). The non-Portuguese did not show more than their proportion of any defects which appeared in any considerable numbers. In addition 8 Portuguese children were reported as being subjected to cruelty in their homes; while 37 or one in four of the Portuguese children said they drank no milk at home, while only 6 non-Portuguese children were so listed. With regard to food also 11 Portuguese children and 6 non-Portuguese were said to be receiving food with insufficient nourishment; while 13 Portuguese and no non-Portuguese were reported as not getting enough food. 13 Portuguese children also were said to be inadequately clad with clothing in poor condition, while none of the other group were so classed. The writer was told of two children whose father made part of his living selling milk, and who fed milk to his hogs but who gave his children none.

These data, though the result of a single study, show plainly that the Portuguese children of Portsmouth are handicapped physically, and that sometimes, though by no means usually, these handicaps may be traced to adverse home conditions. They also show, as might be expected, that children of Portsmouth of whatever nationality are in need of the assistance of a school nurse.

For Fall River we have more accurate and complete data as to mortality. Table 72 gives the deaths of people of Portuguese descent in Fall River in 1920 classified by age groups. One is immediately struck by the large number of deaths of very young children and by the relatively small number of deaths in the older age periods. The marked excess of male deaths is also notable.

TABLE 72

DEATHS BY AGE GROUPS FOR PEOPLE OF PORTUGUESE [1] DESCENT, FALL RIVER, 1920

(STILLBORN OMITTED)

Age at death	Number of deaths	
	Male	*Female*
Under 1	143	86
1–4	47	47
5–9	1	5
10–14	5	3
15–19	1	6
20–24	7	4
25–29	7	6
30–34	3	4
35–39	3	5
40–44	7	6
45–49	7	4
50–54	13	3
55–59	8	4
60–64	5	6
65–69	12	3
70–74	3	2
75–79	1	0
80–84	2	2
85–89	1	0
90–94	1	0
95–99	1	0
	278	196

[1] Computed from Fall River Register of Deaths for 1920.

Table 73 shows the birth-place of the parents of decedents (with stillborn included) in Fall River in 1920.

TABLE 73

BIRTHPLACE OF PARENTS OF PORTUGUESE DECEDENTS OF 1920
IN FALL RIVER

(STILLBORN INCLUDED)

Birthplace	Fathers	Mothers
Azores	430	444
Portugal	35	28
Fall River	11	21
Madeira	14	9
Unknown	9	4
U. S. outside of Fall River	7	2
Syria	2	0
Italy	2	0
Brazil	2	1
Hawaii	1	1
Bermuda	1	1
Ireland	0	1
Canada	0	1
England	0	1
	514	514

This table incidentally reveals how recent has been the immigration of the Portuguese. Of the 514 pairs of parents only 19 fathers and 24 mothers were native-born (including those born in Hawaii). The general death rate of Fall River in 1920 was 14.7.[1] There were in that year a total of 1771 deaths (exclusive of stillborn), of which 469 were of Portuguese descent and 1302 were non-Portuguese. The total population of Fall River was 120,458 of whom 22,431 were of Portuguese descent and 98,027 were non-Portuguese. From these data we figure a crude Portuguese death-rate of 20.9 as against a rate for the non-Portuguese of 13.3. Moreover 228 of the Portuguese deaths and 271 of the

[1] For this and other rates cf. *supra*, p. 240.

non-Portuguese were deaths of infants under one year of age. From our discussion of infant mortality it has been evident that the mortality among infants is extremely high among the Portuguese. If we were to deduct infant deaths from the total deaths of both groups we should have a rate for the non-Portuguese of 10.5 and for the Portuguese of 10.7 or practically the same.

An examination of our table showing the age distribution of the Portuguese population of Fall River shows that it is abnormal. Table 74 shows for Portuguese and non-Portuguese the number and proportion in each age group.

TABLE 74

AGE DISTRIBUTION OF PORTUGUESE AND NON-PORTUGUESE POPULATION [1] OF FALL RIVER—BOTH SEXES COMBINED—1920

Age Groups	Non-Portuguese		Portuguese	
	Number	Per cent	Number	Per cent
Under 5	9,888	10.1	3,752	16.7
5– 9	10,166	10.4	3,123	13.8
10–14	9,739	9.9	2,385	10.6
15–19	8,903	9.1	2,132	9.5
20–44	36,647	37.4	8,480	37.8
45 and over.........	22,684	23.1	2,559	11.4
Totals	98,027	100.0	22,431	99.8

While the Portuguese are seen to have a larger proportion of young children than the non-Portuguese they also have a very much smaller proportion of aged. By using the same method employed in the first part of this chapter [2] we may

[1] Computed from the original schedules of the 14th Census.

[2] The Newsholme method was used in correcting the crude death-rates for the Portuguese and non-Portuguese populations of Fall River, but instead of the age classes, under 5, 5-14, 15-24, 25-44, 45-64, 65 and over, it was necessary because of the nature of the published data to use the following age classes: under 5, 5-14, 15-19, 20-44, 45 and over. The grouping of all persons 45 and over probably involves a slight error in computing the factors of correction, but it is believed that this error does not impair the general validity of the comparison made in the text.

obtain factors of correction which will eliminate the difference in age and sex distributions between these two groups.

We find these factors of correction to be 1.065 for the Portuguese and 1.000 for the non-Portuguese. Multiplying the crude death-rates by these factors of correction eliminates influences due to abnormal age and sex distributions, and gives us a " corrected " death-rate per 1000 for the Portuguese of 22.3 and for the non-Portuguese of 13.3. Deducting the infant deaths in both groups we have a corrected death-rate for the Portuguese of 11.4 and for the non-Portuguese of 10.5. In other words, if the Portuguese had a " standard " age and sex distribution, their general death-rate would be 22.3 instead of 20.9, and their death-rate with infant deaths excluded would be 11.4 instead of 10.7. We find, then, the corrected general death-rate of the Portuguese to be 67.7 per cent higher than that of the non-Portuguese; and the corrected death-rate, with infant deaths excluded, to be 8.5 per cent higher. It must be remembered that in this case we are comparing the mortality of the Portuguese with that of a group made up not only of " the old stock " but also of foreign-born and native-born of French-Canadian, Irish, Italian, Syrian and other stocks.

It is interesting to compare the above apparent evidence of morbidity among the Portuguese with Hoffman's opinion expressed in 1899 as to the effect upon health of the coming of the Portuguese to America. He says: " But this strain (of negro blood) must be considered as unimportant from a physiological point of view, and does not to my mind represent a factor detrimental to the health or longevity of these people at the present time." [1] In the same article Hoffman quotes death-rates by nationality in Fall River for the years 1891-7 as follows: All nationalities 23.0, Portu-

---

[1] Hoffman, *op. cit.*, p. 330.

guese 11.7, Canadians 10.5, Irish 29.2. He admits that the age distribution at that time favored the Portuguese but says that that is not a sufficient explanation of these marked differences in mortality. He concludes:[1] " The conclusion is warranted that on the basis of the local mortality statistics of the Western Islands; on the basis of the mortality statistics for the Hawaiian Islands; . . . on the basis of the returns for the city of Fall River, and on the scanty material in the possession of insurance companies, the mortality of the Portuguese, especially Western Islanders, is below the general mortality of the Portuguese in Portugal, and considerably below the mortality of the Irish and Germans in the United States." It will be remembered that Hoffman calls attention to the fact that at the time of writing the Portuguese in the United States came chiefly from the islands of Fayal, San Jorge and Flores, and that he discusses a possible racial factor differentiating the inhabitants of these islands from other Portuguese, but is inclined to disregard it. Shall we attribute the contrast between our present results and those found by Hoffman to a change in age distribution, to a change in economic conditions, or to a change in racial type as the St. Michael Portuguese have come in? If this were the only evidence found for differences in type between the immigrants from the different islands, the present writer would be inclined to shun the racial hypothesis; but added to the other evidence we have presented there is at least a strong presumption in its favor.

All our evidence points to the conclusion that the Portuguese add not only to the problem of infant mortality in New England but to that of mortality in the upper age groups. It must be admitted, however, that our evidence would be more convincing if we had a parallel study of some other nationality comparable with the Portuguese and living under similar conditions.

[1] *Ibid.*, p. 334.

It is frequently said that the Portuguese being low-grade immigrants are improvident and marry at an extremely young age. Statistics for Portsmouth and Fall River do not altogether bear out such a statement. Table 75 shows the average age at first marriage of 941 individuals whose marriages were recorded in the town records of Portsmouth as occurring between 1885 and 1919 inclusive. In addition there were some dozen individuals married for the first time whose age was not recorded.

TABLE 75 [1]

AVERAGE AGE AT FIRST MARRIAGE—PORTSMOUTH, R. I., 1885-1919

Type	Number	Average age	Age not given
Native-born non-Portuguese men...	342	26.3	4
Portuguese men (native or foreign).	99	25.0	0
Other foreign men...............	24	29.1	1
Native-born non-Portuguese women.	350	23.6	6
Portuguese women...............	100	21.3	0
Other foreign women	26	27.4	1

This table shows that Portuguese women are married on the average 3.7 years younger than Portuguese men; and that the corresponding difference between the sexes among the native-born non-Portuguese is a year less. Also that Portuguese men are married 1.3 years younger than native-born non-Portuguese; and Portuguese women 2.3 years younger than native-born non-Portuguese. Other foreign-born of both sexes marry later than either Portuguese or native-born, but their number is small.

It is quite possible, of course, that Portuguese in the Azores marry younger than in this country. Portuguese having a lower standard of living naturally marry younger than do natives. In view of common report of extremely young marriages, however, the writer is surprised to find as little difference as is shown. The writer has seen one Portuguese woman who was married at 15, but the town records show at least one marriage of a native woman at the same age.

[1] Computed from the Register of Marriages, Portsmouth, R. I.

Table 76 for Fall River separates the Portuguese into native and foreign-born.

TABLE 76

AVERAGE AGE AT FIRST MARRIAGE, FALL RIVER, MASS.,[1]
OCTOBER I, 1918—OCTOBER I, 1919

Type	*Number*	*Average age*
Native non-Portuguese men	635	25.50
Native Portuguese descent, men	30	21.26
Portuguese foreign born	210	29.87
Non-Portuguese foreign-born men	218	29.99
Native non-Portuguese women	671	23.44
Native Portuguese women	47	19.53
Portuguese foreign-born women	209	21.75
Non-Portuguese foreign-born women	223	27.48

In this table the fact that second and third marriages are omitted accounts for the fact that the totals for men and women do not correspond. Differences between men and women of the same nativity group are, of course, also accounted for by mixed marriages. The table shows that the thirty Portuguese men born here were married on the average more than four years younger than were the bulk of the native-born men. The difference between the age at marriage of native non-Portuguese women and that of the native-born of Portuguese descent is nearly as great as that in the case of the corresponding groups of men. On the other hand, we find scarcely any difference in the age at marriage of foreign-born Portuguese men and that of other foreign-born men; and a difference of more than four years in favor of later marriage by Portuguese men as compared with native-born non-Portuguese men. Foreign-born Portuguese women, however, marry younger than either native-born or foreign-born non-Portuguese. The contrast between them and other foreign-born women is one of more than five years and is the most striking of the table. The late marriage of the whole group of foreign-born is also

[1] Computed from the Marriage Register of Fall River, Mass.

notable. The easiest explanation of these data seems to be that the controlling factor is economic, but that granted sufficient means with which to start a family, the Portuguese marry younger than other nationalities. There is no suggestion of child marriage, however.

Our study has discovered no very significant data on mixed marriages among the Portuguese. In Portsmouth in thirty-five years' time 13 cases of mixed marriage where one of the parties was of Portuguese descent were recorded. Eleven of these thirteen cases were personally known to the present town clerk and his opinion was that they had, with one or two exceptions, resulted in happiness and attractive children. One case where the results were apparently the opposite is known to the present writer. In Fall River during the year studied, 36 apparent mixed marriages occurred. It was impossible to tell the nationality of the non-Portuguese party to these marriages in every case but Irish, Italian, English, French Canadian, Polish, Syrian and native American parties were found. The Portuguese party was the man only slightly more frequently than it was the woman. On the whole we do not find evidence for much intermarriage with the Portuguese. It is unfortunate that Drachsler's important study of intermarriage in New York City [1] did not include sufficient numbers of Portuguese to be of significance. He found a very high percentage of intermarriage with the Portuguese but their number was very small.

Educational Achievement

We have already given evidence that the Portuguese are an illiterate people. We have seen that in the District of Ponta Delgada more than half the women and nearly two-thirds of the men who married in 1917 were unable to sign the marriage papers.

---

[1] *Cf. supra*, chap. ii, pp. 31-32.

We have seen that this high degree of illiteracy is characteristic both of emigrants in general from Portugal and of immigrants to the United States from Portugal.[1] While there can be little doubt that emigration to the United States tends to reduce this illiteracy it can have but small effect upon the adult population. We have made special investigations of this matter only in Portsmouth. The Census schedules for Portsmouth for 1920 show the literacy of 169 male Portuguese heads of families and of 161 of their wives to be as follows: 56 men and 74 women able either to read or to write or both; 113 men and 87 women able neither to read nor to write. Defining illiteracy to mean ability neither to read nor to write we find that 66.9 per cent of male heads of families and 54.0 per cent of their wives were illiterate.[2]

The Immigration Commission found that except for the Turks the Portuguese had a larger proportion of illiteracy (inability to read) than any other nationality.[3] Only Bulgarians, Spaniards, Turks and Cubans ranked lower than the Portuguese in their ability to speak English.

The advance sheets of the Census of 1920 show that in Fall River 11.9 per cent of all persons ten years of age and over, 25.5 per cent of foreign-born persons of that age, 3.2 per cent of all persons 16 to 20 years of age inclusive, and 15.2 per cent of males and 16.3 per cent of females 21 years of age and over were illiterate. By every one of these measures Fall River is seen to be the most illiterate of all the 66 Massachusetts cities with 10,000 or more population except one. This one city with greater illiteracy was in each case Easthampton except that New Bedford showed a large proportion of persons 16 to 20 years of age who were illiterate.

---

[1] *Cf. supra*, chap. iv, pp. 114-116.

[2] Computed from the original Census schedules in Washington, D. C.

[3] United States Immigration Commission Report. 61st Congress, 3rd Session. Washington 1911, Vol. I, p. 446.

The three large Portuguese centers of Fall River, New Bedford and Taunton always showed a high ratio of illiteracy. There is no question that the presence of the Portuguese is a very large factor in this unfortunate situation. We should hardly expect children coming from families where neither parent could read or write, where the attainment of even the merest rudiments of an education has been the exception rather than the rule, to show either marked interest in or marked success in their school work. In such families the daily conversation is not concerned with topics of the day because there is no newspaper, and school is too often looked upon as a convenient place to send the youngest children to get them out from under foot, and as a handicap to the older children delaying their entry into remunerative occupations on the farm or in the mill. It will be all the more interesting, therefore, to inquire into the actual educational attainment of Portuguese children in the schools of Portsmouth and Fall River.

Table 77 below shows the number of Portuguese, and non-

TABLE 77

PORTUGUESE AND NON-PORTUGUESE CHILDREN IN PORTSMOUTH [1]
SCHOOLS, BY GRADES—1919-20

	Portuguese Descent	Non-Portuguese	Totals
Grade 1	93	25	118
Grade 2	44	26	70
Grade 3	66	14	80
Grade 4	38	14	52
Grade 5	23	25	48
Grade 6	14	26	40
Grade 7	9	16	25
Grade 8	4	12	16
Grade 9	2	5	7
	293	163	456

[1] Completed from the original school record books.

Portuguese children in each grade of the elementary and grammar grades in Portsmouth. Portsmouth has no high school and we have no data as to how many Portuguese children from Portsmouth were attending high school in Fall River or Newport. They were certainly few in number.

The Portuguese of Portsmouth make up 41.6 per cent of the total population but as the above table shows they send nearly two-thirds (64.3 per cent) of the total children who go to school. This accounts for the waning interest of the " old stock " in good schools. The table also shows that while, as is usual, the number of pupils declines as the higher grades are reached, this decline is more noticeable among the Portuguese than among other children. In the first grade they outnumbered the non-Portuguese nearly four to one, while by the fifth grade they are themselves outnumbered and in the higher grades the excess of non-Portuguese is considerable.

Table 78 below shows the number of each nationality (by language of parents' native land), of children enrolled in the Fall River elementary schools in December 1914. While a table constructed in 1920 would no doubt show some changes in the relative importance of the different nationalities, this table gives a rough idea of the types of children with whom the Portuguese are associated, and of the distribution of the Portuguese among different classes. The table does not include pupils in the parochial schools and thus omits large numbers of French-Canadians and some of other groups. Disregarding this fact, we note that in public schools the Portuguese are numerically second only to children of American-born parents, with the English third and the French-Canadians fourth, while Hebrews, Italians, Poles and Irish follow in the order named. Few Portuguese attend parochial schools.

TABLE 78

PUPILS IN ELEMENTARY SCHOOLS—DEC., 1914,[1] BY NATIONALITY
AND GRADES, FALL RIVER, MASS.

Nationality				Grades						
	1	2	3	4	5	6	7	8	Spec.	Totals
Armenian			1							1
Bulgarian					1					1
Danish	1		3				1			5
Dutch				1	1					2
English (U. S.)	676	590	359	739	587	526	262	280	25	4554
English (other)	253	314	365	395	404	273	234	141	24	2403
Flemish	1		1		1				6	9
French	436	291	323	329	245	122	51	17	134	1948
German	11	4	7	12	6	5	4	3	1	53
Greek	1	3	5	1	3		1		2	16
Hebrew	121	119	86	124	122	96	72	54	12	806
Irish	20	16	29	30	51	34	29	14		223
Italian	97	82	90	70	40	19	7	3	5	413
Norwegian	1	1	1	2		1			2	8
Polish	112	68	61	61	40	13	2	2	19	378
Portuguese	725	624	726	377	201	53	12	3	128	2849
Russians	24	13	24	11	7	5	7	1		92
Scotch	6	3	8	14	15	13	7	10		76
Swedish	2	4	5	3	5	4	1	1		25
Syrian	19	14	17	5	5		1		8	69
Chinese					2		1			3
Finnish									1	1
Rumanian	1									1
Ruthenian		1								1
	2506	2147	2609	2177	1736	1164	692	542	364	13937

A glance at the table also shows great differences among
nationalities in the proportion of children found in the
higher grades. We have figured for the more important
nationalities the percentages of total children in school who
are found in the sixth, seventh and eighth grades taken together. In descending order they are Hebrew 27.5 per cent,
children of English-speaking foreign-born parents 27.0 per
cent, children of English-speaking native-born parents 23.7
per cent, French 9.7 per cent, Italian 7.0 per cent, Polish 4.5
per cent and Portuguese 2.4 per cent. The Portuguese thus
make distinctly the worst showing in this respect. That
three times as large a proportion of Italians as of Portu-

[1] From Fall River School Survey.

guese, and more than eleven times as large a proportion of Jews as of Portuguese, remain for the work of the upper grades is surely significant. How far this difference is due to a difference in natural ability, and how far to the effects of the mores of illiteracy, economic status et cetera, this table does not indicate. We have already shown that this exodus from the schools is not peculiar to the Portuguese, but it is much more noticeable among them.

The same contrast is brought out more clearly still by table 79 which shows the nationality of pupils in Fall River High Schools in December 1914. If we may assume that Portuguese children of high school age in Fall River made up at the end of 1914 approximately the same proportion of all children of that age, which they did in 1920, then they were nearly one in five (19.3 per cent). As the Portuguese population has probably increased somewhat since then, we probably do the Portuguese some injustice in making this assumption. Still the influx since that date has not been very great. Our table, however, finds but four Portuguese enrolled in the high schools or but .3 per cent of the total number of children in the high schools. According to our assumption this is but one sixty-second of their normal proportion. In 1920 there were 20 Portuguese children attending the now centralized High School of Fall River. Of these eleven were in the first year, five in the second year, three in the third year and one was a senior. Thus the Portuguese have multiplied their number of high school pupils by five in less than six years time. The Portuguese are still a very small proportion of all high school pupils but they have increased their percentage from .3 per cent to 1.2 per cent, or four-fold.

The conclusion which one will draw from such figures will depend largely upon the temperament and prejudices of the observer. If he is inclined to fix his attention upon the

TABLE 79

" Nationality " of Pupils in High Schools,[1] Fall River, Mass., Dec., 1914

(BY LANGUAGE OF PARENTS' NATIVE LAND)

Nationality	Grades					
	9	10	11	12	P. Grad. Spec.	Totals
Armenian	2					2
Chinese			1			1
Danish			2			2
English (U. S.)	343	260	131	134	8	876
English (other)	109	76	19	10	2	216
French	18	13	12	4		47
German	3	1	1			5
Hebrew	30	34	19	16	4	103 [2]
Italian	2	1				3
Polish	2					2
Portuguese	3	1				4
Russian	3	4	4	1		12
Scotch	7	3	3		1	14
Swedish	1	2	1	2		6
Syrian	1					1
Welsh	2					2
Totals	526	395	193	167	15	1296 [2]

shockingly small number of Portuguese children who reach the secondary school he tends to accept the explanation of inherent racial inferiority. If, on the other hand, he notes the increase in the enrollment of Portuguese children he becomes more hopeful. The situation is similar to that we shall soon show with reference to the use of the Public Library. A people with low mentality or lacking in ambition do not attend high school. On the other hand a people with normal mentality but coming from homes where the traditional thing to do is to begin work at the age of four-

[1] From the Fall River School Survey, Chap. i, p. 4.

[2] There appears to be a discrepancy here between the figures given in the columns for the Hebrews and the total Hebrews recorded in the grand total. The figures in the columns have been accepted and the totals corrected accordingly.

teen and where the parents are more often than not illiterate
—such a people also do not attend high school. We have
figured below the ratio between the number of pupils of a
given nationality in high school in 1914, and the number of
foreign-born of that nationality according to the Census
of 1920. As a measure of interest in higher education such
a procedure is open to two obvious sources of error. In
the first place the number and proportion of each nationality
in the total population may have changed in six years. In
the second place the proportion of the different nationalities
which is made up of children of high school age may vary.
Nationalities also differ in the proportion between the native-
born and foreign-born among those of a given descent.
These difficulties are of considerable importance and would
lead us to dispense with our table were it not that the contrasts it discloses are so marked that they must be of significance despite these sources of possible error. Our table
includes all nationalities with 800 or more representatives
among the foreign-born except the Irish for whom no figures

TABLE 80

RATIO BETWEEN THE FOREIGN-BORN OF A GIVEN LANGUAGE [1] GROUP
(CENSUS OF 1920), AND THE NUMBER OF PUPILS OF THAT
GROUP ENROLLED IN THE FALL RIVER HIGH
SCHOOLS, DEC., 1914

Language group	*For every pupil in the high school there were foreign-born individuals in Fall River*
English	41
French (Canadian only)	231
Italian	314
Polish	1262
Portuguese	2995

were available, and the Hebrews and Russians for whom
the figures in the two sources were not comparable. Our

[1] Computed from the Fall River School Survey, chap. i, p. 4, and
advance sheets of the United States Census for 1920, pp. 23-4.

table probably does some injustice to groups of recent immigration including Italians, Polish and Portuguese, and correspondingly favors the English and French. As it stands, however, the table implies that the Portuguese to equal the record of the English should have 292 pupils in the high schools instead of 4. Similarly, to equal the record of the French-Canadians they should have 52; of the Italians 38; and 9 or 10 to come up to the Poles. We know, however, that in 1920 the Portuguese had passed the 1914 ratio of the Poles, but we do not know how many Poles there were in Fall River high schools in 1920.

Turning from the school statistics for Fall Fiver as a whole, to schools in Portsmouth and to five elementary and grammar schools in or near our special district in Fall River, we first note the nationality of school children in these latter schools in January 1915, shown in table 81.

TABLE 81

"Nationality" of School Children Near District Studied,[1]
Fall River, Mass., Jan., 1915

(BY LANGUAGE OF PARENTS' NATIVE LAND)

			Schools			
Language	*McDonough*	*Robeson*	*Broadway*	*Longfellow*	*Columbia*	*Totals*
English (U. S.)..	51	61	13	19	14	158
English (other)..	30	18		32		80
French..........	32	43	14	52	7	148
Hebrew	168	195	3	5	7	378
Irish...........	23			1		24
Italian..........	1	2	2	2		7
Portuguese	89	125	180	233	166	793
Scotch..........	6			1		7
Polish	20	59			7	86
Russian		4	5		1	10
Syrian	5				2	7
German	2	1				3
Greek		3				3
Bulgarian	1					1
Danish	1					1
Norwegian	1					1
Totals	430	511	217	345	204	1707

[1] From Fall River School Survey, p. 4.

The distribution of nationalities may have changed slightly since 1915 but probably not greatly. This table was the basis for the choice of Robeson and McDonough schools for a study of scholarship. Since the object of our study is to compare the scholarship of the Portuguese with that of other nationalities, it seemed best to select schools where the heterogeneity was considerable. The Broadway school has the largest proportion of Portuguese pupils (82.9 per cent) but that leaves too few of other nationalities with which to compare them. In the Robeson school on the other hand the Portuguese make up but 24.5 per cent of the school population. They are indeed outnumbered by the Hebrews but have twice as many representatives as do the next largest group—the English-speaking of American parentage. The choice of the McDonough school was dictated by the fact that that is the only school in the district where pupils in the upper grades may be found. The distribution of nationalities there is not greatly different from that in the Robeson school, however. It was impossible to determine the number of each nationality other than Portuguese in these two schools in 1919 partly because of the inability of the writer to distinguish the names of some nationalities, but chiefly because of the frequent changes of names especially by the Hebrews.

It may be interesting in passing to note the contrast between the situation of a Portuguese child who attends the Columbia or Broadway school with that of one in the Robeson school. The former finds himself surrounded by class and playmates nearly all of his own kind, whereas the latter has a choice of eight nationalities besides his own— four of them being found in considerable numbers. The former situation may make for harmony, but the latter presumably promotes more rapid adaptation to the life of the city.

Table 82 compares the average scholarship of Portuguese and non-Portuguese children in the four lower grades of the Robeson school and in the four upper grades of the Mc-Donough school.

TABLE 82

COMPARATIVE SCHOLARSHIP OF PORTUGUESE AND NON-PORTUGUESE [1]
CHILDREN, FALL RIVER, MASS., 1919-20

(FOR SELECTED CLASSES)

School	Grade	Portuguese Children		Non-Portuguese Children	
		Number	Av. standing	Number	Av. standing
Robeson	1	24	80.0	72	80.4
	2	39	79.2	64	80.3
	3	32	75.0	62	78.5
	4	32	75.0	43	76.6
McDonough..	5	70	70.2	73	74.4
	6	53	68.8	51	70.1
	7	16	62.6	33	70.8
	8	5	72.2	27	79.5
Totals	all	271	72.6	425	76.7

As in similar tables in this study the Portuguese were determined by their names. In the case of this particular table this was the only check upon " nationality " as the parents' names were not given on the records. Doubtful cases were very few, but there is, of course, the possibility that a very few names of Portuguese were included with the non-Portuguese. In contrast with similar tables for Portsmouth the Portuguese are here compared with other immigrant nationalities including Hebrews, English, Polish and French, the relative importance of which was presumably in the order named. Nevertheless in every grade the Portuguese are rated lower than their fellows. The differences against the Portuguese children range from .4 points in the first grade to 8.2 points in the seventh. The considerable difference in the two highest grades is in spite of

[1] Computed from the class record books.

the probability that the Portuguese are a somewhat selected group in those grades. The numbers are small, however.

It is particularly worthy of note that in this table we are comparing the Portuguese with a group in which the number of Hebrews is large. We have already seen that the Hebrews send their children to school longer than do other nationalities, and they are well-known for their love of education. It is quite possible, therefore, that our comparison is here quite as severe upon the Portuguese as is that in Portsmouth, where the non-Portuguese are largely native-born of " the old stock ". This latter comparison is shown in the following table.

TABLE 83 [1]

COMPARATIVE SCHOLARSHIP OF PORTUGUESE AND NON-PORTUGUESE
CHILDREN, PORTSMOUTH, R. I., 1919-1920

School	Grade	Portuguese Children		Non-Portuguese Children	
		Number	Av. Standing	Number	Av. Standing
Mine.............	4	4	82.3	1	82.0
B. Ferry	4	6	70.8	2	80.5
Newtown	4	13	77.8	7	81.7
McCorrie	4	4	73.7	2	85.0
Vaucluse	4	2	80.0	2	88.5
Gibbs	4	6	75.3	1	96.5
Chase	4	3	83.3		
		—	—	—	—
Total............	4	38	76.9	15	83.9
Newtown	5	23	67.2 [2]	24	80.2
Quaker H........	6	unknown			
	7	10	79.0	15	75.7
	8	4	68.8	13	75.8
	9	2	80.0	6	76.7
		—	—	—	—
Grand total		77	73.9	73	79.0

Table 83 was computed from the class records of all the schools of the town except that for grade 6, supplemented by conversations with nearly all the teachers. The scholarship ratings were usually secured from records direct, but in a

[1] Computed from class record and teachers' estimates.

[2] Two or three obvious defectives with extremely low standing reduce this average considerably.

few cases were supplied by the teachers from memory. While the former method is preferable the number of children in the cases was so small as to make, in the writer's judgment, the teacher's word almost as reliable as the written record which is merely the expression of her opinion at best. In grades 1-3 where the Portuguese far outnumber the non-Portuguese, no scholarship rating is recorded for the pupils. It is important to remember that in Portsmouth a child recorded as non-Portuguese is with very few exceptions a native-born child of native Anglo-Saxon parentage. The grade four comparisons are probably the fairest we have; for in the higher grades the Portuguese drop out, and those few remaining are probably a more highly selected group than are their non-Portuguese classmates. On the other hand the Portuguese children have had time to become adjusted to the school and to their classmates, by the time they reach the higher grades.

In every grade except the seventh the Portuguese are outranked by the non-Portuguese. The differences range from one of 3.3 points in the ninth grade where the numbers are small, to one of 13 points in the fifth grade where defective Portuguese who should be removed to special classes pull down the average of their fellows. For the entire group we find a difference of 5.1 points as against a difference of 3.9 points in Fall River. The fact that these differences are, with a single exception of one grade in Portsmouth, universal, is a strong argument in favor of their reality. Whether they are due to the handicaps under which the Portuguese children live, or to real differences in native ability is more difficult to determine. That it is a handicap to be born into a home where parents and perhaps older brothers and sisters are illiterate needs no emphasis. To the present writer the above differences in scholarship hardly seem greater than one would expect under such circumstances. It hardly seems necessary to resort to that easy but dangerous explanation by race differences, to explain the backwardness of the Portuguese. It is quite open to enthusiasts for this explanation, however, to reply that the backwardness and illiteracy of the whole Portuguese nationality may be due to racial inferiority. It is no part of the purpose of this study to answer that difficult question.

Another measure of backwardness is to compare the average age of Portuguese and non-Portuguese children in the schools. We have done this for the higher grades in Fall River, as shown in table 84.

TABLE 84

AVERAGE AGE OF CHILDREN IN UPPER GRADES,[1] McDONOUGH SCHOOL, FALL RIVER, MASS., 1919-1920

Grades	Portuguese		Non-Portuguese		Years
	Number	Av. Age	Number	Av. Age	Difference
5	89	11.5	97	11.3	.2
6	80	12.2	75	11.5	.7
7	31	12.5	41	12.1	.4
8	12	12.9	27	12.9	.0

Here we find slight differences only, but again in every case they are against the Portuguese; except that there is no difference in the eighth grade. Table 85 shows similar facts for Portsmouth except that there we have data for all grades. The retardation is seen to be greater in the rural district than in the city in every grade except the seventh where there is a very slight difference in favor of the Portuguese in Portsmouth. Some of this retardation of Portuguese children may be due to the fact that a few of them come to this country during childhood without having had much if any schooling. How important a factor this is it is impossible to say. In the city such children would probably be put

[1] Computed from original school records.

TABLE 85

AVERAGE AGE OF CHILDREN IN SCHOOL,[1] PORTSMOUTH, R. I., 1919-20

Grades	Portuguese		Non-Portuguese		Difference
	Number	Av. Age	Number	Av. Age	
1	93	6.8	25	6.1	.7
2	44	8.2	26	7.35	.85
3	66	9.5	14	8.9	.6
4	38	10.8	14	9.4	1.4
5	23	11.3	25	10.2	1.1
6	14	12.7	26	11.7	1.0
7	9	12.8	16	12.9	— .1
8	4	14.5	12	13.6	.9
9	2	14.5	5	13.8	.7
Total	293		163		.7

into special classes but Portsmouth does not have such classes. It may also be that in Portsmouth children are required to be absent from school more than in the city where truancy laws are better enforced. Or finally it may be that the fact that in the city we are comparing Portuguese with other immigrant groups rather than with native-born may account for the difference.

While the Immigration Commission found a large proportion (45.9 per cent) of Portuguese retarded in school, they also found eight other nationalities with a higher percentage of retardation.[2]

To get an idea of the relative time lost from school by Portuguese and non-Portuguese children in each of our communities, we have computed tables 86 and 87, covering the grades where the children are of ages when their help on the farm or in the home might be of use to the family, but when most of them are still under the legal age for fac-

[1] Computed from the original school records.

[2] United States Immigration Commission Report. 61st Congress, 3rd Session. Washington 1911. Vol. II, p. 36.

TABLE 86

ABSENCES FROM SCHOOL—GRADES FIVE, SIX AND SEVEN,[1] McDONOUGH
SCHOOL, FALL RIVER, 1919-20

Grades	Non-Portuguese						Portuguese					
	Pupils		Days Absent		Av. Days		Pupils		Days Absent		Av. Days	
	B	G	B	G	B	G	B	G	B	G	B	G
Five	35	40	603	562	17.2	14.0	36	41	402	525	11.2	12.8
Six	16	27	140	288	8.7	10.7	26	31	221	471	8.5	15.2
Seven	18	13	217	130	12.1	10.0	10	8	102	153	10.2	19.1
Totals	69	80	960	980	13.9	12.2	72	80	725	1149	10.1	14.4

TABLE 87

ABSENCES FROM SCHOOL—GRADES FIVE, SIX AND SEVEN,[1] PORTSMOUTH,
R. I., 1919-20

Grades	Non-Portuguese						Portuguese					
	Pupils		Days Absent		Av. Days		Pupils		Days Absent		Av. Days	
	B	G	B	G	B	G	B	G	B	G	B	G
Five	13	13	138	108	10.6	8.3	12	10	283	211	23.6	21.1
Six	19	9	152	78	8.0	8.7	6	7	110	127	18.3	18.1
Seven	4	12	79	72	19.7	6.0	4	5	91	33	22.7	6.6
Totals	36	34	369	258	10.2	7.6	22	22	484	371	22.0	16.9

tory employment. Table 86 shows that in Fall River Portuguese boys lost, during the school year, slightly less time than the non-Portuguese, while the girls lost practically the same amount of time as the non-Portuguese. This comparison is, as previously noted, between Portuguese children and those of many other nationalities or descents. Since the numbers involved are not large the differences seen are without significance. In Portsmouth, however, we find a greater contrast between the two groups, both girls and boys among the Portuguese losing over twice as many days from their studies as their non-Portuguese schoolmates did. The time lost by non-Portuguese was less than in Fall River while that lost by Portuguese was considerably greater than in the city. There are several possible explanations for these differences. In the first place it is to be expected that

[1] Computed from original school records.

the rural Portuguese should keep their children out of school more than do their city brethren because children can be more useful on the farms than in the city. Secondly, the fact that rural non-Portuguese children lost less time than those in the city is probably due to the fact that the former are chiefly children of native-born parents of Anglo-Saxon stock. In the third place school-attendance laws are probably somewhat better inforced in urban than in rural communities. Finally it is possible that other causes for absence besides employment may have been more numerous in Portsmouth than in Fall River. These other causes would include sickness and the difficulty in getting to school because of weather conditions. Whatever the causes an average loss of 22 days out of the school year by Portuguese boys of the fifth, sixth and seventh grades in Portsmouth is a real handicap. Portuguese children are not regular attendants at Portsmouth schools, and the teachers say that the cause is very often the desire of the fathers to make use of the children's labor on the farm.

Still another measure of the use which the Portuguese make of their educational opportunities is the number of cards which they take out, and of books which they borrow at the public libraries. Table 88 attempts to estimate the extent to which the Portuguese make use of the Fall River Public Library, by considering the proportion of the total number of card holders which are Portuguese. To secure this information the writer classified the card-holders into Portuguese and non-Portuguese using the names as the basis for classification. Our table considers only card-holders 12 years of age and over. Children under 12 use the Juvenile Department of the Library. The list of names now in use dates from 1911 when all card-holders were re-registered as fast as they came to the library. The number given in the table under 1911 includes, therefore, both re-registra-

TABLE 88

FALL RIVER PUBLIC LIBRARY,[1] NUMBER AND PROPORTION OF PORTUGUESE AND
NON-PORTUGUESE ADULT CARD-HOLDERS AND OF NAMES ADDED
FROM 1912 TO AUGUST 3, 1920

Names	Portuguese	Per cent	Non-Portuguese	Per cent	Total
On books 1911	59	.9	6651	99.1	6710
Added 1912	14	.6	2262	99.4	2276
" 1913	16	.9	1727	99.1	1743
" 1914	50	2.5	1953	97.5	2003
" 1915	55	3.1	1695	96.9	1750
" 1916	30	2.4	1477	97.6	1513
" 1917	53	3.7	1372	96.3	1425
" 1918	46	4.3	1031	95.7	1077
" 1919	76	5.4	1335	94.6	1411
" to Aug. 3, 1920..	48	7.1	624	92.9	672
Totals	453	2.2	20127	97.8	20580

tions and new registrations for that year. The numbers
for succeeding years are presumably chiefly of those applying for the use of the library for the first time, although
doubtless old borrowers continued to come for re-registra-
tion after 1911. Our data is, of course, subject to the possible error caused by misclassification of Portuguese, due to
the fact that they had anglicized their names. The library
attendant who registers most of the applicants expressed the
opinion, however, that very few of the Portuguese who use
the library had adopted English names. Even where the
family name is changed the Portuguese given name is
usually retained. The true number of Portuguese card-
holders may, therefore, be slightly larger than the recorded
number, but only slightly. It is possible also that very occasionally an Italian name may have been taken for a Portuguese name or vice versa. This too can have occurred
only very rarely and the possibility of error was equally
great in the direction of over-stating as of understating the
number of Portuguese names.

Even making allowance for these possible errors our

[1] Computed from the list of card-holders.

table shows that the Portuguese do not make use of the public library to the same extent that natives and other aliens do. In 1920 453 Portuguese names, constituting but 2.2 per cent of the total number of names, were on the records. In the same year the Portuguese population 15 years of age and over in Fall River made up 16.2 per cent of the total population of that age group.[1] Thus the Portuguese who actually applied for the use of the library made up but about one-seventh of their normal proportion. The optimist may note, however, that even this small proportion was more than double that of 1911, and that there was a fairly regular increase in the proportion of Portuguese names added as time went on. Up to August in 1920, indeed, 48 new Portuguese names had been added which number was 7.1 per cent of the total number of names added during the first seven months of that year.

This situation is partly explained by the inability of many adult Portuguese to speak English. The library possesses some books in the Portuguese language and library attendants say that borrowings by adult Portuguese are largely confined to these books. In 1920 99 books written in Portuguese were given out. A second explanation is the high degree of illiteracy among the Portuguese already noted. Other possible factors are the meager education which even the Portuguese educated in American schools received; the fact that the Portuguese very often live in sections of the city at some distance from the library; that they are poor and feel out of place in the library; and, some would add, that they are less intelligent than the majority of the population of the city.

The list of children taking books from the Juvenile Department of the Fall River Library does not give the data

---

[1] Computed from table 43, *supra,* p. 199.

on which the names were listed; consequently no table comparable with the table for adults can be constructed. Of a total of 1264 names listed July 31, 1920, 77 were clearly Portuguese. In other words about 7 per cent of all children who use the library are Portuguese, whereas the Portuguese children 5 to 14 years of age make up 21.7 per cent of all children of that age group. Portuguese children, then, the majority of whom are able to speak English, make about a third the use of the library which they normally should make. We do not know whether the use of the library by the Portuguese children is increasing or not.

Portsmouth has a very small library open two days in the week. In the summer of 1920 there were at this library a total of 425 active cards. Of these 347 were taken out under non-Portuguese names and 78 under Portuguese names. The Portuguese using the library were, however, almost all children. Only 31 of these 78 Portuguese children had actually borrowed books during the first half of the year 1920, but these 31 had averaged to take 15.6 books each during the period. As there were in Portsmouth, according to our study, 482 Portuguese children between the ages of five and nineteen, it does not appear that the use of the library had become habitual with them. The Portuguese population five years of age and over made up in 1920 42.0 per cent of the total population of that age group. Portuguese card-holders made up but 18.4 per cent of total card-holders, or less than half their normal proportion. This showing is, however, considerably better than that in the city.

The Portuguese seem to be making about as much use of the opportunities afforded for evening school instruction in the city schools as do others of foreign descent. The Report of the Public Schools of Fall River for 1920 shows the following numbers of voluntary pupils in the evening schools according to language groups: Portuguese 128, French 135, Italian 6, Syrians 5, Hebrews 2, and one each of Polish, Welsh and Belgians;[1] while among "illiterate minors" in the evening schools the Portuguese made up no less than 268 out of a total of 346 pupils. An examination of about half the enrollment cards for the evening classes of the Bradford Durfee Textile School showed 34 Portuguese out of approximately 600, or only one in eighteen. The day classes of this school which require usually two years of high school preparation attract very few if any Portuguese students. A number of the clubs in which the Fall River Americanization Committee have established classes in English and Citizenship, have been Portuguese organizations and they were considered remarkably successful.

Summarizing our data on the educational status and attainment of the Portuguese in our two communities we may say: (1) that the Portuguese adults have a very high degree of illiteracy which is by no means eliminated by night schools; (2) that Portuguese children rarely remain in school after the legal age for employment has been reached; (3) that Portuguese children attain an academic standing several points below that of non-Portuguese with but few exceptions; (4) that they are somewhat retarded in school as compared with other children; (5) that they lose more time from school especially in Portsmouth than do non-Portuguese children; (6) that minors are conspicuous in voluntary evening classes and classes for illiterates; but (7) that relatively few Portuguese take advantage of the opportunity offered by the State Textile School for more specialized training, and extremely few enter High School. (8) There is some evidence, however, that as time goes on the Portuguese are slowly improving their educational status

---

[1] *Op. cit.*, p. 59-60.

in the schools, and (9) their use of the advantages of the public library. These conditions, however, are to be considered as characteristic of Fall River and Portsmouth and not necessarily of all Portuguese communities. Indeed it is only fair to add that a superficial investigation of some of these conditions in New Bedford disclosed at least one important contrast. The Principal of the High School estimated that between ten and fifteen per cent of all pupils in his school were Portuguese, and added " some of the best are Portuguese." Such apparent contrasts as this and that noted elsewhere [1] with reference to the low infant mortality of Portuguese in Provincetown, emphasize the necessity of confining our own conclusions to the particular types of Portuguese and the particular localities which we have studied.

The Criminal Record of the Portuguese

There are few aspects of the life of immigrants in America more difficult to appraise than their criminality and morality. Among the more important difficulties which one meets in such an attempt are the following:

1. Standards of morality and of criminality differ from place to place.

2. Standards of morality differ greatly among native American communities and those made up of one or more foreign nationalities. This difficulty does not preclude comparisons of criminal acts committed by different nationalities so long as the same standard is used for all groups; but it does prevent the student from measuring the criminal intent of a nationality by its criminal record.

3. Immigrants are frequently ignorant of the law. Such ignorance while no defense at law, should be taken into consideration by the sociologist.

[1] *Cf. supra*, p. 156.

4. Comparisons between the criminality of different nationalities must often be made without considering the varying age distribution of the groups compared.

5. Particular conditions difficult to ascertain may increase the arrests of a particular nationality in a given period.

6. Prejudice against a nationality or against the foreign-born in general may result in an abnormal number of arrests or convictions of a particular group.

7. On the other hand policemen and judges sometimes make allowances for differing standards of morality among immigrant groups, and fail to arrest or convict for minor offenses so long as those offenses are confined to immigrant localities.

The present writer does not pretend to have avoided all these difficulties. The first has been met by considering only our two communities and by treating them separately. The second remains an inevitable difficulty and prevents us from doing more than compare criminal records. We cannot evaluate the criminal intent of the Portuguese. The third difficulty also remains but is more important in vitiating the record of arrests for violation of minor city ordinances than that of arrests for major crimes. The fourth we can fortunately overcome by using our special data on the age distribution of the Portuguese as compared with that of the general population. The fifth difficulty did not exist at the time of our study in the opinion, at least, of the Chief of Police of Fall River, except that the year 1919 witnessed a strike of doffers who are largely Portuguese. Fortunately arrests growing out of this strike are easily identified. As to the sixth difficulty we can only say that no such prejudice against the Portuguese was evident at the time the study was made. The Chief of Police informed the writer that the Portuguese were neither more nor less criminally inclined than other citizens. The opinions of other citizens so far as gathered seemed so varied as to leave one with the impression that perhaps the Chief was right. The seventh difficulty is perhaps the most serious of all, especially in the measurement of sex morality. Social workers among the Portuguese of New Bedford, for example, informed the writer that the standards of sex morality among many of the Portuguese were very low. When it was replied that criminal records in Fall River did not bear out this claim, they answered that most offenses of this nature were unknown to the general community and that arrests for them were infrequent. For example it was reported that illegitimate births were often reported as legitimate et cetera. Serious as is this difficulty it does not appear that it affects the validity of the record of arrests as a measure of criminality when other than minor sex offenses are considered. Neither should too great weight be attached to the opinions of the social workers quoted above. Others expressed opposite opinions.

The following data, then, are to be considered with due caution. Especially is it to be noted that they are not presented as a measure of the criminal intent of the Portuguese. They merely measure the extent to which Portuguese as compared with non-Portuguese are arrested in our communities. Very many of those arrested were discharged or received suspended sentence, but on the whole a comparison between arrests rather than between convictions seems preferable. Table 89 gives for each offense the total number of arrests, the number and per cent of Portuguese arrests, and the average age of Portuguese so arrested. The data are for Fall River in the year 1919.

TABLE 89

PORTUGUESE ARRESTS IN FALL RIVER, 1919, BY NATURE OF ACCUSATION

Accused of	Total Arrests	Port. Arrests	% Port.
Drunkenness	827	43	5.2
Assault and Battery	169	45	26.6
Neglect of family	179	35	19.5
Larceny	155	28	18.1
Breaking Lord's Day Law	111	27	24.3
Auto Law	137	16	11.7
Receiving Stolen Property	37	14	37.8
Disturbing Peace	70	14	20.0
Bastardy	28	10	35.7
Intimidation (Labor Law)	24	8	33.3
Breaking and Entering and Larceny	110	7	6.4
Malicious Mischief	17	7	41.2
Adultery	17	6	35.3
Stubbornness	18	5	27.7
Fornication	23	5	21.7
Assault with weapon	16	5	31.3
Contempt of court	33	5	15.2
Liquor Law	17	8	47.1
City Ordinance	33	4	12.1
Lewd and Lacivious Cohabitation	15	4	26.7
Gaming	23	4	17.4
Violation Weights and Measures Law	11	4	36.3
Food Law	21	3	14.3
Milk Bottle Law	6	3	50.0
Practicing Medicine Unlawfully	5	3	60.0
Robbery	2	2	100.0
Lewdness	11	2	18.2
Dangerous weapon	13	2	15.4
Unlicensed dog	3	2	66.7
Insane	8	2	25.0
Board of Health	2	2	100.0
Statutory Rape	15	2	13.3
Sodomy	2	2	100.0
Taking auto	7	2	28.6
Bondsman	3	1	33.3
Breaking and entering intent to rob	7	1	14.3
Federal Law	59	1	1.7
Polygamy	1	1	100.0
Assault intent to rob	3	1	33.3

Violating probation	4	1	25.0
Perjury	2	1	50.0
Admitting minor to dance hall	2	1	50.0
Idle and disorderly	8	1	12.5
Surety to keep peace	1	1	100.0
Cruelty to animals	1	1	100.0
Escaped	5	1	20.0
Desertion	1	1	100.0
Incest	1	1	100.0
Sub-totals	2265	347	
Other offenses	203	0	
Totals	2468	347	14.1

Computed from Police Records of the City of Fall River—1919. The classifications in this table were made on the basis of names, and there is therefore the same possibility as in the other tables that the number of Portuguese may be slightly understated. The writer believes, however, that the actual error involved is very small.

A glance at table 43 [2] will show that Portuguese men aged 20-44 made up in 1920 20.2 per cent of all men in Fall River between those ages. As men rather than women and young men rather than children or those past middle age con-

TABLE 90

ARRESTS IN FALL RIVER, 1919, CLASSIFIED ACCORDING TO TYPE OF OFFENSES—PORTUGUESE AND TOTAL ARRESTS

Offenses	Total	Portuguese	% Portuguese oj Total
Against Property			
Serious	15	2	13.3
Minor	339	52	15.3
Against persons (n.o.c.)			
Serious	5	0	00.0
Minor	203	51	25.1
Sex Crimes	157	33	21.0
Violations of City and			
Federal Ordinances	662	113	17.1
Drunkenness	827	43	5.2
Against family	180	35	19.4
Miscellaneous minor	80	18	22.5
	2468	347	14.1

[1] *Cf. supra*, p. 199.

stitute the most criminally inclined element in any community, this figure is the significant one for our purposes. In other words, when we find Portuguese making up more than a fifth of those arrested for any crime or group of crimes, we know that that crime was in 1919 at least somewhat characteristic of the Portuguese. Turning to table 90 we note that when all types of offenses are considered the Portuguese contribute but 14.1 per cent of the arrests, or considerably less than their normal proportion. If, however, arrests for drunkenness are omitted the Portuguese are found in nearly their normal numbers—18.5 per cent. They are underrepresented in the commission of the most serious crimes both against property and against persons, and in that of minor offenses against property. They committed practically their proportion of sex crimes and offenses against the family, and somewhat more than their share of minor offenses against persons, and miscellaneous crimes; and were slightly under-represented in the commission of offenses which violated city or Federal ordinances. In arrests for drunkenness, like many other south Europeans, they are conspicuous by their absence. Since there were but 20 arrests for serious offenses either against persons or against property in 1919, it is perhaps a fair conclusion to say that the Portuguese are, judging from statistics of arrests, slightly less criminal than their numbers would lead us to expect when arrests for drunkenness are disregarded. Their normal record in the commission of sex crimes is due chiefly to the fact that but two were arrested for rape, and their showing is bad with reference to all the other sex offenses.

Some data on arrests in the town of Portsmouth were obtained from the County records in Newport, the Portsmouth arrests being identified by the name of the constables making them. Only 120 arrests were recorded as made in Portsmouth between January 1st, 1916 and September 21st,

1919. Of these only 16 or 13.3 per cent were of persons bearing Portuguese names. Reference to table 41 [1] will show that 158 out of 411 men aged 15-44 in Portsmouth in 1920 were Portuguese. That is to say, the Portuguese had 38.4 per cent of the younger men of the community. So measured the Portuguese record is very good indeed, but in the writer's opinion this comparison is of little value because a very large proportion of the arrests were for speeding in automobiles, and were very often arrests of non-residents passing through Portsmouth en route for Newport or Fall River. The truth is that both Portuguese and non-Portuguese of Portsmouth seldom get into trouble with the authorities. No doubt many crimes for which arrests would be made in the city go unpunished in Portsmouth, but the community is essentially law-abiding. As to the extent of sex immorality among the residents of Portsmouth the writer knows nothing.

Table 91 shows the juvenile arrests recorded in Fall River for the year ending Nov. 30, 1919 with the Portuguese distinguished, and also by sex. We note that children of Portuguese descent contributed 96 out of a total of 493 arrests, or 19.5 per cent. Portuguese boys and girls aged 10-14 made up 19.8 per cent of all boys and 19.5 per cent of all girls of that age group in 1920. Their proportion among children 15-19 was practically the same.[2] We may therefore say that Portuguese children contributed practically their normal proportion of juvenile arrests in 1919. The detailed figures for kinds of offenses are in most cases too few to be of significance.

Whether we consider adult or juvenile arrests, therefore, we get no striking contrasts between the Portuguese and other inhabitants with reference to their criminal record.

[1] *Cf. supra*, p. 197.

[2] *Cf.* table 43, *supra*, p. 199.

TABLE 91

JUVENILE ARRESTS, FALL RIVER, MASS. FOR THE YEAR ENDING, NOV. 30, 1919 [1]

Offenses	Total			Portuguese		
	Male	Female	Total	Male	Female	Total
Dangerous weapon	2		2			
Assault and Battery	5	1	6	2	1	3
Assault—indecent	1		1	1		1
Assault (weapon)	2		2			
Auto law	1		1			
Breaking and attempted entry	4		4			
Breaking, ent. and larceny	164		164	17		17
Breaking, ent., int. larceny	2		2	1		1
Bd. Health	4 [2]		4	4		4
Concealed weapon	1		1			
Carrying revolver	1		1			
City ordinance	17		17	3		3
Night walker		1	1		1	1
Contempt Court	1	1	2			
Defacing building	3		3	3		3
Deserter	1		1			
Dist. Peace	3		3	3		3
Escaped	2		2			
Fornication		2	2			
Rifle to minor	1 [3]		1			
Revolver to minor	1 [3]		1			
Gaming	3		3	3		3
Idle and disorderly		2	2			
Indecent exposure	1		1			
Larceny (attempted)	2		2			
Larceny	95	19	114	18	7	25
Lewd cohabitation	1	1	2			
Lewdness	1	2	3			
Lord's Day	22		22	5		5
Malicious mischief	37		37	12		12
Parole violation	3		3			
Probation violation	12	3	15	1	1	2
Rec. stolen prop.	5		5			
False alarm	1		1			
Runaway	22		22	3		3
Airgun to minor	1 [3]		1			
Stoning train	3		3			
Stubbornness	16	10	26	5	3	8
Trans. reg. bets.	1		1			
Trespass	3		3	2		2
Taking horse	3		3			
Unnatural act	1		1			
Vehicle law	2		2			
Wayward child		1	1			
Totals	450	43	493	83	13	96

[1] Computed from Police Records, Fall River, Mass.

[2] Recorded as " 3 " in report but presumably error.

[3] As these are offenses against minors rather than by minors they have been deducted in figuring percentages.

Such contrasts as we note are rather due to the inconspicuousness of the Portuguese in the commission of one or two offenses, notably drunkenness among adults. Many informants have commented, however, upon the amount of " moonshine " which is manufactured and sold by the Portuguese especially in the rural districts. No facts need be presented, however, to prove that they are not monopolizing that industry. In certain sections of Fall River, Portuguese homes may almost be identified by the grape vines covering often the entire available space in the yard. Mill owners also complain that the Portuguese habitually steal cloth from the mills, frequently winding it around their bodies to escape detection. Some of these mill men maintain that such thefts need not necessarily appear in the police records for, except for occasional clean-ups, it has been found impossible to prevent this petty theft. On the other hand other informants have especially stressed honesty and reliability as traits of the Portuguese especially in Portsmouth. It would, of course, be very desirable if our data on arrests covered a longer period of time. The Secretary of the Society for the Prevention of Cruelty to Children in Fall River, stated to the writer that Portuguese cases make up more than their proportionate share of those which come to his attention, but added, that he felt that the explanation was usually ignorance rather than deliberate neglect upon the part of parents. Sexual immorality he felt sure was prevalent among these people, but almost invariably the parties were married before the birth of a child. This and similar evidence from other informants leads one to suspect that while police records may give a somewhat too favorable picture of Portuguese morality, their misdeeds are those of an ignorant people with relatively low standards rather than the serious offenses characteristic of some other nationalities.

Achievement in Miscellaneous Fields

Many other important social characteristics and activities should be treated to make up anything like a complete picture of Portuguese achievement or failure to achieve. Most of them do not lend themselves, however, to the use of the statistical method we have employed thus far in this study. Moreover, to know the Portuguese character and the more intimate aspects of his life which are not a matter of record, one should speak his language, should live in his home, and attend his church services, club meetings and social and recreational gatherings. No attempt has been made to mingle thus intimately with the Portuguese and we must frankly admit the lack of such acquaintance. Such insight as has been gathered into these aspects of Portuguese life in Fall River and Portsmouth, has come through interviews with Portuguese leaders—lawyers, farmers, physicians, priests et cetera.

The Portuguese are reported as not taking great interest in politics. In Fall River there are probably less than a thousand registered voters of Portuguese descent and the Portuguese do not hasten to secure citizenship. When naturalized they are said to divide their allegiance between the different political parties somewhat impartially. A study of this matter made in Rhode Island in 1907, showed among 2508 foreign-born Portuguese men over 21 years of age in the state, 473 who were legal voters, 85 non-voters and 1950 aliens. The corresponding figures for Portsmouth were 33 voters, 3 non-voters and 239 aliens.[1] Such figures without information as to the length of time that the aliens have been in this country are not of great significance, however.

The Immigration Commission studying 564 foreign-born male Portuguese employees, found only 5.5 per cent who had

[1] Rhode Island Bureau of Industrial Statistics, *op. cit.*, pp. 419 and 425.

either been naturalized or taken out their first papers. This was the smallest proportion found among any of the " new immigration."[1]

Neither have the Portuguese organized co-operative societies as have some other immigrant groups. They have innumerable benefit societies, social clubs and athletic organizations, however. The benefit societies have members in the rural districts as well as in the city and usually pay a $500 death and burial benefit and perhaps seven dollars a week during illness. These benefit societies go far to relieve the community of the care of Portuguese poor. Some of these organizations are large and like the St. Michael's Portuguese Benefit Society and the Azoreana, own buildings of their own. The latter organization has more than two thousand members. Other well-known organizations are St. Joseph's Portuguese Benefit Society, the Portuguese Fraternity of the United States of America, the Portuguese Catholic Society of Our Lady of Lourdes, the St. Pedro Portuguese Society, the St. Isabel Society, and the St. Catherine Ladies Society. A large number of social clubs with or without benefit features also exist, whose chief interests are said to be card playing, boxing and wrestling. These societies, together with the social activities centering in the churches, are the distinctively Portuguese recreational centers.

In addition to these recreational activities of their own the Portuguese belong to a few organizations where they come into contact with other nationalities and with native-born. Among these should be mentioned the labor unions where the Portuguese are especially strong in the doffers union, and have developed a leader of their own who has gained a reputation for leadership even outside of Fall River.

[1] United States Immigration Commission Report. 61st Congress, 3rd Session. Washington 1911. Vol. I, p. 484.

Approximately a fifth of the membership of the Fall River Boys Club, which includes adults as well as boys under 14, are Portuguese. Adults pay a fee of $6 a year for the use of the varied facilities of this club and boys 10 cents a month. A large proportion of the adult Portuguese members of the Boys Club are given memberships free of charge, however, by the American Printing Company. Outside of these non-paying members, the Secretary of the Club reports that the Portuguese come chiefly for boxing and wrestling with the object of becoming professionals in these sports. Indeed this tendency toward professionalism is said to be one of the regrettable features of much of the recreational activities in the city. Of the 600 members of the Boy Scouts very few are Portuguese, although those who have joined are reported to be good scouts. The fact that many of the Troops have their headquarters in Protestant churches has hindered the use of this organization by the Portuguese.

The Church also plays a large part in the lives of this people. In Portsmouth one Catholic Church with a Portuguese priest serves all the Catholics of the town. In Fall River there was but one Portuguese parish nineteen years ago. To-day there are six with fourteen priests and 21,000 communicants. Practically all church-going Portuguese in these communities are Roman Catholics but there are a very few Protestants. Priests report that it is sometimes hard to hold the Portuguese who come to this country, especially those who came while the church in Portugal was still state-supported. It has taken time to educate them to make their churches here self-supporting. It is also said that the Portuguese from the mainland who have come in considerable numbers recently, and who have been through the revolution with its anti-church emphasis, are frequently irreligious and do not support the church in this country. Most of the Portuguese from the Azores, however, are deeply devoted to their church which as we have seen is so large a factor in their social as well as their religious life in the islands. Processions are still held through the streets of Fall River but their importance to the people has waned somewhat and at least one priest uses his influence to minimize the superstitious ritual amounting almost to image worship which is attached to such occasions. His own parish, however, occasionally celebrates Saints' days with such processions which some of the people demand. While some of the priests have recently come to this country and do not even speak English others are educated men of real culture who seem honestly to seek to aid their people in adapting themselves to their new environment.

It can hardly be unfair to the Portuguese of these communities to close our account of their achievements and their failures with a few examples of their superstitions. It is not unfair because these superstitions, though admittedy not characteristic of the entire group, are nevertheless evidence of that fundamental characteristic of the large majority —ignorance—which perhaps more than any other cause explains their characteristic problems and shortcomings. Admitting many other factors which play upon their lives we may say that Portuguese children die because of ignorance; Portuguese adults are exploited because of ignorance; their women continue their lives of toil and endless child-bearing because of ignorance; their children are backward in school through ignorance; and very many of the other tragedies of their lives are the product of ignorance. Superstitions are evidences of ignorance, causes of disaster and hindrances preventing an escape from ignorance.

The following examples will show that the Portuguese of Fall River believe in magic and the evil eye and employ Witch Doctors to effect cures quite after the fashion of many primitive peoples. Many of these superstitions are by no means confined to the Portuguese but are shared by Italians and other immigrant peoples of the city. The examples are given just as they were collected for the writer through the help of a group of women who come into intimate contact with the Portuguese in their homes.

Witch Doctors may be employed either in case of illness, distress, poverty, bad luck or love affairs. The child born after the death of the father comes to have the greatest power. To gain the greatest benefit from the treatment absolute obedience to directions must be given. Lack of faith may interfere with the result.

The witch is able either personally or through pigs or donkeys to cast a bad influence over the child in the cradle. To prevent this it is well to place over the covers an old coat turned inside-out—sleeves and all—especially when the child is sleeping. Allowing the baby to be placed on the back of a donkey is especially harmful, this or the kissing of a mirror may prevent him from ever learning to talk.

The pregnant woman must never step on or over a rope or the unborn child may be strangled with the cord about its neck.

Anyone, man or woman, may possess the " evil eye ", but the one born on the fifteenth of the month is to be most carefully avoided. The person may not always know that she is ' so gifted ' and may exert the bad influence unconsciously. If she knows it and ' if sorry ' she may lessen the power of ' electricity which flies from the eye ', by wearing colored glasses. The evil influence may be prompted by love, hate, envy or the pure love of mischief. The careful mother will protect the child in every way possible. There again the old coat inside-out over the crib while the baby is sleeping is a great help. A small coral or ivory hand with index finger extended will direct the evil eye away. This may be tied to a ribbon about the child's neck or anywhere on the body, over or under the clothing or even on the cap. With this may be worn ' the horn of plenty ' and a gold key to bring wealth and prosperity.

Patients may treat their own wounds if where they may be

seen, but not if anywhere on the body that necessitates the use of a mirror, as the reflection from the mirror poisons the wound.

In case of illness the parents may care for the child, but the child may not care for the parents. This is equally true of hair-cutting or shaving. Even if the child is an expert barber he may not cut the hair of or shave his father.

Parents must not play games with their own children which allow the child to strike the parents—such as games of tag. This will bring bad luck to both parents and children.

Instead of seeking the advice of a physician for a baby with malnutrition or other ailments not understood, many of the mothers will resort to 'the pumpkin treatment'. A female pumpkin must be secured which is to be boiled with a pound of sugar. With this concoction the baby is to be bathed on three successive days, always rubbing from down up. After the third application the remains of the pumpkin must be turned into a napkin and taken by the mother to the salt water. With her back to the water the napkin must be thrown into the water and she must walk away without once turning to look back. Nor is the child ever to be taken past the spot where she stood.

One mother consulted a 'Witch Doctor' in order to cure the attachment between her son and a young woman in the neighborhood. She was told to go to a certain place and get a certain amount of earth and in the middle of the night, when the lady was asleep, to throw this earth at the door of the house. With each handful so thrown she was to say 'You shall not marry my son; you shall not marry my son; you shall not marry my son.' In this particular case the charm did not work—the marriage took place—but the faith in the 'Witch Doctor' was in no way diminished.

With these examples of Portuguese superstitions we shall close our discussion of the Portuguese of Fall River and Portsmouth, conscious that many aspects of their lives have been inadequately treated. We have already made the point that the Portuguese problem varies among each of the various types of Portuguese. We must also stress the obvious fact that within each of these types there are great individual differences. The Portuguese are dirty but hundreds of homes are spotlessly clean. They are ignorant but Angela Mello is at the head of her class. They are industrious but the second generation is often lazy. They are superstitious but it was a Portuguese physician who most despised their superstitions. They have too large families but not universally. The St. Michael Portuguese seem to be the lowest grade, but our most attractive farm photograph is the home of an illiterate farmer from that island. Whatever conclusions we shall draw in the concluding chapter, therefore, must be understood as applying only to the majority of one type of Portuguese immigrants living under specified conditions in two specified communities in New England.

CHAPTER VII

LIMITATIONS AND CONCLUSONS

1. Perhaps the most important outcome of our study of the Portuguese is at once a conclusion in itself, and a limitation upon most of the other conclusions which we shall draw. For we have seen that the Portuguese are not a homogeneous group. By this we do not mean simply that the Bravas are a distinct type, nor merely that the Portuguese from the mainland are to be distinguished from those from the Azores and Madeira. In addition we have found that among the islanders themselves at least two types are to be found—the Fayalese and the Portuguese from St. Michael's. We have also found that this difference in type is associated with social differences of some importance. We have admitted that the evidence of the existence of these types is in single instances insufficient to be convincing; but the cumulative effect of evidence from many sources constitutes a very strong presumption that the differences are real. Thus we have noted that Flemings settled in Fayal in considerable numbers but not, so far as we know, in St. Michael's; that Negroes possibly were brought in larger numbers to St. Michael's than to Fayal; that travellers in the islands have contrasted the relative prosperity of parts of Fayal with the backwardness of some of the other islands including St. Michael's; that some of these travellers noted the presence of the Teutonic type in Fayal though some maintained that it has disappeared; that Portuguese vital statistics show a higher birth and a higher death rate for

the Ponta Delgada District (St. Michael's and St. Mary's) than for the Horta District (including Fayal); that the Horta District is also notable for its relatively small percentage of illiterates; that ships' manifests show much larger percentages of blue eyes and light hair among emigrants from Horta than among those from the other island districts; that the early immigrants to parts of New England were chiefly from Fayal and that these Fayalese are said to have been peculiarly healthy with a low death rate, while the St. Michaelese of to-day are characterized by an abnormally high rate. And finally we have seen that the Fayalese, though few in numbers in our communities, have a higher standard of living than their brethren from St. Michael's. This latter statement is, however, subject to the qualification that the Fayalese have been in this country longer than the St. Michaelese.

The discovery of the heterogeneity of the Portuguese limits somewhat the value of our study. It means that our data on the Portuguese in general and on the Azoreans relate to a somewhat varied group. It also limits somewhat the value of our community studies, though not seriously, for we have evidence that Fall River has attracted predominantly the Portuguese from St. Michael's, and we know just how large a proportion of the Portuguese of Portsmouth came from that island. For all practical purposes we may call our community studies, studies of the St. Michael Portuguese. It must be borne in mind, then, that the following conclusions refer to the St. Michael Portuguese only.

The fact that the Portuguese are made up of a number of types also makes the more necessary, studies to supplement this one. Before we can characterize the Portuguese immigrants as a whole we need at least the following studies: (1) of communities of mainland Portuguese; (2) of communities of Bravas; (3) of communities where the Fayalese predominate; (4) of communities of Portuguese fishermen like Provincetown, Massachusetts; (5) of communities of Portuguese in California; (6) of communities in the Azores and on the mainland with special attention to homes where members of the families are in America; (7) a study of the anthropology of the Portuguese of the Islands. When such studies are made we may be able to draw somewhat more general conclusions as to the effect of the immigration of the Portuguese upon America.

Our study of the St. Michael Portuguese of Fall River and Portsmouth is also confessedly incomplete. Particularly it lacks an intimate picture of the personal and social life of the Portuguese such as can only be secured by living with them, speaking their language, visiting their churches and clubs, and so entering into their real life. In addition it is unfortunate that we do not have a psychological study of the Portuguese in our communities based upon the intelligence tests. Such a study would be of value despite the grave doubt whether the army intelligence tests really measured the innate intelligence of the immigrants or indeed of the soldiers in general.[1]

2. Returning to our tentative conclusions we note secondly that the Azorean Portuguese have received considerable infusion of negroid blood at four different periods in their history. We cannot demonstrate the social importance of this

---

[1] *Cf.* especially *Memoirs of the National Academy of Science* (Washington, 1921), pp. 701-4, where the scores made by foreign-born soldiers are correlated with their length of residence in the United States. A difference of the equivalent of something over two years mental age was found between men who had been in this country five years or less and those who had been here over twenty years. Until evidence is presented showing other causes for this contrast, it is legitimate to ask whether it is not due to the fact that the tests were measuring an acquired adaptation to the conditions of the tests rather than simply innate intelligence.

infusion. We have seen that there is some reason to doubt that it accounts for the excessive infant mortality of the Portuguese of Fall River and elsewhere.

3. Our study has emphasized the ignorance and illiteracy of the Portuguese. Whether their misfortunes are traceable to low innate intelligence or not, many of them are traceable in large part to ignorance. High infant mortality, lack of interest and meager attainment in education, low wages and economic exploitation, superstition and fatalism, cheap amusements, and unrestrained fecundity—these are some of the Portugues characteristics attributable largely to the fundamental factor of ignorance.

4. The Portuguese have a shockingly high birth rate. Their families increase too rapidly and the improper spacing of pregnancies spells early death for children and narrow lives for mothers. Indeed the normal state of young married Portuguese women is well-nigh constant child-bearing. This seems to be both an index and a cause of ignorance and poverty. It is associated with the high infant mortality and low standard of living of these people. The birth rate declines, however, in the second generation.

5. The Portuguese also have an abnormally high death rate especially but not solely in the years of infancy and early childhood. While economic factors undoubtedly tend to increase this evil we have reason to conclude that ignorance, superstition and improper spacing of pregnancies are the fundamental causes.

6. The Portuguese are typically unskilled laborers who begin life on American farms on a very low plane and receive low wages in the mills. At the cost of the health and happiness of the entire family, however, they save money and make considerable economic progress as measured by ownership of property. Eventually their material standard of living rises as they remain longer under American in-

fluence. Its rise is seen to be correlated with type of occupation, and with a relatively small size of the family, as well as with length of residence here. As yet the Portuguese have not often attained the professions, and their occupations are still, despite some progress, those of unskilled or semi-skilled laborers.

7. Portuguese children leave school almost invariably at the earliest possible moment and almost never attend high school. They make lower grades than their associates both in Portsmouth and Fall River, are somewhat retarded, and lose considerable time from school especially in Portsmouth. In all these respects they compare unfavorably with the non-Portuguese. They also make relatively little use of the public library though this use is increasing. Nevertheless, in the writer's opinion, these evidences of educational backwardness are hardly greater than would be expected of children coming from homes more often illiterate than not, where education is no part of the family mores, and where more income now is desired and sometimes greatly needed. Our data therefore leave unanswered the fundamental question whether the Portuguese are naturally inferior or whether their poor showing is chiefly due to tradition and lack of incentive and opportunity.

8. The Portuguese are also found to marry somewhat earlier than do non-Portuguese, but child marriage is rare. Employment of mothers in the mills is not unusual and is almost universal on the farms.

9. In all the above respects the contrasts between the urban and the rural Portuguese are not great. The typical home in the country is on a lower plane than that in the city, but exceptionally attractive homes are more numerous in the country, where also are found the most wretched hovels. On the whole life in Portsmouth is perhaps more beneficial to the Portuguese than life in Fall River. They find there

a simple rural environment to which it is relatively easy for them to adapt themselves. In that environment they largely control their own destinies, and they have met with reasonable material success. But the same high infant mortality, the same reckless fecundity, the same backwardness in cultural advancement, characterizes them in Portsmouth as in Fall River. In the city they have the handicap of a more complex environment, and the cotton mill probably utilizes less of their untrained capacities than does the more varied work on the farm. On the other hand they have in the city the advantage of greater cultural opportunity, and of the assistance of a good many fairly well organized social agencies. Their greatest ills, being largely attributable to ignorance, follow them to either community.

10. There seems no doubt that for the great majority of Portuguese, immigration to New England has meant an improved status. Granting that they are poverty-stricken here, that they live far below our standards of comfort and decency, that women often work outside the home and that children leave school as soon as the law allows, that homes are unattractive and wages low; nevertheless their lot is far better than in the homeland, except perhaps in its picturesqueness. America gives the Portuguese a small wage but a higher one, a poor house but a better one, a meager sixth grade education but more than they know enough to want, and it is universal and compulsory.

11. What does the coming of the Portuguese mean to Fall River and Portsmouth? Immediately it means industrious labor on the farms, and perhaps less industrious labor in the mills. But it also means all the evils of an ignorant population. The presence of these people undoubtedly handicaps the public schools, complicates the work of public health organizations, increases the births where they should be fewest, and the death rates at all ages but especially of

little children. It also makes possible economic and political exploitation whether by unscrupulous natives or by their own leaders. Indeed the presence of the Portuguese goes far to account for the poor record of our two communities in official statistics and for the not altogether enviable reputation which they may have among sociologists. If Fall River could dispense with the Portuguese to-morrow she would probably benefit.

12. But the Portuguese are a permanent element in our two communities. Moreover if they should leave, a substitute labor supply would have to be found. Whether the securing of this labor supply would compel the payment of higher wages than are now offered in the mills the writer does not know. There are, of course, plenty of cotton-mill communities without Portuguese. Portsmouth would probably miss the Portuguese more than Fall River, for there are few enough men to-day willing to struggle with New England farmland at its best. As a people willing to work abandoned farms and able to make a living from them the Portuguese seem to be a real asset. If they could be induced to leave the city for the farms in large numbers, and if greater efforts could be made to aid them—to promote their assimilation and educational progress—they would constitute productive and useful rural citizens. There seems to be evidence that they have proven their worth on Cape Cod. But the movement from city to farm is not marked. They are to-day a permanent and a backward element in our city (Fall River) population.

13. The above paragraphs do not rate the Portuguese high. But it must be noted that they speak of the Portuguese as they are to-day. If the backwardness of the Portuguese proves to be the result, not of inborn racial inferiority, but of social handicaps, the future may value them more highly even in Fall River. We have found a little

reason to hope that there will be improvement, for we have already witnessed some improvement. The Portuguese have demonstrated their ability to save out of their meager incomes; their standard of living has been seen to rise with longer residence in the communities; the birth and infant mortality rates fall in the second generation; a somewhat larger proportion of children attend high school to-day than did six years ago, and a somewhat greater use is made of the Public Library. Moreover the Portuguese of our two communities are recent immigrants and have perhaps scarcely had time to show what the long-time effects of their new environment and their new opportunities will be. We have had hints also that they have done somewhat better in other communities. They have advanced further in New Bedford schools than in those of Fall River, and we know that for a number of years the Portuguese infant mortality rates in Provincetown were not high. Such facts suggest that we must allow more time to elapse before drawing final conclusions, for New Bedford and Provincetown are older settlements than Portsmouth and Fall River. On the other hand contrasts between Fall River and New Bedford or Provincetown may be due to the presence of different types of Portuguese. We need more light.

We have tried to present some facts as to the effect of the coming of the St. Michael Portuguese upon Portsmouth and Fall River; and as to the effect of these communities upon them. The facts are admittedly inconclusive. They will therefore leave the pessimist discouraged as to the future of these communities and these people. They will similarly give the optimist hope that much may be done for and by the Portuguese when their handicaps shall have been removed and when they shall be truly of America as well as in America.

BIBLIOGRAPHY

1. American Child Hygiene Association. Statistical Report of Infant Mortality for 1920, in 519 Cities of the United States. Baltimore, Md. 1921.
2. Aronovici, Carol. Housing Conditions in Fall River. Fall River. (Undated).
3. Ashby, Hugh T. Infant Mortality. Cambridge, England, 1915.
4. Ashe, Thomas. History of the Azores.
5. Baker, C. Alice. A summer in the Azores. Boston, 1882.
6. Beazley, C. Raymond. Prince Henry of Portugal and His Political, Commercial and Colonizing Work. American Historical Review, Jan. 1912, Vol. XVII, pp. 252-267.
7. Bell, Aubrey F. E. The Future of Portugal. Contemporary Review, April, 1919, Vol. CXV. pp. 568-571.
8. Bell, Aubrey F. E. In Portugal. London, 1912.
9. Bennett, Arnold. Some Impressions of Portugal. Harpers Magazine, Jan. 1922. Vol. XCIV, pp. 201-215.
10. Biddle, A. J. Drexel. The Land of the Wine. 2 vols. London, 1901.
11. Biddle, A. J. Drexel. The Madeira Islands. Philadelphia, 1896.
12. Bolt, Richard Arthur. Fundamental Factors in Infant Mortality. Annals of the American Academy of Political and Social Science, Nov. 1921. pp. 9-16.
13. Borden, Alanson et al. Our Country and Its People. Boston, 1899.
14. Boyd, Captain. A Description of the Azores or Western Islands. London, 1834.
15. Brassey, Lady Anne. (Allnutt.) In the Trades, Tropics and the Roaring Forties. New York, 1885.
16. Brewster, William T. A Corner of Old Europe. Harper's Magazine, July, 1918, Vol. CXXXVII. pp. 209-219.
17. Bryce, James. South America. New York, 1913.
18. Callender, E. B. Islands of the Hawks. Travel, Nov. 1911. Vol. XVIII. pp. 24-27; 50-52.
19. Caswell, L. E. The Portuguese in Boston. The North End Mission Magazine July, 1873, Vol. II, pp. 57-73.
20. Clare, Constance Leigh. A Letter From a Portuguese Country House. Living Age, Vol. CCLV, pp. 590-599. December 7, 1907.

21. Clare, Constance, Leigh. Another Letter from a Portuguese Country House. Living Age, Vol. CCLXII, pp. 414-423.
22. Corrêa, A. A. Mendes. Origins of the Portuguese. American Journal of Physical Anthropology, Vol. II, pp. 117-145.
23. Crawfurd, Oswald. The Greatness of Little Portugal. National Geographic Magazine, Vol. XXI, pp. 867-883. Oct. 1910.
24. Crawfurd, Oswald. Portugal. Living Age, Vol. CCLVI, pp. 515-530. Feb. 29, 1908.
25. Crawfurd, Oswald. Portugal Old and New. London, 1880.
26. Cunha, V. de Braganca. Eight Centuries of Portuguese Monarchy. New York, 1911.
27. Davenport, Charles B. Comparative Social Traits of Various Races. School and Society. Vol. XIV, pp. 344-348.
28. Davis, William H. Infant Mortality in the Registration Area for Births. American Journal of Public Health. April 1920, Vol. X, pp. 338-341.
29. Denis, Pierre. Brazil. London, 1911.
30. Drachsler, Julius. Intermarriage in New York City. Columbia Studies in History, Economics and Public Law. Vol. XCIV, No. 2, New York, 1921.
31. Dublin, Louis I. Infant Mortality in Fall River, Mass. Publications of the American Statistical Association, New Series, Vol. XIV, pp. 505-520.
32. Dublin, Louis I. Mortality Statistics of Insured Wage-earners and Their Families. Metropolitan Life Insurance Company. New York, 1918.
33. Dwight, Helen C. First Aid to Thirty Thousand Children. Child Labor Bulletin, Feb. 1917, Vol. V, pp. 213-215.
34. Ellis, A. B. West African Islands. London, 1885.
35. Ellis, Leonard Bolles. History of New Bedford. Syracuse, 1892.
36. Encyclopedia Americana. Article on Azores.
37. Encyclopedia Britannica. Article on Azores.
38. Evans, Morris. Black and White in South East Africa. London, 1911.
39. Eye-witness. Narration of the Political Changes and Events Which Have Taken Place Recently in the Island of Terceira. London, 1829.
40. Fall River, Mass. Board of Health. Annual Reports for 1919, 1920, and 1921.
41. Fall River, Mass. Board of Police. Annual Report for Year Ending Nov. 30, 1919. Boston, 1920.
42. Fall River, Mass. District Nursing Association. Annual Reports for the Years Ending March 31, 1919, 1920, and 1921.

42 *a*. Fall River, Mass. Public Library. Report of the Trustees for the Year Ending Feb. 28, 1920.

43. Fall River, Mass. Public Schools. Fifty-fourth and Fifty-fifth Annual Reports for the years 1919 and 1920.

44. Fall River, Mass. Women's Club, Civic Department. Report on Infant Mortality. Fall River, 1915.

45. Fenner, Henry N. History of Fall River. New York, 1906.

46. Finch, Earl. The Effects of Racial Miscegenation. In Universal Races Congress, 1911. London, 1911.

47. Forsyth, David F. Children in Health and Disease. Philadelphia, 1909.

48. Furlong, Charles Wellington. Two Mid-Atlantic Isles. Harper's Magazine, Nov. 1916, Vol. CXXXIII, pp. 801-813.

49. Furlong, Charles Wellington. With Columbus in the African Isles. Harper's Magazine, Nov. 1917, Vol. CXXXV, pp. 745-757.

50. Furlong, Charles Wellington. On the Crest of the Lost Atlantic. Harper's Magazine, Feb. 1917, Vol. CXXXIV, pp. 331-342.

51. Great Britain, Foreign Office, Historical Section. Handbook 116. Azores and Madeira. London, 1920.

52. Grosvenor, Edwin A. The Races of Europe. National Geographic Magazine, Dec. 1918. Vol. XXXIV, pp. 441-536.

53. Guilfoy, William H. The Influence of Nationality upon the Mortality of a Community. New York City, Department of Health. Monograph Series, no. 18, Nov. 1917.

54. Haeberly, Arminius T. The Azores. National Geographic Magazine, June, 1919. pp. 514-545.

55. Henriques, M. Borges de. The Portuguese of Boston. The North End Mission Magazine, July, 1873, Vol. II.

56. Henriques, M. Borges de. A Trip to the Azores. Boston, 1867.

57. Hibbs, Henry H. Jr. Infant Mortality: Its Relation to Social and Industrial Conditions. New York, 1916.

58. Higgin, Louis. Spanish Life in Town and Country.

59. Hoffman, Frederic L. The Portuguese Population in the United States. Publications of the American Statistical Association. Vol. VI. no. 47, pp. 327-336, Sept. 1899.

60. Howard, Stanley E. The Fall River Sliding Scale Experiment of 1905-1910. American Economic Review, Vol. VII, pp. 530-552, Sept. 1917.

61. Hume, Martin. The Woods and Gardens of Portugal.

62. Hunter, Estelle B. Infant Mortality in Waterbury, Conn. Children's Bureau, Infant Mortality Series, no. 7.

63. Hurd, D. Hamilton. History of Bristol County. Philadelphia, 1883.

64. Iliowizi, Henry. In the World of the Azores. Harper's Monthly, Vol. CIV, pp. 85-94.

65. Independent, editorial, Dec. 28, 1914. Vol. LXXX, p. 486.

66. Johnston, Sir Harry H. The Negro in the New World. London, 1910.

67. Johnston, Sir Harry H. The Portuguese Colonies. Nineteenth Century and After, March 1912, Vol. LXXI, pp. 497-510.

68. Johnston, Sir Harry H. The World Position of the Negro and Negroid. Universal Races Congress, 1911, pp. 328-336.

69. Kerhallet De, Captain C. P. The Azores or Western Islands. Washington, 1874.

70. Keller, Albert Galloway. Colonization. New York, 1908.

71. Koebel, W. H. Madeira: Old and New. London, 1909.

72. Koebel, W. H. Portugal, its Land and People. New York, 1909.

73. Koebel W. H. South America. London, 1913.

74. L. P. T. Azorean Economics and the Peasantry. The Nation, Vol. LXXIII. pp. 354-356, Nov. 7, 1901.

75. Lathrop, Julia C. Income and Infant Mortality. American Journal of Public Health, April, 1919, Vol. IX, pp. 270-274.

76. Lincoln, Edward A. et al. A Survey of the Schools of Fall River, Mass. (manuscript) Fall River, 1917.

77. Literary Digest. Portuguese in America. Vol. LX, p. 40.

78. Living Age. (Unsigned article) August 6, 1910, Vol. CCLXVI, pp. 348-354.

79. Lyman, Payson Williston. Fall River, Massachusetts. New England Magazine, May, 1901, Vol. XXX, pp. 291-312.

80. Macdonald, A. J. M. H. Trade, Politics, and Christianity in Africa and the East. London, 1916.

81. Mangold, George B. Child Problems. New York, 1910.

82. Mangold, George B. Problems of Child Welfare. New York, 1914.

83. Marsh, A. E. W. Holiday Wanderings in Madeira. London, 1892.

84. Marsh, C. Wainwright. Sketches and Adventures in Madeira, Portugal and the Andalusias of Spain. New York, 1856.

85. Massachusetts, Commonwealth of. Annual Report of the Trustees of the Bradford Durfee Textile School, for the Year Ending Nov. 30, 1920.

86. Massachusetts, Commonwealth of. The Decennial Census of the Commonwealth, 1915. Boston, 1918.

87. Massachusetts, Commonwealth of. Department of Labor and Industries. Annual Reports.

88. Mees, Jules. Histoire de la Decouverte des Iles Açores et de L'origine de Leur Denomination D'Iles Flamandes. Gand, 1901.

89. Meyer, Ernest Christopher. Infant Mortality in New York City. Rockefeller Foundation, New York, 1921.
90. Moore, Isabel. In Unknown Portugal. Atlantic Monthly, July, 1907, Vol. C, pp. 100-108.
91. Morse, Stephen H. Portugal. New York, 1891.
92. Murray, Charles Augustus. Travels in North America. London, 1839.
93. National Academy of Science. The Army Intelligence Tests. Memoirs, Vol. XV. Washington, 1921.
94. Nelson, Thomas. Remarks on Slavery and the Slave Trade of the Brazils. London, 1846.
95. New Bedford, Massachusetts. Annual Report of the City Clerk, for the Year 1920. New Bedford, 1921.
96. New Bedford Board of Trade. New Bedford Massachusetts—its History. New Bedford, 1889.
97. Ogburn, William F. Study of Rents in Various Cities. Monthly Labor Review, Sept. 1919, Vol. IX.
98. Palmer, George T. and Blakslee, G. Arthur. Infant Mortality in Detroit. American Journal of Public Health, June 1921, Vol. XI. pp. 502-507.
99. Pease, Z. W. History of New Bedford. New Bedford, 1889.
100. Peixotto, Ernest. North Portugal and its Romarias. Nov. 1915- Vol. LVIII, pp. 620-634.
101. Peterson, O. M. Is There African Blood in the White Race of Europe and America? Scientific American Supplement, Feb. 18, 1905, Vol. LIX, pp. 24, 362-3.
102. Portsmouth, Rhode Island. Tax Book with the Reports of Town Officers Including Statistics for the Year 1920. Newport, 1920.
103. Republica Portuguesa, Censo da Populacao, 1911, Vol. I, Part I.
104. Republica Portuguesa, Ministerio das Finances, Direccao Geral de Estatistica, Reparticao Central, Estatistica Demografica, Movemento da Populacao, 1917.
105. Ramsey, L. F. Levada-Walking in Madeira. Living Age, Vol. CCCVII, pp. 656-663.
106. Reuter, Edward Byron. The Mulatto in the United States. Boston, 1918.
107. Rhode Island State Board of Health. Child Welfare Division. Is Rhode Island a Thoughtful Father to the Children? Providence, 1920.
108. Rhode Island Bureau of Industrial Statistics. Annual Report for 1907 Part I. Number of Families of Specified Size, Occupying Specified Number of Rooms, etc. Providence, 1907.
109. Richardson, Norval. Commuting from Mont' Estoril to Lisbon. Scribner's Magazine, Vol. LXXI, pp. 547-555.

110. Ripley, W. Z. Races of Europe. New York, 1899.
111. Ross, Edward A. The Old World in the New. New York, 1914.
112. Roundell, Mrs. Charles. A Visit to the Azores. London, 1889.
113. Rugg, Harlold O. Statistical Method Applied to Education. New York, 1917.
114. Sandham, Henry. St. Michael's of the Azores. Century Magazine, Dec. 1915, Vol. XCI, pp. 223-231.
115. Schultz, Alfred Paul. Race or Mongrel. Boston, 1908.
116. Silva, Jose B. D'Andrada E. Brazil. London, 1826.
117. Smith, M. Josephine. Portuguese Silhouettes. Travel Magazine, April, 1913. pp. 17-20; 54-57.
118. Sobel, Jacob. Need for Protecting Maternity and Infancy. American Labor Legislation Review, March, 1921, Vol. XI, pp. 74-79.
119. Taylor, Ellen M. Madeira, its Scenery and How to See It. London, 1882.
120. Thomas-Stanford, Charles. Leaves from a Madeira Garden. London, 1909.
121. U. S. Bureau of the Census. Birth Statistics for the Registration Area, 1920. Washington, 1922.
122. U. S. Bureau of the Census. Decennial Censuses of the U. S. from 1850-1920 inclusive.
123. U. S. Bureau of the Census. Twentieth Annual Report on Mortality Statistics for 1919. Washington, 1921.
124. U. S. Bureau of Immigration. Annual Reports of the Commissioner General of Immigration, 1899-1920.
125. U. S. Bureau of Labor Statistics. Bulletin, no. 175. Summary of the Report on the Condition of Woman and Child Wage-earners in the United States. Washington, 1916.
126. U. S. Bureau of Labor Statistics. Bulletins, no. 239, 262, and 288. Wages and Hours of Labor in Cotton Goods Manufacture and Finishing. Washington, 1918, 1919 and 1921.
127. U. S. Bureau of Labor Statistics. Monthly Labor Review for May, 1919. Average Amount and Percent of Expenditure, etc. for Families of Fall River, Mass. p. 154. Vol. VIII.
128. U. S. Bureau of Labor Statistics. Monthly Labor Review. Nov. 1919. Cost of Living in the United States. Clothing and Miscellaneous Expenditures. Vol. IX, pp. 1-19.
129. Do. Dec. 1919. Family Incomes. Vol. IX, pp. 29-41.
130. Do. August, 1919. Family Expenditures. Vol. IX, pp. 303-327.
131. Do. January, 1920. Family Expenditures. Vol. X, p. 91.
132. Do. October, 1920. Changes in the Cost of Living in the United States. 1913-June, 1920. Vol. XI, p. 689.
133. U. S. Immigration Commission Report, 61st Congress, 3rd Session. Washington, D. C., 1911. Vols. I, II and XXII.

134. U. S. Children's Bureau. Infant Mortality Series, nos. 2-12. Washington, 1915-1920.

135. U. S. Senate Document, no. 645, Vol. I, p. 217. Sixty-first Congress, Second Session, Senate Documents. Women and Child Wage-earners in the United States.

136. Verdery, Katherine. Madeira, An Island of Enchantment. Travel Magazine, Feb. 1913, pp. 31-33; 54-56.

137. Verrill, Charles H. Infant Mortality and Its Relation to the Employment of Mothers in Fall River, Mass. Transactions of the 15th International Congress on Hygiene and Demography. Vol. III, pp. 318-337. Washington, 1913.

138. Vorse, Mary Heaton. The Portuguese of Provincetown. The Outlook, Feb. 25, 1911, Vol. XCVII, pp. 409-416.

139. Walker, Walter Frederick. The Azores. London, 1886.

140. Weatherly, Ulysses G. Race and Marriage. American Journal of Sociology, Jan. 1910. Vol. XV, pp. 433-453.

141. Webster, John W. M. Description of the Island of St. Michael. Boston, 1821.

141. Weeks, Lyman H. Among the Azores. Boston, 1882.

143. Weston, Silas. Visit to a Volcano. Providence, 1856.

144. Woodbury, Robert M. Infant Mortality Studies of the Children's Bureau. Publications of the American Statistical Association. June, 1918, Vol. XVI, pp. 30-53.

145. Young, George. Portugal, Old and Young. Oxford, 1917.

146. Yule, G. Undy. An Introduction to the Theory of Statistics (6th ed.) London, 1922.

VITA

THE author was born on the seventh of November, 1886, in Worcester Massachusetts. He graduated from the Classical High School of that city in 1903 after a five year course. For the following eight years he was employed in the paper business, and for six of these years he was acting superintendent of the Whitney Manufacturing Company. Entering Clark College in 1911 he was graduated in 1914. He was Bancroft (Worcester) Scholar during the first year of his graduate work at Columbia University (1914-1915), and received the degree of Master of Arts at the end of that year. He was Richard Watson Gilder Fellow in Sociology at Columbia 1915-1916. He attended seminars in Sociology under Professors Franklin H. Giddings and Alvan A. Tenney. He attended lectures under Professor Giddings and Professor Tenney, and also under Professors Robert E. Chaddock, Henry R. Seager, John B. Clark, James H. Robinson and James T. Shotwell.

From 1916 to 1917 he was Assistant Secretary of Carnegie Institute of Technology, and during the second half of that year was also Acting Registrar and Instructor in Sociology. From 1917 to 1918 he was Instructor in Economics and Sociology at Ohio State University, and from 1918 to 1919 was Assistant Professor at the same institution. From 1919 to 1920 he was Assistant Professor of Economics and Sociology at Wellesley College. From 1920 to date (1923) he has been Associate Professor of Economics and Sociology and Head of that Department at Wells College. In 1923 he was appointed Professor at the same institution.